Educat

Advice   tury

Canada

Women wh   early 1950s
undoubted   pproach to
child rearir   rigid, scientific appro   t and child
care.

Katherir   d begins in
the first d   rate among
infants, sn   d a massive
governmer   ex tasks of
motherho   mented appropriate   ig every aspect of motherhood from pregnancy and childbirth to nursing and
toilet training. As the century advanced, mothers were inundated with
advice, in government pamphlets, health journals, women's magazines,
and child-care manuals. Focusing on the period from 1900 to 1960,
Arnup provides thorough documentation of this barrage from the experts and assesses its changing messages and its impact on women's
daily lives. She reveals that child-rearing literature has transformed
women's experiences of pregnancy, birth, and motherhood.

Arnup's special contribution is her illumination of the shift in child-
care advice in the period following the Second World War. No previous
book, furthermore, has assessed the effects of this kind of literature
on women's lives. Her study offers new material to scholars in women's
studies, Canadian history, and sociology. It will be of interest also
to all mothers who have felt confused or manipulated by the advice
of experts.

KATHERINE ARNUP is Assistant Professor, School of Canadian Studies,
Carleton University.

KATHERINE ARNUP

Education for Motherhood
ADVICE FOR MOTHERS IN TWENTIETH-CENTURY CANADA

UNIVERSITY OF TORONTO PRESS
Toronto Buffalo London

© University of Toronto Press Incorporated 1994
Toronto Buffalo London
Printed in Canada

ISBN 0-8020-2861-6 (cloth)
ISBN 0-8020-7361-1 (paper)

∞

Printed on acid-free paper

Canadian Cataloguing in Publication Data

Arnup, Katherine, 1949–

Education for motherhood: advice for mothers
in twentieth century Canada

Includes bibliographical references and index.
ISBN 0-8020-2861-6 (bound)   ISBN 0-8020-7361-1 (pbk.)

1. Motherhood – Canada.   2. Child rearing – Canada.
I. Title.

HQ755.7.A75 1994   306.874'3   C94-930093-4

University of Toronto Press acknowledges the financial assistance to
its publishing program of the Canada Council and the Ontario Arts
Council.

This book has been published with the help of a grant from the
Social Science Federation of Canada, using funds provided by the
Social Sciences and Humanities Research Council of Canada.

To Dora, Jesse, and Kate

Contents

viii Contents

Acknowledgments

This book has been many years in the making. It began as my doctoral dissertation, completed in 1991 in the Department of History and Philosophy at the Ontario Institute for Studies in Education. Thanks first to my thesis committee: Johan Aitken, Linda Siegel, and Alison Prentice. To Alison, in particular, I owe an enormous debt of gratitude, for her willingness to take a risk with me, and for always having the time to talk, to listen, and to read my work.

Scholarships from the Ontario Graduate Scholarship program and the Social Sciences and Humanities Research Council of Canada enabled me to pursue my initial studies on a full-time basis. A post-doctoral fellowship from the Social Sciences and Humanities Research Council of Canada helped me to complete the necessary revisions. My parents, Dora and John Arnup, provided 'no strings' financial assistance at key points along the way. In addition, for five years I taught women's history at Trent University. My students at Trent provided valuable insights into the history and practice of motherhood. My sisters, Carol and Jane Arnup and Judy Dickson, and my friends Shelley Gavigan, Joan Gilroy, Margaret Hobbs, Didi Khayatt, Joan Sangster, and Ingrid Wellmeier offered encouragement, advice, and lunch-time companionship throughout the lonely writing process. During the lengthy pre-publication process, my editor at University of Toronto Press, Laura Macleod, was unwavering in her enthusiasm and support.

My mother's enduring interest in my work extended far beyond the call of maternal duty. She provided emotional and financial support, continually reminding me that I *would* one day be finished. Her love and our shared experience of mothering continue to sustain me in my work and in my life.

Thanks are also owed to the women who shared the stories of their child-rearing years with me. During the cold and snowy winter of 1986, they welcomed me into their homes, offering me tea and treats. Despite their fears that they had 'nothing very important to say,' they constantly amazed me with the power of their memories and with the strength and complexity of their lives as mothers.

Special thanks are due to my family. My daughters, Jesse and Kate, provided countless diversions from the tedium of research and writing. Last, I thank Susan Genge, with whom I have shared the joys, the frustrations, and the hard work of motherhood.

The Experience of Motherhood

Two days before I am due to leave the hospital with my new baby, I go down to the nursery to check on the procedures for being discharged. The nurse in charge looks up my file.

'Mrs Arnup?' she asks.

'Yes.'

'You haven't bathed your baby yet.'

'No.'

'You have to bathe your baby before you can go home. Have you been to the baby bath class yet?'

'No, but I already know how to bathe a baby.'

'That may well be, but you still have to bathe her here before you can go home.'

'You mean I can't check out until I bathe her?'

'That's right. Now ... which class will you be coming to? Eleven or one?'

'Eleven.'

'And you'll come back down to bathe her at four?'

'Yes. And then can I go home on Tuesday?'

'Of course.'

Jesse's two-month check-up at the doctor. I transport her, still sleeping, across town to the office. She lies peacefully in my arms until we are called for our turn.

'And how's Jesse today?' the doctor asks. 'Her eyes seem to be a bit gummy.'

I look down to see eyes still half shut with 'sleepy dust.'

'She just woke up,' I explain.

'Well, it looks like a plugged tear duct to me. Put these drops in her eyes every three hours and press down right here. It should clear up this way. If not, we'll have to send her to a specialist and have a tube put in.'

I return home, to poke and prod, use arms and legs to hold down a fighting child, as I struggle to put drops in her eyes. The next day I abandon the project. Her eyes are clear and bright, no sleepy dust in sight.

Jesse's four-month check-up. The doctor sets her on the scales, returns to plot her weight on the chart, then shakes his head.

'Bottom tenth percentile,' he says. 'She's just not gaining fast enough.' He looks at me sternly. 'Are you doing too much?'

'Doing too much,' I splutter, completely caught off guard. 'Well, I'm a full-time PhD student, and I'm editing a journal, and I'm taking care of Jesse. But I don't think I'm doing too much.'

'Well, see that you don't. I want you to start feeding her every two hours. Day and night. And bring her back in two weeks to be weighed again.'

I return home in tears, certain that I have been starving my child, determined to do my duty and offer my breasts every two hours, ready to set aside all other claims on my time. Never thinking that perhaps her size might have something to do with my less-than-five-foot frame. Certain that doctor knows best.

Journal extracts, 1982

The choice of maternal advice literature as the subject of this book is by no means an accidental one. Two months before I began my PhD program, I gave birth to my first child. The experience altered the course of my life and work more profoundly than I could ever have imagined. Suddenly, after nine months of happily anticipating the 'new arrival,' I was a mother, with a crying, hungry, wet-bottomed infant to care for. And I knew nothing – or so I thought. And so, like so many new mothers, I read. Penelope Leach. Dr Spock. Sheila Kitzinger. I listened intently to every order from my doctor, following his advice with what amounted to religious fervour.

After four months of this regimen, I began to emerge from the fog of new motherhood. I was shocked by the degree to which expert advice had taken hold of my life. I scarcely took a move without consulting a manual. I worried about Jesse's weight, her waking in the night, her seemingly endless demands. Slowly my analytical faculties began to return. I began to ask questions. Where had all this advice come from? How did these experts really know they were right? How had women ever managed to raise their children in the days before the experts? These and a myriad of other questions formed the starting-point for my investigation into the historical and social construction of motherhood.

This is not an attack on expert advice. Rather, it is an attempt to situate child-rearing advice in its historical and social context. By examining the origins of and changes in this advice, I will demonstrate that there is seldom one right answer to our questions concerning the best way to raise our children. I would hope that my work might help to empower women to deal with the tremendous volume of information and advice that faces new mothers today, to question the validity and objectivity of the advice, and to seek help from a variety of sources, including friends, family, and, of course, Dr Spock.

The experience of motherhood is one that has been shared by the vast majority of women throughout history. Even today, despite tremendous demographic and social changes taking place in our society, most women still give birth to at least one child during their lifetime. Yet the experience of mothering has been largely omitted from traditional accounts of history. This book begins to address that untold story.

Infant Clinic, Earlscourt Avenue, Toronto, August 1914

Infant Clinic, Memorial Institute, Toronto, August 1914. The sign invited mothers to 'come and have your Baby Weighed.'

Earlscourt Baby Show, Toronto, July 1918

Breast-feeding, November 1942

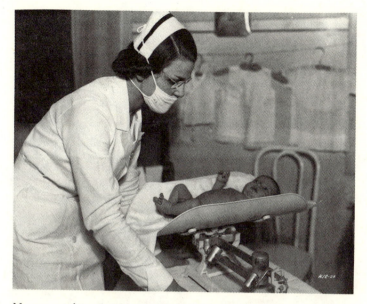

Nurse weighing unidentified baby, Ottawa, December 1939

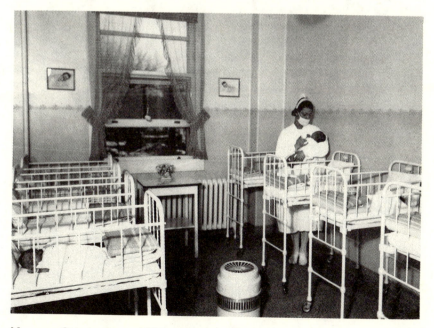

Nursery, Ottawa General Hospital, December 1939

'When preparing the formula have everything you require near at hand. It is of the utmost importance that every utensil be scrupulously clean. Wash your hands well before preparing the formula.' Ernest Couture, *The Canadian Mother and Child* (1940), 130. Photograph taken Ottawa, December 1939

'Canadian mother waves good-bye to her children left at day nursery while she works at part-time job.'

City Nurse J.H. Shaw conducting baby clinic at the Dixon Community House, Peterborough, Ontario, September 1943

Nurse Beatrice Kitchen of St Luke's Mission Hospital holding Quaga while Soudlo, the baby's mother, prepares powdered milk formula, Pangnirtung, Northwest Territories, August 1946

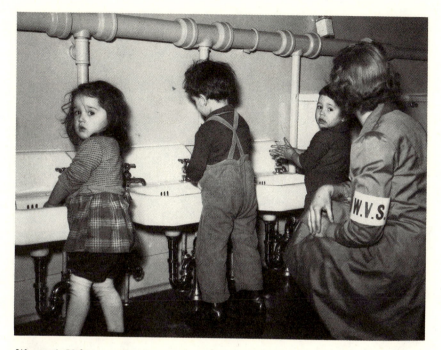

Women's Voluntary Service assistant helping children wash hands at day nursery in the Givens Street School, Toronto, February 1943

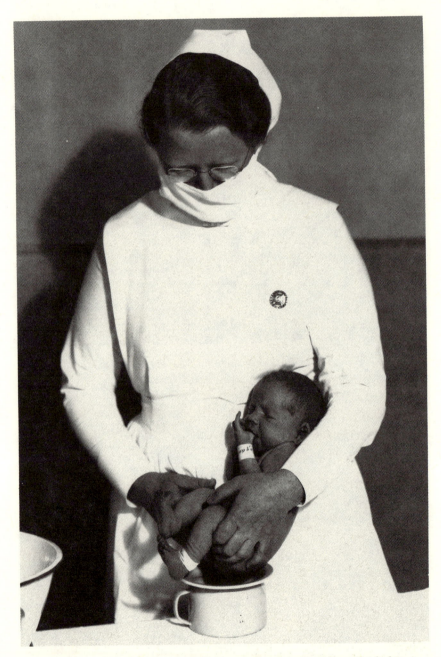

'With patience, a baby can be trained at an early age to regular toilet habits.'
Ernest Couture, *The Canadian Mother and Child* (1940), 97. Photograph taken
Ottawa, January 1940

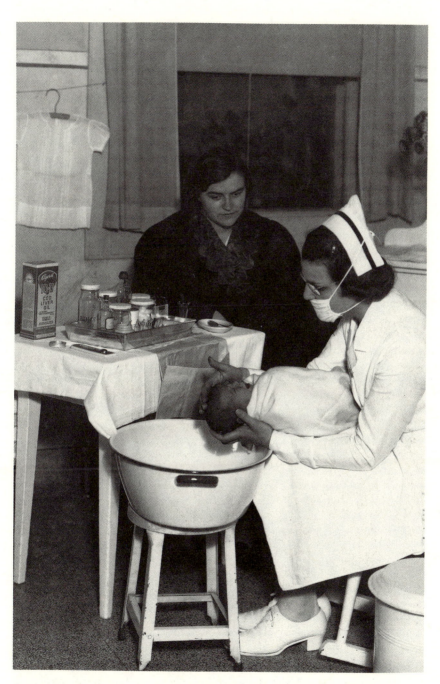

'Instructing Mother how to bathe and hold baby,' Ottawa, December 1939

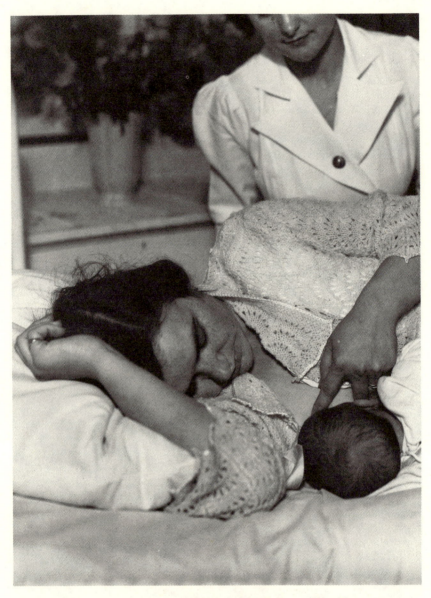

'Teaching baby to nurse rightly. Mother should lie in comfortable position while nursing the baby.' Ottawa, December 1939

'First call for dinner,' Ottawa, December 1939

A 'typical' middle-class family in the 1950s, Port Bruce, Ontario, summer 1953

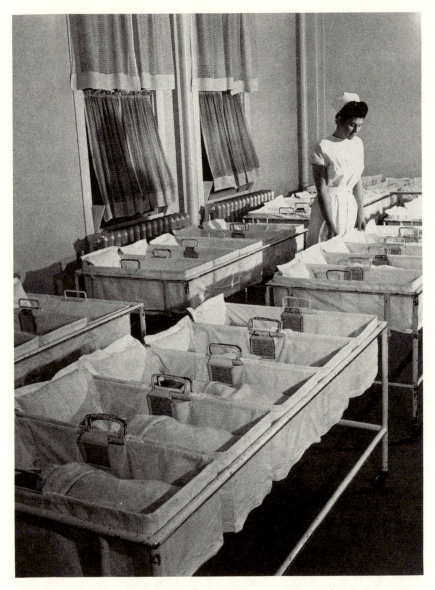

Nursery in the Ottawa Civic Hospital, March 1946. 'Hospital nurseries are well ventilated and regulated as to temperature.'

A Victorian Order nurse showing a woman how to bathe a baby, Ottawa,
March 1946

Woman attempting to 'toilet train' baby, Ottawa, March 1946. 'Babies should be trained in regular voiding habits almost from the beginning. This illustration shows the best method.'

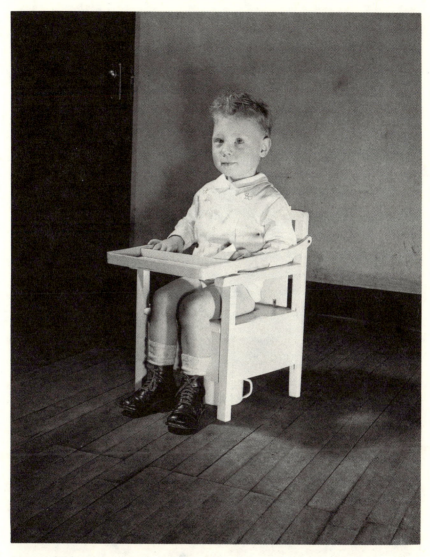

Young child sitting on early toilet training device, Ottawa, March 1946. 'The child trained from birth in regular voiding habits and provided with a small "toidey" as shown, is able to look after himself in this respect.'

'Typical Canadian Family – Mrs. William Meadows of Hull, P.Q., washes clothes in washing machine in kitchen of her four-room apartment.' Hull, Quebec, September 1947

EDUCATION FOR MOTHERHOOD

Introduction

The conditions of motherhood in Canada have changed dramatically over the course of the past two centuries. Beginning with conception and continuing throughout pregnancy, childbirth, and child rearing, the experience of motherhood has been shaped and determined by technological and medical advances and by ideological and political shifts. Changes in the technology of both contraception and abortion have enabled women to exercise some control over when, and indeed if, they bear children. Contraceptive devices, outlawed under the provisions of the Criminal Code until 1969,[1] are now readily available at birth-control clinics and corner stores. Abortion, no longer included in the Criminal Code,[2] has become a more or less routine, albeit controversial, medical procedure performed under local anaesthetic in hospitals and clinics across the country. Shifts in sexual mores and practices, ranging from the so-called sexual revolution to the growth of the lesbian and gay movements, changes in family forms, and the development of new reproductive technologies have resulted in dramatic transformations in both the context and the methods of procreation. Childbirth itself has been transformed from a family-centred event that took place within the confines of a woman's own home, attended by a midwife, female friends, or relatives, to a medical event that takes place within a hospital, supervised and controlled by doctors and nurses, and from which family members have been, until recently, entirely excluded. Child rearing, the exclusive preserve of women and their 'maternal instincts' during the nineteenth century, has become the terrain of experts, as doctors, nurses, social workers, and psychologists have made it their business to advise women on the best way to rear their children.

Tremendous demographic changes have also had a significant impact on the lives of Canadian mothers. Despite the legal prohibition of the sale or distribution of contraceptive information and devices, the birth rate in Canada declined dramatically during the latter part of the nineteenth century. The result was that, although the number of hours per day spent in child care and housework has remained constant, and, in some instances, even increased,[3] women spent fewer years of their lives involved in the processes of pregnancy, childbirth, and child rearing. Equally dramatic changes have taken place in the areas of maternal and infant mortality. Although there have been tremendous regional, class, and racial disparities, this century has witnessed a significant decline in the risks associated with childbirth and dramatic improvements in child and maternal health in Canada. The result of these demographic changes has been longer, healthier lives for most mothers and their children.

Despite these transformations, the central image of motherhood remains largely unchanged. Motherhood. The very word conjures up images of women and children glued together in a divinely ordained symbiotic relation. Whatever else may change, whatever additional tasks women may perform inside or outside the home, children remain part of the picture – children waiting to be fed, held, nurtured – mothered. As Adrienne Rich has noted, 'whatever the known facts, it is still assumed that the mother is "with the child." It is she, finally, who is held accountable for her children's health, the clothes they wear, their behavior at school, their intelligence and general development.'[4] As well, motherhood is often perceived to be a transhistorical condition, bridging epochs and cultures, as permanent and unchanging as God in His heaven and the sun in the sky.

Recent feminist analysis has been concerned with challenging this image of motherhood. During the latter part of the 1960s, radical feminists began to explore and to examine the origins of many of the oppressive aspects of motherhood. Motherhood, they asserted, was not always fun. Children could be sick, whiny, demanding – even boring. Shulamith Firestone, in her classic work *The Dialectic of Sex*, stated her case boldly: 'The heart of woman's oppression is her childbearing and childrearing roles.'[5] Arguing that child rearing inevitably becomes a trap for women, Firestone called for a rejection of motherhood itself.[6]

In their haste to expose the problems associated with modern motherhood, Firestone and many of her contemporaries ended up quite literally 'throwing out the baby with the bath water.' While they challenged the notion that women must *of necessity* perform the labour associated with child rearing, they failed to examine changes which have taken place in child-rearing arrangements across cultures and throughout history. In an ironic twist of fate, they fell prey to the very form of biological determinism they sought to avoid. Accepting the views of much of social and political theory that define women's relegation to the private sphere as the inevitable result of women's role in reproduction, many radical feminists felt that the only way for women to escape the problems of motherhood was to eschew the condition altogether.

Such an approach fails to recognize the changes which have taken place in the conditions of mothering. In so doing, it grants to biology far too grand a role in determining human behaviour. In this book, I begin with the understanding that reproductive biology is profoundly shaped, influenced, and, at times, determined by the social organization of society. While only women can bear children,[7] this biological fact alone cannot account for the current practices of woman-centred child rearing within the nuclear family. On the contrary, our 'modern' methods of child rearing represent only one form of the social organization of reproduction and socialization.[8] Changes in reproductive and household technology, in fertility patterns, family size, and patterns of divorce and remarriage, coupled with drastic changes in ideas about maternal practices, underlie the shifting social organization of the bearing and rearing of children.

In her ground-breaking work *Of Woman Born*, Adrienne Rich distinguishes between the experience of motherhood – 'the *potential relationship* of any woman to her powers of reproduction and to children' – and the '*institution* [of motherhood], which aims at ensuring that that potential – and all women – shall remain under male control.'[9] By separating the biological act of mothering from the structures and ideology that surround it, Rich enables us to examine motherhood as a construct, much like religion, compulsory heterosexuality, or the family, all of which tend to be seen as 'givens' in our society. In this way, we can examine and perhaps criticize particular aspects of the institution of motherhood without devaluating the joy and pleasure that the experience of mothering brings to many women.

Much of this book is an examination of the ideology of motherhood, as it is reflected in the child-rearing advice given to new mothers. In the chapters that follow, I explore the changes that have taken place in this advice over the course of this century. I also consider the ways in which this advice has shaped and determined the everyday experiences of women's lives. My focus, then, is on two different but related issues: the changes that have taken place in advice on child rearing during this century, and the impact that these changes have had on women as the primary caretakers of children.

In contrast to recent books on child rearing which employ the gender-neutral term 'parent,' I have chosen to speak almost exclusively about mothers. While infant and child care need not, of course, be done solely by women, the vast majority of the tasks involved in the rearing of infants and small children have been and continue to be performed by women. To use a term such as 'parenting,' in recognition of the fact that either sex could (in some ideal world) care for their offspring, masks women's important contribution as mothers.

Most of the experts upon whose work I draw directed their advice towards women, in recognition, presumably, that it was women who would be charged with the responsibility for carrying out their instructions. On occasion, authors would direct their comments towards 'parents,' referring, for example, to the importance of 'parent education.' While such usage might appear to reflect an acknowledgment that either parent could perform child-care tasks, in practice it was virtually always women who were expected to implement the experts' directives.

It is likely that women have always needed to learn how to be mothers. In earlier centuries, however, much of this knowledge was passed along through female support networks, from mother to daughter, from elder to younger sister, from friend to friend.[10] By the late eighteenth century, books, too, were available to enlighten the new mother. Books on infant feeding and care written specifically for mothers appeared in Britain and the United States as early as the 1760s.[11] Written primarily by mothers and other lay people, these early child-care manuals were collections of homespun wisdom based in large measure on common sense and practical experience. In contrast to those volumes, child-rearing manuals of this century are presented as scientific tracts, written by officials in various levels of government and members of the medical, nursing, and psychological professions – people whose knowledge of children was and is frequently based on a professional rather than a parental relationship.[12]

Many factors caused women to turn to outside experts for help and counsel. The process of urbanization, hastened by the Industrial Revolution in the latter half of the nineteenth century, meant that increasing numbers of women were separated from other family members, facing childbirth and the early years of motherhood virtually alone. Furthermore, the declining birth rate meant that far fewer women had the direct experience with babies that came through assisting with younger siblings. For many twentieth-century mothers, particularly women in the urban middle class, the initial experience with a newborn came with the birth of their first child.[13] Thus, science and its discoveries offered help in what had become alien territory for many women.

The advent of mass-circulation magazines and the growth of government child-welfare departments meant that for the first time a large and significant body of 'scientific' advice literature designed to teach women the best ways to rear their children was available to the vast majority of Canadian mothers. Increased literacy rates secured a readership far beyond the limited, largely middle- and upper-class audience of nineteenth-century manuals. Virtually every issue of popular magazines like *Chatelaine* included at least one article on infant and child care. In addition, divisions of child welfare at all levels of government and social-welfare agencies like the Canadian Council on Child and Family Welfare produced and distributed free pamphlets and books on a wide range of subjects related to child rearing. After the Second World War, inexpensive commercial child-care manuals were available to offer advice for mothers of the post-war baby-boom. It is that body of literature which represents the primary source material for this book.

Advice literature has provided historians and contemporary observers with both a wealth of information and a host of methodological problems.[14] In recent years, many authors have relied upon prescriptive literature to make inferences about child-rearing practices in the past.[15] It is tempting, for the manuals document in great detail many aspects of child-rearing behaviour deemed to be appropriate in a given historical period. The methodological problem lies, however, in determining whether these dicta were ever put into practice, or, indeed, whether more than a few parents were even aware of them. We cannot merely assume that advice manuals provide an accurate representation of either official wisdom on child rearing or parental behaviour without ever putting those assumptions to the test. Rather, we must closely scrutinize advice manuals as we would any historical document, considering such issues as authorship, distribution, and readership. In addition, we must try to determine whether recipients of an advice manual were actually exposed to its contents. Did they read it or simply put it on the shelf unopened? If they read it, did they try to follow the advice? If they did, how did it affect their child-rearing practices? These are among the empirical questions that I address in the chapters that follow, and, in particular, in the final chapter of the book.[16]

Throughout this century, the material reality of mothers' lives differed widely according to class, racial, and ethnic status, as well as by region and historical period. Access to hospital and medical facilities, to food, housing, and other necessities of life differed greatly. All of these elements affected how mothers lived their lives and how they raised their children. In short, there was no unitary experience of motherhood for Canadian women. There was, however, a dominant view of 'good mothering,' a developing ideology of appropriate Canadian child-rearing practices. This common ideological construct was developed and propagated through the advice literature, much of which was generated federally or in central Canada, primarily in Toronto. Federal government publications and the monthly letters produced by the Canadian Council on Child and Family Welfare were frequently distributed by provincial departments of health to women in remote areas of the country. Thus, most of the publications that I have examined were readily available to women across the country.

Where I have considered local or provincial public health initiatives, I have focused primarily on the city of Toronto and on the province of Ontario. While the experiences of Toronto mothers cannot simply be generalized to mothers across Canada, in many respects, in terms of English Canada, Toronto and its child-welfare measures served as a model for other cities in Canada. As Neil Sutherland has noted, 'Toronto in the late nineteenth and early twentieth centuries led the nation in most forms of social experimentation,' despite the fact that it was not Canada's largest city at the time.[17] Thus, health- and child-care measures that were implemented in Toronto were often held up as the ideal – if not the reality – for all Canadian mothers and children.

Although I present a historical overview of the changing attitudes towards mothers and children during the nineteenth century, the study concentrates on the years 1900 to 1960. In the first chapter, I document the rise of infant and child health as key social and political issues during the first two decades of this century. That chapter sets the historical stage for the examination of child-rearing advice during the period between 1920 and 1960, which comprises the core of this book.

I have chosen this time frame for a number of reasons. First, the end of the First World War represents a watershed in Canadian history, as Canada emerged from the Great War 'a nation transformed.'[18] On the home front, the end of the war saw the establishment of the federal Department of Health, a key organization in the development of advice literature and in the provision of services for women and children. During the interwar years, health departments at all levels of government sought to combat high levels of infant and maternal mortality and to improve the health of Canadians. In addition, the child-study movement established a foothold in Canada through such institutions as the St George's School for Child Study (later the Institute of Child Study), whose director, Dr William Blatz, gained worldwide recognition as a leading expert in child development. The Second World War marked a hiatus in many government health programs as the nation once again turned its attention to the battlefield. Many Canadian mothers found themselves in the paid labour force for the first time in their lives, and, in a limited number of cases, their children were cared for in publicly funded, licensed child-care facilities. That was to change at war's end, however, as the elimination of day-care centres and tax incentives for working wives, coupled with an extended period of prosperity, made the family wage a real possibility for a substantial proportion of the population, and reinforced once again the centrality of full-time motherhood for Canadian women. I conclude my investigation in 1960, at the end of a decade that many critics have regarded as the most profoundly pro-natalist of the twentieth century.[19] The year 1960 also marked the beginning of the decade which was to see the birth of the civil-rights and student movements, as well as a renewed women's movement, all of which would, in their own ways, question many of the principles held dear in those earlier decades.

All previous studies of Canadian motherhood and child-rearing practices have confined their analysis to the period prior to the Second World War. Extending the period of analysis to 1960 enabled me to examine the dramatic shift in child-care advice from a rigid, health-oriented focus in the interwar years to the more relaxed, 'permissive' approach of the post–Second World War years. These decades also witnessed the transition from home to hospital as the appropriate site of childbirth and from family and friends to doctors and psychologists as the appropriate advisers on infant and child care. While it is beyond the scope of this study to account fully for these shifts in child-rearing advice, I document the critical role which the professionalization of medicine and health care played in the early decades of this century. Doctors, armed with the latest medical and scientific discoveries, launched a concerted attack on the 'old-fashioned' methods of infant and child care. From the promotion of 'scientific' child care to the systematic attack on information-sharing between women, doctors exerted increasing control over access to health- and child-care information as the century progressed. During the post-war economic boom, as national health improved with increased knowledge and enhanced nutrition, psychological concerns began to emerge as central issues on the child-rearing agenda. Psychologists and health-care professionals, trained in the emerging fields of psychology and psychiatry, began to promote a 'permissive' mode of child rearing that concentrated on the child's emotional as well as physical well-being. No longer solely concerned with rates of infant mortality, child-care experts could focus on how the child 'felt' – whether he was happy and well adjusted – and once again they determined that the most effective means to achieve the child's happiness was through the attentive care of a full-time mother.

The book is organized thematically, reflecting the central themes contained in the prescriptive literature itself. In chapter 1, I examine the historical roots of child-rearing advice, focusing on the problem of infant mortality and the initiatives that were taken by both the private and the public sectors to reduce the high rates of infant deaths, for it was in relation to this concern over infant deaths that the campaign for maternal education was undertaken. In chapters 2 and 3 I examine the two major solutions that were offered to the twin problems of infant and maternal mortality – education for motherhood and the medicalization of motherhood – using the advice literature itself to illustrate these themes. As well, in chapters 3 and 4 I focus on specific details of the advice, looking at a range of topics including prenatal care, birth, infant feeding, and habit training. Within each of these topics I consider the changes in advice to mothers that occurred during the first six decades of this century. In the final chapter, I assess the impact of this advice on the lives of Canadian mothers, using both oral and literary sources. On the basis of my research and of my own experiences as a mother, I also attempt to evaluate the experts, offering suggestions to both historians and mothers on a realistic approach to child-rearing advice. The use of my experiences should not be seen to contradict my central argument that motherhood is a socially constructed and changing phenomenon. Rather, it reflects my commitment to locate myself in my research and writing and to ground my theory in the day-to-day reality of women's lives.

In my examination of motherhood in Canada, I have chosen to focus primarily on the advice concerning the rearing of infants and preschool children. During the early decades of this century, the infant and pre-school years were viewed as critical ones in the campaign to raise 'a strong and healthy race.'[20] Accordingly, developing an understanding of these early years is essential to an analysis of the ideology and practice of motherhood. Other aspects of maternity have received considerable scholarly attention in Canada in recent years. In a series of articles published over the course of the past fifteen years, and in an excellent book co-authored with Arlene McLaren, Angus McLaren has documented the history of birth control and abortion in Canada.[21] The experience of childbirth, and in particular the transition in the site of parturition from home to hospital, has been ably documented by several Canadian authors.[22] In chapter 3, I draw upon and extend beyond that work, as I examine changing prescriptions of prenatal care and childbirth during the pre- and post-Second World War period.

Less work has been done on the history of childhood and child-rearing practices in Canada. Neil Sutherland's *Children in English-Canadian Society*, first published in 1976, remains the only comprehensive work in the area. Concentrating on the period from 1870 to 1920, Sutherland examines changing attitudes towards children and the social programs that were instituted to improve their health and living conditions. Sutherland and his colleagues at the University of British Columbia are currently engaged in a large-scale research project designed to reconstruct the history of Canadian children, using oral history and archival sources.[23] In contrast to this book, which takes as its starting point the experience of motherhood, the work of Sutherland and his colleagues concentrates on child rearing almost exclusively from the point of view of children themselves.[24]

Two authors have dealt specifically with the experience of motherhood in Canada during the interwar years. In a ground-breaking article on the subject, and in her chapter on motherhood in *The New Day Recalled*, Veronica Strong-Boag describes the intrusion of experts into the child-rearing practices of Canadian mothers during the interwar years.[25] Strong-Boag uses the examples of the Dionne Quintuplets, the work of Dr William Blatz at the St George's School for Child Study, and the Little Blue Books by Dr Helen MacMurchy to demonstrate the degree to which child-care experts came to dominate maternal practice during this period. While Strong-Boag's work has been an important influence on my own scholarship, the present book draws upon a much broader range of sources than Strong-Boag's initial work, and extends the period of analysis into the decades after the Second World War.

In her doctoral thesis and in an article which draws upon that work, Norah Lewis examines the advice on child care offered to parents in British Columbia during the interwar years.[26] In contrast to both Strong-Boag's and my own published work on the subject,[27] Lewis sees expert advice as having a largely salutary effect on parents and children alike. Lewis notes, for example, that during the interwar years, 'for the first time in history, infants had a good chance of surviving to adulthood if parents adopted the new scientific approach to child care.'[28] Like Neil Sutherland, her colleague and former supervisor, Lewis views the public health movement as an almost unqualified good for the nation's citizenry. As a result, she tends to turn a blind eye to the negative impact these scientific advisers may have had on the lives of mothers.

Neither Lewis nor Strong-Boag attempts to assess the degree to which mothers either sought out or followed expert advice. In this regard, this study breaks important new ground, as it is the first Canadian book to move beyond analysis of the content of advice literature to a consideration of its effects on maternal practice. Determining the actual numbers of women who attempted to implement these ideas is a difficult enterprise. While a limited amount of data is available on rates of breast-feeding, hospitalization for childbirth, and attendance at prenatal clinics, most mothering took place behind closed doors in the realm of the private home. Thus, it is virtually impossible to determine with any certainty the degree to which most women actually put into practice the prenatal and child-rearing advice they received. In the chapters that follow, I incorporate available data on maternal practices; because of the limitations of such data, however, the picture of maternal life will always be a partial one.

While it is impossible to determine how *most* Canadian mothers brought up their children, we must nonetheless be careful not to treat women as the passive recipients of expert advice. Rather than seeing women as victims of the experts, as, for example, in Deirdre English and Barbara Ehrenreich's *For Her Own Good: 150 Years of the Experts' Advice to Women*, I have tried to document the ways in which women attempted to control and change the circumstances of their own lives. To do this,

I have considered women's role in seeking out, sifting through, and, on occasion, rejecting expert counsel. In the chapters that follow, I demonstrate that hundreds of thousands of Canadian mothers were exposed to child-rearing literature. They wrote to government agencies requesting information, and help; they visited prenatal and well-baby clinics, infant-care lectures, and medical offices; they wrote thousands of personal letters to child-care experts, asking for help with their children. The information that I gained through interviews, letters, and other first-hand accounts suggests that many women tried, not always successfully, to implement the advice that they received. However wrong-headed this advice may appear to us, in the harsh light of our current scientific and medical knowledge, we must bear in mind the reasons why women stood ready to ask for and to embrace such solutions. As I document in the pages of this book, in the past Canadian mothers faced the very real danger of dying in childbirth. Their children faced the very real danger of falling victim to disease, infection, and early death. Those dangers alarmed both government officials and mothers alike. Their responses may have differed, but their concerns were the same – the health and well-being of Canadian mothers and children. In the following chapter, I turn my attention to the ways in which the issues of maternal and infant health were framed in the early years of this century.

1

Waging War on Infant Mortality

There is something wrong with the place where children die.
Helen MacMurchy, 1910[1]

Infant mortality is to-day one of the great national, social and economic problems. The future of every nation depends on its children, their physical, intellectual and moral strength.
Alan Brown, 1918[2]

Why did infant mortality emerge as 'one of the great national, social and economic problems' during the early years of the twentieth century? To answer this question, we must briefly consider the enormous changes to Canadian society wrought by the Industrial Revolution. During the second half of the nineteenth century, Canada, like most countries in the Western world, had undergone a process of industrialization. With the development of industry, commerce, and government came the growth of cities, as people moved from rural areas in search of work. Rapid urban population growth, particularly in Ontario and Quebec, outstripped available municipal services, for this growth was almost entirely unplanned and haphazard. Lacking adequate sanitation, sewage disposal systems, and clean water supplies, cities soon became centres of disease.[3] Babies died from contaminated milk supplies, and adults and children alike were victims of epidemics of smallpox, diphtheria, typhoid, tuberculosis, and other contagious diseases.[4]

For babies and small children, the picture was particularly bleak.[5] In 1901 the City of Toronto, for example, reported that 160 of every thousand babies died before reaching the age of one.[6] The situation continued to deteriorate as the first decade of this century wore on:

in 1907, 196 of every thousand babies were reported to have died, or an average of one in five.[7] Montreal claimed the highest infant mortality rate in North America, as one in three babies died before reaching its first birthday.[8] While these rates may have been somewhat inflated as a result of the under-registration of births coupled with more accurate reporting of infant deaths, the figures nonetheless suggest that an alarming number of babies were dying.[9]

The problem of infant mortality had, of course, existed throughout history. In fact, in earlier days, babies' lives were considered to be so fragile that parents often waited to name their children until they reached their first birthday, referring 'to their newborn infants as "it" or the "little stranger."'[10] The medieval practice of giving the same name to two siblings on the assumption that at least one of them would die also supports this notion of the fragility of infant life. More common still in the sixteenth, seventeenth, and eighteenth centuries was the practice of naming a newborn after a sibling who had already died.[11] The historical debate still rages as to whether the high infant mortality rate in Europe during earlier centuries meant that parents did not really *care* about their babies.[12] Historian Lawrence Stone argues that 'to preserve their mental stability, parents were obliged to limit the degree of their psychological involvement with their infant children.'[13] A number of historians of the family have even suggested that high infant mortality rates were the *result* of maternal indifference and neglect. Edward Shorter has argued that traditional mothers 'did not *care* and that is why their children vanished in the ghastly slaughter of the innocents that was traditional childrearing.'[14] In the same vein, Lloyd deMause describes 'the history of childhood' as 'a nightmare from which we have only recently begun to awaken. The further back in history one goes, the lower the level of child care, and the more likely children are to be killed, abandoned, beaten, terrorized, and sexually abused.'[15] These authors are taken to task by Stephen Wilson, who challenges their 'ethnocentric' or 'chronocentric' approach to historical subjects. In the work of many historians of the family, Wilson argues, 'the behaviour of mothers of the past is judged by the standards of today, and little attempt is made to appreciate that behaviour in its own context.' Parents' failure to attend their infants' funerals, for example, might be indicative *not* of parental indifference but rather of profound grief.[16]

Documenting parental concern is a difficult matter, particularly in an era when the vast majority of the population could neither read nor write. Little work has been done in the Canadian context, but autobiographical evidence from the nineteenth century clearly indicates both a high rate of infant death and the deep sadness mothers experienced at the loss of their children. Letitia Hargrave, the wife of an officer of the Hudson's Bay Company living in York Factory, Northwest Territories, described the devastating impact of the death of her young son in 1843, as follows: 'Altho I think of it [the child's death] constantly I will never be able to write with composure . . . Poor Hargrave [her husband] was terribly distressed, but he soon got well again. I thought I never [would].'[17] In an article based on the diaries and letters of Elizabeth Simcoe, Mary O'Brien, and Letitia Hargrave, Linda Siegel argues that 'parents displayed a great deal of affection toward their children,' and 'were deeply grieved at the loss of a child.'[18]

Mothers frequently expressed thanks to God for the 'miracle' of their babies' survival. One nineteenth-century mother made a routine note at the end of an otherwise cheerful diary entry: 'I wonder if our happy little family circle will be unbroken at the end of another year.' The same mother marked her daughter's fifth birthday with the following observation: 'Tomorrow my darling will be five years old. I thank God that he has spared her to us and such a healthy little girl as she is and has always been.'[19] Despite their best efforts, however, women like Mrs Merkeley could often do little to save their infants from disease and death.[20] For such help they would have to wait until politicians and scientists 'discovered' the problem of infant mortality.

While there is evidence to suggest that a degree of concern over infant mortality had existed within the European scientific community since at least the middle of the nineteenth century,[21] few concerted efforts were being made to overcome the problem. One British economist, writing in 1882, complained that, 'in spite of the steady appearance of articles in learned periodicals on the subject of infant death rates in large towns in Britain,' infant mortality 'remained "far too wide and vague an idea to rivet the attention of the public."'[22] This situation was to change dramatically by the opening years of the twentieth century.

There are several reasons for this shift. Until the middle of the nineteenth century, the infant mortality rate corresponded with a high general mortality rate. Plagues and disease were sorry facts of life and people faced early death with a mixture of sadness and resignation. By the latter part of the nineteenth century, rapid developments in the fields of bacteriology and immunology, spurred on by the demonstration of germ theory by Louis Pasteur in 1876, led to a decline in the general death rate throughout the Western world. Babies, however, continued to die from gastro-intestinal infections, the result of contaminated milk supplies and inadequate refrigeration, and from respiratory infections, often associated with premature birth. Thus, the infant mortality rate remained high while the general death rate declined. For the first time, perhaps, it appeared that something *could* be done about infant mortality.

The growing concern over infant mortality also reflected a changing view of the value and importance of population. In the nineteenth century, the views of Thomas Malthus concerning the dangers of excessive population held sway in international scientific and political circles alike.[23] As Alan Brown, physician-in-chief of Toronto's Hospital for Sick Children for over thirty years, noted in 1918, 'formerly, and in fact only till recent years, it was considered that the nation with the highest infant mortality rate was the most fortunate.'[24] Malthusian views were sustained by the writings of Darwin, whose observations on the survival of the fittest in the natural world were translated into the human sphere by Social Darwinists. In their view, high rates of infant death represented nature's efforts at weeding out the sick and weak. As Brown was to argue, however, many of the sickly babies survived, only to take a toll on society's resources later: 'Elimination even if selective, does not necessarily remove those calculated to prove inferior citizens. Many survive with enfeebled constitutions and weakly health, who in after years help to swell the lists of pauperism and spend their lives in squalor and misery and become a charge upon the state.' 'Infant mortality,' he concluded, 'should not be a question of the survival of the fittest, for it is our task to see that every baby is made fit.'[25] In an article which appeared the following year, Brown pointed to a shift in thinking, noting that 'the State has begun to view the individual from an economic standpoint, and to realize that money spent in various ways to keep the individual well, improve his environment and promote his development, means a corresponding decrease later in the cost of providing for defectives and delinquents.'[26]

The growing social-reform and feminist movements of the late nineteenth and early twentieth centuries were also instrumental in promoting a concern over infant mortality. Social reformers sought to foster an attitude of caring towards society's less fortunate members. Arguing that the poor and sick needed help and encouragement rather than punishment, they worked on a wide range of issues including child-welfare work and the campaigns against prostitution and drink.[27]

In many respects, child-welfare work exemplified their concerns, for babies were clearly innocents who could not be held responsible for their plight. Furthermore, babies held out special promise for the new society which social reformers believed they were building. For these men and women, children represented the hope of the future.

Infant- and child-welfare work held a special appeal for members of the women's reform movement, who saw themselves as bringing their mothering skills to bear on the public sphere. The following story, from Dr Helen MacMurchy's first report on infant mortality, submitted in 1910, illustrates the appeal that reformers made to middle- and upper-class women's maternal feelings:

In San Francisco last summer, a wealthy woman looked at her maid's baby and saw how pale and thin he was in contrast with her own chubby child. She found that the poor child was being boarded by the Associated Charities, and they could not afford to buy certified milk. She brought the matter before a College Women's Association, to which she belonged – the Association of Collegiate Alumnae. They took the matter right up, planned a campaign, issued 2,000 Coin Cards with this on one side:

'When the fog rolls in from the ocean, and the wind begins to blow,
And you pack up your belongings for the seashore or the snow;
Won't you leave behind some money for milk that's clean and pure,
For the little helpless babies of San Francisco's poor?'

The other side of the card stressed the importance of certified milk in reducing infant mortality. Through this appeal, $55.44 was raised in two days. 'What did it?' asked MacMurchy. 'The kind eyes of the wealthy mother that looked on the other baby.'[28] MacMurchy, herself a professional woman, saw nothing incongruous in the fact that the wealthy woman's maid was paid too little to provide adequate food for her own child.

Members of the women's reform movement were actively involved in a number of campaigns to improve conditions for women and children in society.[29] For many, this activism was prompted by experiences with sickness or death in their own families. Adelaide Hunter Hoodless, for example, became involved in reform activity after her young son died as a result of drinking contaminated milk. Recognizing that even middle-class women lacked adequate knowledge of the importance of proper hygiene and nutrition, Hoodless dedicated her life to the establishment of domestic-science classes in Canada in the hopes of preventing similar tragedies through the provision of scientific training for women.[30]

Through pressure from the social reform and women's movements, governments were forced to acknowledge the human dimension of the problems of infant and child welfare. Gradually, however, leaders of government and the military in both Europe and North America were realizing that infant mortality had a *political* significance as well. In Britain, the issue of infant mortality came to the fore when recruitment for the Boer War revealed the poor quality of the nation's health. As many as one-third of the possible recruits were rejected as unfit for military service.[31] Recruitment for military service in Canada during the First World War stirred up similar fears, as a substantial proportion of potential recruits had to be rejected on the basis of ill health.[32]

These health concerns were compounded by the devastating effects of the Great War. Canada sustained some 250,000 casualties, of which 60,661 were fatal.[33] With a total population of only 8,148,000,[34] this represented a significant proportion of the population lost to war. The Spanish influenza epidemic struck a further blow, as an estimated 50,000 Canadians died from the disease brought to Canada by the returning troops.[35] Leaders of the day could not escape the significance of these figures. Something had to be done about the state of the nation's health. And the place to begin was with the nation's babies. In a 1922 editorial in the *Canadian Medical Association Journal*, R.E. Wodehouse reminded medical men: 'The large percentage of defectives revealed by the late war not only in our own country, but in all others where medical inspections were made of recruits for the army awakened not only our profession but all thoughtful minds to the necessity for a more careful medical oversight of all children during their early years of growth.'[36]

Even before the devastation of the Great War, government officials throughout Europe and North America had begun to recognize the connection between poor national health and the soaring rates of infant deaths and to implement measures designed to reduce infant mortality. Although the first conference on infant mortality was not held until 1905,[37] limited reform activity had been taking place since the 1890s. In France, Dr Leon Dufour established a Goutte de Lait, a facility which provided sterilized milk for women unable to breast-feed. These milk depots, as they were known elsewhere, became a model for such services in both England and North America.

In the United States, under the direction of philanthropist Nathan Straus, milk depots were established in New York City as early as 1893. In several large urban centres, infant-welfare clinics were set up to offer help to new mothers.[38] Infant mortality was one of the first issues seized upon by the United States Children's Bureau when it was established by President Taft in 1912. Under the able leadership of Julia Lathrop, the Children's Bureau conducted studies of infant mortality and produced educational literature on prenatal and infant care. To promote its work, the bureau sponsored baby weeks across the country, and was instrumental in the declaration of 1918 as 'Children's Year' in the United States.[39]

The movement in Britain incorporated many of the experiments begun on the continent and in the United States.[40] In major centres across Britain, an array of institutions, ranging from milk depots to schools for mothers were established.[41] Despite such a range of activities, however, it appears that the most frequently established measures were of an educational nature: leaflets, lectures, consultations at clinics, and visits by 'lady health visitors.' All of these measures were designed to instruct mothers in the correct styles of 'mothercraft.'[42]

In their efforts to combat infant mortality, Canadians drew upon both European and American models. At the same time, however, Canadian officials assumed leadership roles in the field of child welfare and participated in establishing an international climate of relief.[43] One of the key Canadian contributions was the investigative work done by Dr Helen MacMurchy.[44] In 1910, William Hanna, the provincial secretary of Ontario, appointed MacMurchy, a graduate of the Faculty of Medicine at the University of Toronto (1901), former teacher, school medical inspector, and his personal friend, to investigate the problem of infant mortality.[45] The story of MacMurchy's appointment is suggestive of the ambivalence of at least one Canadian authority towards active intervention. According to a 1920 article in MacLean's, MacMurchy approached Hanna to ask if he would send a Canadian representative to a conference on infant mortality to be held at Yale University on 11 November 1909. Hanna agreed to send MacMurchy, who, upon her return, told Hanna that she would like to write a report on the subject. "'Well", said Hanna, who was really becoming quite interested himself, "you write it, and however foolish it is I suppose we'll have to publish it."'[46]

MacMurchy claimed that her report, released in 1910, represented 'the first instance in which a Government ordered a Special Report to be made' on the subject of infant mortality.[47] MacMurchy prepared three reports in all, each one fifty per cent longer than the preceding one.[48] The reports, published in 1910, 1911, and 1912, helped to shape the infant-welfare movement in Ontario, and, indeed, throughout the Western world. In her 1912 report MacMurchy noted that requests for previous editions of the report had been received from 'London, Liverpool, Edinburgh, New York, Boston, Philadelphia, Washington, Chicago, Australia and New Zealand.' In addition, the Chicago Board of Health had asked for fifty copies of MacMurchy's 1911 report to be used by its nurses in their efforts to reduce infant mortality.[49] One indicator, perhaps, of the popularity of the reports is that within one year of the release of the 1911 report it was already out of print. In the *MacLean's* article referred to above, the author reported that 'some time after [the 1910 report was released], an American doctor inquired of the Bureau of Vital Statistics, Washington, for the best information obtainable on Infant Mortality. "The best book on Infant Mortality," she was told, "has been written by a Canadian and it's a Government Report."'[50]

Like many of her contemporaries, MacMurchy offered a stern warning about the political significance of infant deaths: 'We are only now discovering that Empires and States are built up of babies. Cities are dependent for their continuance on babies. Armies are recruited only if and when we have cared for our babies.'[51] Concern over infant mortality had a eugenic dimension as well. The birth rate among native-born Canadians, and particularly middle-class Canadians, had declined steadily since the late nineteenth century. The birth rate among the immigrant population, however, remained high. Combined with the influx of immigrants during this period, this meant an overall decrease in the population of British descent. The result was that during the last decade of the nineteenth century, the number of residents in Canada who were British-born actually *decreased* while the number of European and Asian residents nearly doubled.[52] This situation appears to have caused widespread fears of what contemporary ideologues termed 'race suicide.' The following excerpt from MacMurchy's first report reveals the ethnocentrism which underlay that concern: 'EVERY YEAR NEARLY TEN THOUSAND CHILDREN IN ONTARIO, under the age of five years, go to their graves. We would think ten thousand emigrants a great addition to our population. It is a question if ten thousand emigrants from anywhere would equal in value to us these ten thousand little Canadians of Ontario, whose lives are sacrificed to our carelessness, ignorance, stupidity, and eager haste to snatch at less valuable things.'[53]

Infant mortality, then, was not merely a matter of the tragic deaths of infants. The future of the nation – the white Imperial Nation – was deemed to be at stake. MacMurchy offered a dire forecast for the country that dared to ignore this equation:

The lines are fallen unto us in pleasant places, but our goodly heritage will go to the sons of the stranger, unless we put our hands and our minds in earnest to the work of rearing an Imperial race ... The future of our Province, the future of our country, the future of our Empire, the future of our race, is signified by the same sign, and that sign is a child ... The keys that unlock the problem of Infant Mortality, are the keys of National and Imperial hope and power.[54]

Like most professionals active in the public health movement, Mac-Murchy believed fervently in the value of preventive medicine, arguing that up to eighty per cent of infant deaths could be prevented. What was required to solve 'the greatest problem of Preventive Medicine' was an all-out campaign – a war against infant mortality.[55] The battle would have to take place on several fronts, for MacMurchy acknowledged that many factors, including poverty, overcrowding, and malnutrition, contributed to the problem of infant mortality. In recognition of this fact, her reports contained a broad range of proposals, including the registration of births and deaths of infants to facilitate public-health supervision of children, pensions for breast-feeding mothers, the establishment of a bureau of infant welfare, and the employment of doctors and nurses to work in infant-welfare clinics. MacMurchy recommended the hiring of one health visitor per one thousand infants registered per year. Through the visitation program, mothers could be trained in correct procedures of infant care. The production of health-care literature and other 'printed information' would also help in this enterprise. Recognizing that infectious diseases still represented one of the major killers of infants and young children, MacMurchy argued that free diphtheria antitoxin should be provided for the poor. To prevent the spoilage and contamination of milk supplies, free ice should be provided to poor mothers during the summer months. As well, a supply of clean milk should be ensured through legislation and inspection.[56]

Both international studies and the surveys which MacMurchy herself conducted pointed to the central role that poverty played in the problem of infant mortality. 'It is a poverty question largely,' Mac-

Murchy noted. 'Everything we can do to increase efficiency and prevent poverty, will prevent infant mortality too.'[57] Rather than dealing with the question of wages, however, MacMurchy focused on the 'living conditions' of the poor, most of whom were confined to congested urban slums. In keeping with the pastoral ideology of a still largely rural society, MacMurchy argued that 'conditions in the city must be made as nearly like good country conditions as possible.' This was to be achieved through the establishment of more parkland and open spaces and of communities of workers 'on the outskirts of the city.' The poor needed 'more chances for holidays and fresh air funds,' as well as a return to 'more sympathetic neighbourliness,' an area in which MacMurchy felt the health visitor could help.[58]

Despite offering such a range of alternatives, however, in her search for solutions, MacMurchy focused almost exclusively upon mothers, arguing that 'the mother is the only one who can save the baby.'[59] One of the reasons for this emphasis lay in the special role assigned to breast-feeding. MacMurchy stated: 'One thing we know about Infant Mortality. If the baby is nursed by its mother the chances are great that it will live. If the baby is fed in any other way the chances are great that it will die.' 'Mother's milk,' she concluded, 'is the only really safe food for baby.'[60] Countless articles in medical journals of the period attested to the supposed connection between bottle-feeding and infant deaths.[61]

In an age before refrigeration, pasteurization of milk, and the sterilization of equipment used in bottle-feeding, breast-feeding undoubtedly was the safest method of infant feeding. Furthermore, in light of the dramatic increase in the availability and use of commercial baby formula during the late nineteenth and early twentieth centuries, the concerns expressed about bottle-feeding were not unwarranted.[62] The problem lay not in the encouragement of breast-feeding as such, but in the increasing tendency to focus on this solution to the exclusion of other alternatives. Women were to be taught the value of nursing and to be encouraged to set aside anything – be it work in the paid labour force or other family responsibilities – that interfered with that enterprise. MacMurchy explained: 'the way above all others to save the baby and reduce Infant Mortality, is to see that the child is being nursed by the mother, and any occupation that prevents this or makes it hard, is a direct cause of Infant Morality.' MacMurchy argued that the major reason for women's decision not to breast-feed was maternal ignorance. The woman who chose not to breast-feed 'does not know that it makes all the difference to the child. When she does know, she nurses it.' MacMurchy concluded that 'we must give her skilled medical advice' to prevent such mistakes from happening.[63]

In light of her insistence on the importance of breast-feeding, it is not surprising that MacMurchy stood opposed to mothers' working outside the home. She stated categorically that, 'where the mother works, the baby dies,' adding that 'nothing can replace maternal care.'[64] Throughout her report MacMurchy stressed the dangers of mothers' working in the labour force. She noted: 'When trade is depressed and work scarce, when wages are low, and employment intermittent, the rate of infant mortality drops. What explanation is there for that, except that the mother is at home and the baby is nursed, because good wages and easily got work do not tempt the mother to work outside her home?'[65] In such an analysis, MacMurchy and the other Canadian experts were not unique. Carol Dyhouse has documented the extent to which maternal employment – and the attendant failure of working mothers to breast-feed – were blamed for high rates of infant mortality in Britain. Dyhouse concludes that there was insufficient evidence to support this allegation. Furthermore, she cites a 1911 study by the Infants' Health Society in St Bartholemew's which demonstrated that 'the artificially-fed babies of working mothers whose wage bought a slightly better standard of living for their families showed a better rate of survival than did the breastfed babies of mothers in similar social circumstances who stayed at home.'[66] Despite evidence to the contrary, infant-welfare experts in both Britain and North America were prepared to blame maternal employment for many infant deaths.

Not surprisingly, then, nowhere in Helen MacMurchy's recommendations do we find acceptance of such solutions as child-care centres or babysitting services for working women. Those measures would only serve to encourage women to work outside the home. Nor was MacMurchy prepared to recommend changes to women's employment conditions such as shorter working hours, flexible schedules, maternity leaves, or higher wages – changes that might have enabled mothers to work in the paid labour force, thereby providing a better standard of living for their children.

Indeed, MacMurchy was firm in stressing the importance of avoiding all forms of institutional care for children: 'Institutions for infants, Creches, Day Nurseries, Infants' Homes, are not at all the best solution of the problem of Infant Mortality among the poor, deserted and unfortunate. They have been established by the best and kindest people, and with the best intentions; but when they take the baby away from the mother, they sign the baby's death warrant.'[67] While recent work has shown that the infant mortality rate in institutions such as the Toronto Infants' Home and Montreal's Hôpital de la Miséricorde were appalling,[68] these statistics alone did not rule out the possibility of temporary care such as babysitting or day-care centres for working women. For MacMurchy, and other members of the international infant-welfare movement who adhered to a philosophy of maternal responsibility, such alternatives were abhorrent. Leaders in both the private and government sectors were adamant that individual families must retain the ultimate responsibility for their children. Nothing, they argued, could take the place of the mother. In the words of Dr Saleeby, the noted British eugenicist: 'There is no State womb, there are no State breasts, there is no substitute for the beauty of individual motherhood.'[69]

The following passage, published in the *Canadian Practitioner and Review* in 1921, reflects the ambivalence many child welfare officials felt towards state intervention. Haunted, perhaps, by the spectre of communism following the Russian revolution, Helen MacMurchy warned her readers: 'Nothing will be gained by the crude methods of socialism, by taxing the middle class, the intelligent, hard-working, thoughtful, industrious people – the real strength of the nation – out of existence, and replacing them by parasites who expect everything to be done for them and do nothing for themselves or for their children.'[70] Thus, while child-welfare workers assumed an increasing degree of responsibility for the provision of educational services and resources for parents, they took great pains not to usurp the mother's role as caregiver and the father's role as breadwinner. The resulting focus on maternal education and full-time mothering was to have important implications for the social policies that affected the lives of working women.

In the first two decades of this century, and, with a renewed sense of urgency following the First World War, a number of different segments of Canadian society joined the war against infant mortality. Until 1920 voluntary efforts provided the driving force behind these efforts.[71] The National Council of Women of Canada showed an interest in the issue as early as 1895, when a paper on infant mortality was presented to its annual meeting.[72] Two years later the organization took one of the first initiatives on the question, establishing the Victorian Order of Nurses (VON) in 1897. Nurses from the VON visited new mothers in their homes, offering instruction in infant care and feeding. By 1900 the order employed thirty-two nurses, who worked in both rural and urban areas across the country.[73] In rural areas, the Women's Institutes helped to establish health services and provided a range of child-welfare services, making layettes and school lunches, and distributing health information and literature. Child-welfare work was to remain an important priority of the institutes throughout the interwar years. As Helen MacMurchy noted, 'from the Federated Women's Institutes of Canada down to the newest branch in every province the members of the Women's Institutes remain, as they have ever been, the firm and constant friends of all child welfare work. It always occupies a leading place on their programs and everything which will help the children of Canada is supported by them.'[74] In Quebec, Les Cercles des Fermières engaged in similar activities. Other women's organizations involved in child-welfare work included the Imperial Order of the Daughters of the Empire, La Féderation de St Jean Baptiste, and La Féderation des Femmes Canadienne-Française, all of which were involved in maternal and child-welfare campaigns.[75]

Recognizing the key role which a tainted milk supply could play in infant deaths, a number of voluntary organizations sought to improve the quality of milk consumed by Canadian babies. As early as 1901, the Montreal Local Council of Women joined forces with the Foundling Hospital and several local doctors to establish a pure milk depot, modeled on the Gouttes de Lait de Paris. In Toronto, the Pure Milk League, organized by James Acton, established two milk depots which provided inexpensive, certified milk. The league also distributed free milk to those who were unable to pay, organized lectures and published pamphlets on child and infant care, and offered free vaccinations against smallpox. In June 1908 the Canadian Medical Association appointed its Milk Commission, thereby providing expert medical evidence on the problem of tainted milk. The commission's report pointed out the dangers of typhoid, scarlet fever, diphtheria, diarrhea, and tuberculosis which contaminated milk presented, and encouraged the passage of public-health legislation as well as the establishment of additional milk depots.

Following the First World War, the Canadian Red Cross Society also turned its attention towards the issue of child health, assisting in 'the professional training of public health nurses,' 'giving short-term home nursing courses which included much practical material for mothers,' and teaching the importance of health to young children through an expanded program of the Junior Red Cross societies.[76] The children's programs proved to be extremely popular, and, by 1923, the Junior Red Cross Clubs had an enrolment of 75,000 Canadian children.

Corporate enterprises also became involved in the fight against infant deaths, producing promotional literature for their own products as well as pamphlets on the care of infants. The Metropolitan Life Insurance Company, an American-based organization, prepared and distributed infant-care literature to the homes of its policy holders. The company also hired public health nurses to visit policy holders. Established in Toronto in 1911, the service was primarily 'for the acutely ill, often pneumonia cases in those days, and for maternity patients.'[77]

Although a variety of voluntary and corporate organizations became involved in the issues of infant mortality and child health in Canada, the major impetus was provided by the rapidly developing public-health bureaucracy. Between 1900 and 1920, an elaborate system of institutionalized health care developed at all levels of government in Canada. As Paul Bator notes in his exhaustive study of the public health movement in Toronto: 'In the fifty years between the 1880's and the 1920's, the growth of the public health bureaucracies at the federal, provincial and municipal levels constituted one of the major changes in the role of government in Canadian society. During this period, public health work evolved from the status of a periodic preoccupation of a few doctors and lay volunteers into a permanent occupation for experts who daily monitored the health of communities.'[78] In the City of Toronto, the rate of growth was astounding, skyrocketing from one full-time employee in the 1880s to over five hundred people employed in the field of public health after the First World War.[79] Disbursements for the local Board of Health likewise increased astronomically, from $51,476.32 in 1901 to $826,657.86 in 1921.[80]

At all levels of government, departments of health were established, each with its own division of child welfare. In Toronto, the Division of Public Health Nurses was created in February 1914. The Division of Child Hygiene was formed in June of that year. In Ontario, the Bureau of Child Welfare was established in October 1916. As its supervisor, Mary Power, noted, the duties of the bureau were 'to conduct investigations in various communities in respect to infant mortality, to provide literature and advice to mothers in the care of their babies, and in a general way to be a source of help and comfort to anyone who may be in need of assistance in this important variety of life-saving.'[81] The bureau published infant-care literature and sponsored travelling child-welfare exhibits in communities throughout Ontario. In 1919 the Provincial Board of Health was transferred to the Ministry of Labour and Health and several new divisions were created, including Public Health Education, Maternal and Child Hygiene, and Public Health Nursing.

The federal government appears to have been rather slow off the mark on the issue of infant mortality. Memoranda in the files of the Ontario Provincial Board of Health indicate frustration on the part of provincial officials with the failure of the federal government to assume its share of the responsibility. As Dr McCullough, Ontario's chief medical officer of health, noted in 1919: 'Child Welfare in Canada which should also include maternal welfare to be productive of results, requires the combined force of the Dominion, the provinces and the municipalities. It is essentially a Federal problem as much as a provincial or municipal one . . . So far the Federal government has done absolutely nothing in respect to this question.'[82] Finally, in the same year, under pressure from reform elements, including the National Council of Women, the federal Department of Health was formed.[83] The Division of Child Welfare was the first division to be established. Its chief, Dr Helen MacMurchy, was appointed on 10 April 1920.

The aims of the new division included the following:

To save and preserve Maternal and Child Life.
To promote and secure Maternal and Child Welfare.
To maintain and improve the health, strength and well-being of Mothers and Children.
To make known to all the Principles of Maternal and Child Welfare, and the supreme Importance of Home life to the individual and to the Nation.[84]

These goals were to be accomplished through cooperation with all agencies, both government and voluntary, already working in the field of child welfare. Such cooperation was imperative in light of the jurisdictional overlap between the federal government, which was responsible for national health, the provinces, which were responsible for medical care, and municipalities, which were responsible for the provision of many direct services.[85] Formal links were established between various agencies involved in child-welfare work through the Dominion Council of Health, a statutory body created under the Department of Health Act to serve as a liaison between the provinces and the federal Department of Health.[86] The council met twice a year and included the federal deputy minister of health (acting as chair), the chief officer of health for each province, and up to five other members appointed by the Governor-General of Canada. On the first council, the additional members were chosen to represent 'agricultural interests,' 'trades and labour workers,' 'health education,' 'the women of Canada resident in urban districts,' and 'the women of Canada resident in rural districts.'[87]

One of the first initiatives of the Department of Health was to call a Dominion Conference on Child Welfare, held in Ottawa on 19 and 20 October 1920. At that conference, a provisional executive of the Canadian National Council of Child Welfare was formed, with the purpose of coordinating voluntary activities in child-welfare work in all the provinces.[88] At its first annual conference, the name Canadian Council on Child Welfare was adopted.[89] This organization, headed by Charlotte Whitton for most of its years, played a key role in developing child-welfare policies and child-care literature for three decades.[90] Funded by grants from the federal government and from the Canadian Life Insurance Officers' Association, the council's work paralleled and, at times, competed with the work of the federal Department of Health. Indeed, between 1933, when the Division of Child Welfare was disbanded, and 1937, when the Division of Child and Maternal Health was created, the council was solely responsible for the production and dissemination of infant- and child-care information and advice on a federal level. The council played a critical role in the creation and distribution of health information from the 1920s until 1947, when responsibility for distribution of literature was transferred to the Department of Health and Welfare.[91]

Within both the Canadian Council on Child Welfare and the new divisions of child hygiene and child welfare, experts in the field of public health were prominent. Since the formation of the Canadian Public Health Association in 1910, members of that organization had developed a keen interest in child health. By the end of the First World War, the association formed its own child-welfare division, and, under its auspices, began to intervene actively in the campaign to improve the health of the nation's children.[92] Articles on child welfare appeared in virtually every issue of the association's official journal, the *Canadian Journal of Public Health*, and members participated in a national survey of child-health activities in Canada. While membership in the association was open to anyone involved in the field of public health, positions of responsibility were reserved almost exclusively for medical doctors.

While doctors assumed key posts in the various divisions of child welfare, nurses took their place in the front lines of the war against infant mortality. A brief examination of the development of public health nursing in Ontario is illustrative of the role that nurses played. The City of Toronto hired its first public health nurse, Lilly Lindsay, in 1907. She was soon replaced by Janet Neilson, who worked primarily in chest clinics with tuberculosis patients.[93] When Dr Charles Hastings became medical health officer for the city in 1910, he expanded the role of the public health nurses. Under his directorship, nurses working at well-baby clinics and milk stations were transferred to the civic payroll. In 1913 all child-welfare work was centralized with the creation of the Division of Child Hygiene. Registration of all births, begun in 1914, enabled the department to keep track of each baby born in the city. Infant-care literature and information about well-baby clinics could then be sent to each new mother through the mail. In 1914 further expansion enabled the city to decentralize its operations, by placing the thirty-seven nurses in its employ in three district offices located in police stations at Woodbine and Hillcrest and in University Settlement House. Under the able and determined leadership of Eunice Dyke, from 1911 until her resignation in 1932, the Department of Public Health Nursing played an important role in the delivery of health-care services and information to women in Toronto. Throughout the middle decades of this century, nurses also worked in a number of areas in addition to maternal and child welfare, including school nursing, the control and prevention of tuberculosis and other communicable diseases, hospital and health service, and staff and student education.[94]

In rural Ontario, public health nurses worked with the Bureau of Child Welfare, established in 1916 under the jurisdiction of the Provincial Board of Health. The bureau sponsored child-welfare exhibits and prenatal and well-baby clinics in communities throughout the province. In the absence of other trained medical personnel, public health nurses in rural areas were often called upon to perform tasks usually restricted to doctors, including supervision at childbirth and bedside care. As Cynthia Abeele has pointed out, in the remote and rural areas of Ontario, 'mothers and children suffered from deficient health care primarily because of the poverty and isolation that kept medical services out of their reach.' She adds that 'the effectiveness of even the services that *were* presented to them were limited by professional rivalries.'[95] Despite these limitations, however, throughout the middle decades of this century, public health nurses performed a key role in the delivery of both services and information to the mothers and children in urban and rural areas of the nation.

Although infant mortality emerged during the first two decades of this century as a matter of 'Imperial importance,'[96] in practice governments in the Western world adopted few concrete measures for saving the lives of infants. Despite the public outcry concerning infant mortality, social-welfare policies and practices placed moral and physical responsibility for the deaths of babies largely in the laps of their mothers. In accepting and, in fact, reinforcing the responsibility of the individual family, especially the mother, child-welfare experts could ignore other causes of infant deaths such as poverty, inadequate housing, and malnutrition. Thus, solutions which might have proved too costly, such as the establishment of quality infant- and child-care centres, home care, and babysitting services for working mothers, and the provision of free or inexpensive food for mothers and babies were rarely attempted. Such services might have angered war-weary citizens, still adjusting to the new national income tax, implemented as a 'temporary' measure during the First World War. While little concrete aid was offered to Canadian families, massive initiatives were undertaken to ensure that mothers were adequately trained for the important responsibility of bearing and rearing children. It is to those educational initiatives that I now turn my attention.

2

Creating 'An Educational Campaign'[1]

Heaven has inspired in the mother's face something beyond this world, something which claims kindred with the skies, the angelick smile, the tender look, the waking, watchful eye, which keeps its fond vigil over her slumbering babe, these are objects which neither the pencil nor the chisel can touch, which poetry fails to exhalt, which the most eloquent tongue in vain would eulogize, and on which all Description becomes ineffective.
'Maternal Affection,' 1833[2]

The trouble is that the home today is the poorest run, most mismanaged and bungled of all human industries ... Many women running homes haven't even the fundamentals of house management and dietetics. They raise children in the average, by a rule of thumb that hasn't altered since Abraham was a child.
Canadian Home Journal, 1932[3]

These two statements, made one hundred years apart, suggest a tremendous change in attitudes towards mothers. Although not all twentieth-century advice givers were as critical or as gloomy as the *Canadian Home Journal*, the tone of that periodical was typical of the time. From the beatific, all-knowing protectress described in the first passage to the inefficient bungler of the second, mothers *appear* to have experienced a long fall from grace. Why this shift in ideology took place and how it served to support a call for a campaign of maternal education are the subjects I will consider in this chapter.

Contrary to popular opinion, the notion of a specialized maternal role, such as the idealized one presented in the quotation that opens this chapter, is a relatively recent creation. Prior to the Industrial Revolution, the home was a centre of activity, where parents and children, servants, and other members of the extended family all contributed to the survival of the family, whether it was through the family farm or a cottage industry. Women and children were active participants in the family economy and 'a woman was rarely if ever alone with nothing but the needs of a child or children to see to.'[4] Indeed, the prescriptive literature of late eighteenth- and early nineteenth-century America indicates that it was *fathers* who had 'superior intellectual and moral authority' over their children.[5] This authority was supported by the fact that fathers worked in or near the home and were therefore able to take a major role in the education and care of their children. Mothers, like other household members in this preindustrial world, were generally involved in numerous activities besides child rearing. Whether it was helping with the family trade or engaging in commodity production, women were typically far too busy to occupy themselves solely with the bearing and rearing of children.

By the end of the eighteenth century a change had begun to take place in the roles of both men and women. For the first time 'writers began to dwell on the critical importance of proper maternal care during infancy.' Articles, pamphlets, child-care manuals, and handbooks condemned the practice of wet nursing and exhorted mothers to spend increasing amounts of time with their children. At the same time, 'fathers began to recede into the background,' as many of the 'responsibilities that had earlier been assigned to fathers or to parents jointly became transferred to mothers alone.'[6] The maternal ideal had been born.

The primary reasons for this change in parental roles were the commercial and industrial revolutions, which resulted in the gradual shift of the father's workplace from the home to the factory and the marketplace. As fathers and their co-workers and helpers lost ongoing, daily contact with children, responsibility for parenting shifted to mothers. Furthermore, as the domestic system of production declined, 'women were relieved of much of their former economic role.'[7] Isolated within the home, divested of many of their responsibilities, women in the emerging middle class turned their attention increasingly to the business of rearing children.

Among the working class, women and children joined men in following their trades into the factories. Entire families worked side by side, enduring long hours and horrendous working conditions to eke out a living. Under such circumstances, there was little room for a specialized maternal role. But gradually, with the passing of legislation regulating the labour of women and children, the maternal ideal found its way into working-class families as well. Working-class men fought for a wage large enough to support their entire family, and increasing numbers of working-class women embraced the dual roles of housewife and mother.

The process of the establishment of a specialized maternal role was both slow and uneven.[8] But accompanying its emergence was an idealization of maternity as women's highest calling. Not only did women bear and suckle children, but these biological facts were translated into an ideology which dictated that mothers were specially endowed to *rear* children. Women's so-called maternal instinct, largely an elaboration of the nineteenth century, ensured that children should receive the best of care from the adult best suited to offer that care.[9] The shift in parental roles reflected a changing image of children as well, as the mid- and late nineteenth century witnessed a transition from a view of children as wild creatures in need of frequent paternal whippings to a more tender view of childhood as an age requiring the compassionate nurturing only a mother was deemed fit to provide.[10]

Women themselves often embraced this maternal image, since it afforded them a valued occupation at a time when their traditional roles had been eroded. As Celia Stendler noted in her survey of the image of motherhood in women's magazines, during the decade between 1890 and 1900, 'mothers occupied a position of importance which they have never since recovered. This was the day when Mother knew best; there was no book, no scientific authority to shake her maternal self-confidence, and she could tend her flock with the calm assurance that her "instincts" were right.'[11] The maternal role eventually served as a justification for women's political involvement, as many suffragists argued that the corrupt world of politics required the purifying hand of a mother. Exemplary of this view was the declaration by Lady Aberdeen, founder and first president of the National Council of Women of Canada, that the national council's mission was 'in one word, mothering.'[12] Nonetheless, the maternal ideal ultimately served to limit women's experience, as mothers were, for the most part, expected to remain confined within the home until their children had been safely reared.

While the development of the doctrine of separate spheres has been well documented in Britain and the United States,[13] Canadian scholarship in this area is sparse. Although a separation of the spheres of men and women took place in Canada as well, it appears that this transition occurred later in this country, as Canada remained a predominantly rural, even frontier, land throughout much of the nineteenth century. Although recent scholarship on women's work in Ontario suggests that separate spheres on Canadian farms predated the Industrial Revolution, nonetheless, farm women engaged in a wide range of tasks in addition to the bearing and rearing of children.[14] In the growing urban centres of Toronto, Montreal, and Halifax, women in the emerging middle class may have been exposed to the concept of 'woman's place' through women's magazines and novels. Nonetheless, 'thousands of others lived beyond the reach of these journals or were too busy to read them. For such women, the expansion of consumer goods had only begun to make a difference in the decades before Confederation. In British North America's predominantly agricultural, hunting, and fishing communities, the wife's reproductive and productive roles, with their sorrows and rewards, were the basic sources of her identity and gave definition to her daily life.'[15] As the authors of *Canadian Women: A History* note, 'probably relatively few British North American women were greatly affected by the new attitudes towards women's work that were developing in England and New England, where things were patently changing far more rapidly.' If women in the first half of the nineteenth century in British North America 'were not supposed to engage in productive or remunerative work, they did not know it.'[16]

British North American society could not long remain unaffected by the transformations elsewhere, however. Female immigrants from New England and England, for example, brought with them 'their belief in the ideology of "domestic" womanhood' and 'they adhered to it as best they could.'[17] Coupled with the effect of the industrial and commercial revolutions, by the latter part of the nineteenth century, as the primary responsibility for child welfare rested increasingly with women, an ideal of motherhood had emerged in Canada as well.

By the turn of the century, then, the ideal of motherhood held sway in Canada as in Europe and the United States. The British Chemists Company, in its Canadian advertising, described this ideal as follows: 'The relations of mother and child are the highest, holiest, most important in existence. The duties and responsibilities of motherhood are of most vital consideration ... To make the race beautiful, pure, strong and good, is the high and holy mission of MOTHERHOOD.'[18] Placed high on a pedestal, secure within the home, women were engaged in the important task of bearing and rearing children. Endowed with maternal instincts, women were deemed to be uniquely suited for this responsibility. Within a few decades, however, motherhood would become a task for which women required education. Maternal instincts alone would no longer be sufficient to raise the imperial race.

Contradictory as it may appear, the idealization of motherhood had set the stage for the 'mother-blaming' which would begin in the early decades of this century. For this idealization of the maternal role, based on the separate sphere of women's activity, clearly established that it was women who were responsible for their children's health and well-being. If babies were dying, it must be the result of faulty maternal care. Why were mothers to blame, rather than the inadequate medical care, the lack of proper sanitation and refrigeration, and the grinding poverty of many people's lives? Solutions to such major social problems would have been both costly and contentious. Far simpler, and far less expensive to target maternal incompetence. Mothers, after all, were responsible for caring for their children. If babies were dying, surely mothers were to blame. An Ontario government publication, *The Baby*, proclaimed: 'In 1919 in Ontario, 5,999 babies under one year of age died ... A large number of these babies died because their mothers did not know how to care for them.'[19] Furthermore, if the general health of the Canadian population was poor, as the recruitment drives during the First World War had revealed, this too could be traced to inadequate care during the early years. And finally, if mothers were dying during pregnancy or childbirth, once again they had no one to blame but themselves.[20]

The problem of maternal ignorance appeared to cross class boundaries. Writing in the *Canadian Nurse*, S.M. Carr Harris noted that 'the mother with a Master's degree may be quite as much at sea when facing a temper tantrum as the poor uneducated mother.'[21] Another nurse, working in the field of public health in Alberta, complained that 'it is appalling the amount of ignorance there is regarding these matters, even among educated people.'[22] Rich or poor, all women needed education for motherhood.

Why was the maternal instinct, with which women had been so well endowed during the early and middle years of the nineteenth century, no longer sufficient for the twentieth? Experts and social theorists offered a range of answers to this perplexing question. Eugenics represented one of the most compelling responses of the day. 'As flawed and self-serving as the science of eugenics might in hindsight appear,'

Angus McLaren notes, 'it had an enormous appeal in both Britain and North America.' Indeed, 'few scientists or doctors in early twentieth-century Canada were not drawn' to such ideas.[23] Eugenicists, like British author C.W. Saleeby, for example, felt that women's maternal instincts had been blunted by the modern age. Writing in 1911, in a chapter entitled 'The Maternal Instinct,' Saleeby made the following distinction between human and feline mothers: 'We cannot teach a cat anything about how to look after a kitten; but parallel instincts amongst ourselves, though not less numerous or potent, are not perfected, not sharp-cut. In the cat there is no need for education; in woman there is eminent need for it. Indeed it is the lack of education that is largely responsible for our large infant mortality; not that woman is inferior to the cat, but that, being not instinctive but intelligent, she requires education in motherhood.'[24] For Saleeby and other eugenicists, the demise of the maternal instinct was in part the result of women's ventures into higher education. Saleeby argued that a woman's 'whole life before she becomes a mother – nay, even before she chooses her child's father – shall centre in the education of her instincts for motherhood.'[25] Without such a program of education, women measured up poorly when compared with mothers in the animal kingdom. In the following passage, quoted approvingly in Helen MacMurchy's first report on infant mortality, Saleeby castigated women:

The mother cat not merely has a far less helpless young creature to succour, but she has a far superior inherent or instinctive equipment; she knows the best food for her kitten, she does not give it 'the same as we had ourselves' – as the human mother tells the coroner – but her own breast invariably. None of us can teach her anything as to washing the kitten, or keeping it warm. She can even play with it and so educate it, in so far as it needs education. There are mothers in all classes of the community who should be ashamed to look a tabby cat in the face.[26]

It is interesting to note that in her 1912 report, released just two years later, MacMurchy was in fact critical of what she termed the 'blame the mother' attitude that such tracts encouraged. Noting that 'the popular fashion of the day is to "come down on" the mother, to say she "does not know her business," should be ashamed to look a respectable tabby cat in the face, etc., etc., etc.,' MacMurchy countered that the average mother was 'a heroine,'[27] evidently unaware of the contradiction implicit in the fact that she herself had quoted Saleeby's entire passage on the mother cat in her 1910 report. Such contradictions were common in the work of theorists of the day who attempted to both elevate the status of motherhood and castigate individual mothers for their failure adequately to perform their duties.

Indeed, even in her first report, Helen MacMurchy evoked the argument that women could not fairly be blamed for their ignorance: 'We expect the ideal mother to know everything by instinct, without giving her any chance to learn. We might much better expect her to read by instinct, for the alphabet can always be found not far away. We teach reading, and we leave parenthood to come by chance. It does not so come, and there is great need that our people, most of whom are to be parents, should be educated with this great privilege and responsibility and power in view.'[28]

Eugenicists apparently hoped that castigations such as Saleeby's might impel women of the 'better classes' to take up the vocation of motherhood. As we have seen, the falling birth rate among middle- and upper-class women was a cause of rising concern. To stem the tide of 'race suicide,' eugenicists also sought to elevate the role of motherhood, and so make it once again an attractive option for women. Eugenicists thus resorted to both blame and an idealization of the maternal role in their efforts to increase the birth rate among the wealthier families in society.

The indictment of mothers was, in fact, widespread. Maternal ignorance and the need for educating mothers were common features in most discussions of infant mortality, and in the programs of all the voluntary and municipal associations concerned with maternity and child welfare. Whether they believed that women could fairly be blamed for their ignorance, experts agreed that mothers in the twentieth century needed training. Some authors pointed to demographic factors to account for this need. In a vocational textbook for girls written in 1919, E.M. Knox argued that mothers needed more training than women in years gone by because 'times have changed. Your mother, the chances are, was one of nine or ten, whereas you yourself may be an "only," or next to an "only." Your mother nursed her younger brothers and sisters, darned their stockings, turned her hand to everything, whereas you, if you marry, will be almost afraid to handle your children when they come.'[29]

Not only did women face child rearing virtually alone and with little former experience with siblings or other young children, but many theorists argued that mothers faced an increasingly complex job. In contrast to eugenics, with its emphasis on heredity, the emerging fields of paediatrics and psychology stressed the importance of children's early experience for their later development. Nurture, not nature, was the key. Such insights found their way into the pages of popular women's magazines, where articles on infant and child care regularly appeared. A 1928 article in *Chatelaine*, for example, castigated parents for relying on 'that bogey heredity, which is the lazy parent's excuse for his own short-comings.'[30]

The early years were seen as holding particular significance. A nurse writing in *Chatelaine* in 1929 warned: 'The first five months very often determine [the child's] health for life. How important that his mother should give him his best chance of being physically, mentally and socially fit; she alone is able to provide the best food and to a great extent, mould his character.'[31] Frances Lily Johnson noted in the first of a series of articles on child development published in the late 1920s that 'science has found that many, if not all, salient character traits are developed during the years of infancy.' To insure that parents provide the optimum environment for their children, this author urged that they 'make a scientific study of their children.'[32] With the increased emphasis on environmental influences, child rearing became an increasingly complicated job, for which 'a warm heart was simply not enough.' The maternal instinct, sufficient, perhaps, for a simpler day, had to give way to 'maternal insights.'[33] It is ironic that, while experts were prepared to recognize the impact of the environment on a child's development, they employed a very narrow definition of that concept, interpreting environment to be synonymous with the mother-child relationship rather than looking at the impact of other facets of the child's world, such as poverty, inadequate housing, and malnutrition. A broader definition would, of course, have required the provision of services rather than merely an educational campaign.

For many child-care experts, maternal instincts and 'the good old-fashioned way' had, in fact, *never* been sufficient. Writing in a 1926 volume of the *Canadian Nurse*, S.M. Carr Harris asked: 'Was it ... the parental instinct which allowed infanticide for centuries; disgraceful child labour abuses, and the haphazard child treatment we so frequently see today by not merely the ignorant but by many so-called educated parents?'[34] The Canadian Council on Child and Family Welfare's series *Post-Natal Letters* offered a similar evaluation of the 'old ways,' reminding parents that 'the thousands of unfortunate results of such a trial and error method of rearing helpless children can be seen in many of the physically and mentally warped and twisted lives we see around us.'[35] Indeed, one of the ways in which child-care experts attempted to ensure that their advice would be followed was to denigrate traditional methods of child rearing, urging parents to follow the 'modern' way. The following quotation, excerpted from a 1932 *Chatelaine* advice column entitled 'The New Mother,' exemplifies the attitude child-care experts adopted towards both traditional methods of child rearing and the older women who might proffer such advice. K. McAllister, a mother herself, wrote: 'To the young mother, dozens of well meaning friends are anxious to give advice. On this score, the best advice I know was given by my doctor: "Do not listen to old ladies." Superstitious, needless fears, half-truths have been handed down for generations by word of mouth. They are not the best source of information for modern mothers.'[36]

With the shift away from maternal instincts and the traditional methods of child rearing came a call for the instigation of special training in parenthood. While many of the articles referred to 'parental education,' it is clear from their discussion of the *content* of such programs that the intended recipients are mothers. Seldom, for example, are specific child-rearing tasks assigned to fathers. It is mothers who are expected to feed, bathe, and train the baby; and it is mothers who require training in those skills. Frequently, authors would slip between the terms 'parents' and 'mother,' often using the latter term when specific details of child care are discussed. A typical example follows. In her book *The School Nurse*, Lina Rogers explained the need for the educational services provided by public health nurses as follows: 'Far too many parents, even those well-educated, are absolutely ignorant of the simplest laws of health, and what mothers need is a knowledge of the laws of health rather than medicine for their children. The mother as well as the child should be instructed in the personal care of the body, the importance of ventilation, a proper diet, suitable clothing, amount of recreation and sleep, the irreparable damage done by tea drinking, coffee drinking, or candy and pastry eating to a young child.'[37] That shifting between 'parents' and 'mother' characterizes much of the discussion on the importance of education throughout these years.

Articles abounded in medical and popular journals conveying horror over the lack of parental training. S.M. Carr Harris in 1926 noted: 'We are in an age where training for all vocations is demanded. Our doctor, our nurse, our lawyer, our salesman, and even our barber or manicurist have had to undergo training; but our parent – surely our most important social agent – has not hitherto been required to have any training for his job. Society has demanded no standard of qualification, nor offered any systematic facilities for its attainment.'[38] Nearly ten years later, an article in the *Canadian Medical Association Journal* made a similar observation: 'In these modern days one goes to school or college to learn how to raise cows or pigs or chickens in a successful manner, but men and women plunge into parenthood, knowing nothing of baby culture, and babies just grow.'[39]

The emphasis on education continued throughout the middle years of the twentieth century. For example, R.R. Struthers, writing in the *Canadian Public Health Journal* in the 1940s, noted: 'I know of no greater undertaking in life into which the average parent moves with less forethought and preparation than the education and rearing of a child. Some means of educating our young people in the skills of parenthood must be evolved at once if we are to have an emotionally stable population.'[40] In the same vein, the introductory lecture on the importance of homemaking to a 1949 series of prenatal classes reminded those in attendance: 'Motherhood is the greatest of all jobs and yet is one for which we seldom make adequate preparation. Our schools of today are mainly concerned with preparing our young people for a means of earning a livelihood with too little emphasis given to their preparation for this great task of being good parents.' In a classic example of the interchangeable use of the terms parent and mother, the speaker shifted her attention to her real audience: 'We would not care to trust our lives to Doctors or Nurses who did their work by instinct and yet in many instances, Canada's most precious possession, her children, are entrusted to mothers who have little or no preparation for the complex job of motherhood.'[41]

Implicit in such calls for education was the recognition that many women, prior to motherhood, had held jobs in the paid labour force. By the first decades of this century, increasing numbers of single women moved into positions in the expanding clerical and service sectors. Professions, albeit primarily the 'feminized' fields of social work, nursing and teaching, were opening their doors to women. Dr Edna Guest, speaking on the 'Problems of Girlhood and Motherhood' before the Hamilton Social Hygiene Council in 1922, noted: 'Before her marriage she had a job which required training and skill, and which was well paid – but since her marriage she seemed to be messing about at a job which any girl could get with no training, no skill – and no pay.'[42] Many authors maintained that motherhood, too, was a profession, requiring specialized training and preparation. One author advised that 'every expectant mother should prepare to take up her work as seriously as she would if she were choosing a profession.'[43] E.M. Knox, author of *The Girl of the New Day*, a 1919 textbook which described professional opportunities for girls in the post-war period, left motherhood until the last, terming it 'The Queen of Them All.'[44]

In a period of increasing professionalization, it is not surprising that the argument for maternal education should be framed in such a manner. It should be noted, however, that the term profession is usually employed to denote an occupational group which has, *inter alia*, secured a degree of self-regulation, as, for example, the medical profession has obtained, through the powers vested in the College of Physicians and Surgeons. In contrast, the suggestion appeared to be that motherhood, like most of the women's 'professions,' should be regulated by experts who were not necessarily themselves members of the occupation. Mothers would be the guardians of these standards, but they were standards largely imposed upon rather than determined by the members of this fledgling 'profession.'[45]

While the idealization of the maternal role served as a rationale for the focus on mothers, another motive undoubtedly lay under the surface. In the final analysis, it was both inexpensive and convenient to blame mothers for high rates of infant mortality.[46] Thus, educating women for motherhood became the theme of much of the work in maternal and child welfare during the period 1920 to 1960. Through films, radio talks, lectures, prenatal classes, and advice clinics, and especially through the production of pamphlets and booklets at a staggering rate, child-care experts sought to teach women the skills of 'mothercraft.' In the following section of this chapter, I will discuss a range of direct methods of instruction, including lectures, classes, and home visits, before turning my attention to the indirect methods of film, radio, and advice literature.

Perhaps the single most important figures in the educational campaign were the public health nurses employed by municipal and provincial health departments across the country.[47] Staffing well-baby clinics, child-welfare displays, and milk depots, giving lectures in community centres and neighbourhood houses, and visiting new mothers in their homes, nurses carried the message of public health to the women of the nation. In rural areas, the scope of their work was enlarged to include supervision of childbirth and bedside nursing care. In urban areas, however, their work was almost entirely educational in nature.

In Toronto, public health nurses worked in three main areas: well-baby and child-health clinics, school nursing, and home visiting. In the post–Second World War period, prenatal classes were added to the roster of the public health nurse's duties. In all these spheres, education was the keynote. As Dr Charles Hastings, Toronto's medical officer of health from 1910 to 1929, noted: 'Public Health work is so intimately linked up with social work as to be practically inseparable; education is the means by which probably nine-tenths of the permanent, efficient public health work is accomplished.'[48]

Through well-baby clinics, public health nurses came into contact with thousands of new mothers and their babies. By 1923, twenty-three such clinics had been established by Toronto's Department of Public Health. The purpose of these clinics was, in the words of one public health official, to keep 'the well baby well.'[49] On her initial visit to the clinic, a mother consulted with the clinic's doctor, who encouraged women to seek medical attention from their own physicians or from the outpatient clinic at the hospital in cases of illness or distress. On subsequent visits to the clinic, mothers and babies usually saw only the public health nurse, who was responsible for the monthly weigh-ins and for offering instruction in bathing, feeding, and care.[50] Nurses were not supposed to diagnose or prescribe; rather, they provided advice and instruction, encouraging good habits through the baby shows and other competitions that they supervised.

Well-baby clinics represented an important shift from the provision of direct service to an emphasis on education and information. Efforts to reduce infant mortality in the city of Hamilton illustrate this transition. One of the first cities to provide services for pregnant women and nursing mothers, Hamilton established the Babies' Dispensary Guild in June 1911. An outgrowth of the work of the local milk commission, the guild went beyond the milk-depot model, encouraging women to bring their babies for examination by a doctor. Initially doctors prescribed a formula for each baby, and 'nurses mixed the formulas for mothers to pick up at regular intervals.'[51] That practice was both expensive and cumbersome, however, and the guild soon shifted its focus to infant-health clinics. There babies were examined and breast-feeding or certified milk recommended. Nurses provided instruction in food preparation and in various aspects of infant care.[52]

A key element of the work of public health nurses was the program of prenatal and postnatal visits.[53] Beginning in 1914 Toronto's public health nurses began receiving the daily list of birth registrations from the city clerk's office, whereby they were enabled to pay a personal visit to each new arrival. The program of post-natal visits expanded rapidly: during 1922 Toronto's nurses paid 8,974 visits to new mothers.[54] That expansion continued throughout the period under examination in this book. In 1945, for example, nurses visited an average of three hundred expectant and recently confined mothers in their homes each week. An estimated eighty-three per cent of babies born in the city that year were visited at least once by a public health nurse. 'Many are visited regularly,' the author of a brief history of Toronto's public health nurses noted, 'if need for advice as to the best methods of infant care is evident.'[55]

Home visits afforded the Department of Public Health direct access to women's homes, giving the nurses the opportunity to inspect, advise, and instruct. As a 1915 article on the department explained:

Very soon after the advent of each tiny citizen the public health nurse is on the spot taking note of its surroundings. Where the home conditions menace the baby's well-being city philanthropies are called on to adjust them. Work must be found for the father if possible, that the mother may remain with the baby; food must be found for the mother that the baby may be nourished; the house must be made weathertight and sanitary by the landlord; tuberculous members must be removed and premises fumigated. In short the home must be normalized for the baby citizen, as only in the normal home does the baby appear fairly secure of thriving.[56]

While that passage suggests that a range of initiatives would be undertaken should the home conditions appear to warrant intervention, it would appear that educational activities were once again the chief priority. Dr Grant Fleming, Toronto's deputy medical officer of health from 1921 until his death in 1943, explained the purpose of home visits as follows: 'The object of such calls is to find the home where instruction is needed. In many cases the mother is entirely ignorant and needs instruction and demonstration concerning things that we are apt to think a woman knows by intuition, such as how to bathe a baby, how to dress it, all simple if you know how, but if not a real difficulty.'[57]

In addition to offering instruction on bathing, feeding, and dressing the infant, the nurse distributed free copies of *The Care of the Infant and Young Child*, a booklet produced by the Department of Public Health. In 1923 Dr Fleming described the booklet as 'a storehouse of information for the mother,' adding that the material 'has been carefully compiled and is approved by the best authorities.' Providing such information was seen as 'the first step in the education of the young and ofttimes ignorant mother, for our system of education has left largely to chance that women be instructed in this most important duty in life they must take.'[58]

In the early years of infant- and child-welfare work, exhibits at fall fairs enabled health educators to reach many mothers, especially in rural areas. These ranged from simple displays to more elaborate productions which included a well-baby clinic, public lectures, and the distribution of health literature. In Ontario, exhibits were held at the Canadian National Exhibition in Toronto beginning in 1911. A baby clinic, featuring a weigh-in and consultation by medical attendants provided by the city's Division of Child Hygiene, was added in August 1917, and, during the course of the exhibit, several hundred mothers and their babies were examined.[59] In the following year, the exhibit toured from February to October, stopping in twenty-two different centres for stays ranging from one day to two weeks.[60] To facilitate their work in rural areas, in 1920 the Ontario Bureau of Child Welfare established the 'Child Welfare Special,' a specially equipped truck that travelled to fall fairs and baby weeks throughout the province.[61]

As infant mortality rates began to decline during the late 1910s and the 1920s, concern among public-health advocates shifted to the health of pre-school children. By 1922, the city of Toronto's twenty-one well-baby clinics had become child-health centres, offering medical inspection of children and advice for their mothers. Financial pressures during the Depression and Second World War limited the expansion of such services, but child-health clinics proved to be very popular among new mothers in the baby boom period between 1947 and 1963. In 1957, for example, forty-six per cent of the babies born in Toronto had attended a child-health centre. By 1961, Toronto could boast thirty-one child-health clinics in operation within its borders.[62]

Throughout the period under investigation, classes and lectures on infant care were a popular means of reaching new mothers. While these were often held in conjunction with a well-baby clinic, one of the more successful initiatives was a series of classes run by Toronto's Public Health Department in the Eaton's infants' wear department during the Second World War. Subjects such as the baby's bath and the care of the expectant mother were covered and public health literature was available for distribution.[63] When the federal Division of Child and Maternal Hygiene was resurrected in 1937, that division also used lectures as a way 'to educate mothers in regard to the care of children,' employing the services of the division's sociologist.[64]

During the 1940s and 1950s public health nurses turned increasingly to group teaching efforts in order to reach the growing number of new mothers in the post–Second World War period. In 1944 the Victorian Order of Nurses, the St Elizabeth Visiting Nurses' Association, and the Visiting Homemakers combined forces with the health department's nurses to introduce prenatal classes sponsored by the Welfare Council of the Community Chest. Once again, the classes proved to be very popular. By 1950 four series of prenatal classes conducted under the auspices of the Toronto Welfare Council were being held in eleven prenatal centres. A total of 920 expectant mothers attended the classes, an increase of fifty from the preceding year.[65] Prenatal classes were publicized by means of radio announcements and news items in daily and weekly papers, as well as through the display of the poster 'While You Are Waiting for Me' in infant-wear departments and baby shops.

'Little mothers' classes,' conducted in public schools, community centres, and settlement houses, provided a means of reaching both mothers and their daughters – the mothers of the future. Health educators believed that girls would be less likely to hold fixed ideas about child rearing and that this education might filter down to their mothers as girls carried their lessons home. Furthermore, compulsory public education ensured that girls would be readily accessible.[66] Voluntary organizations like the National Council of Women of Canada sponsored 'Little Mother Classes,' which were designed 'to stimulate girls to help with babies in their homes and neighbourhoods, to encourage them to direct their mothers to medical care and to prepare themselves for the eventual career of motherhood.'[67] One textbook of nursing history noted that 'the classes became so popular that other children wanted to join, and were permitted to do so if they could borrow a baby.'[68]

During the 1920s the classes in Toronto became known as Junior Health League Classes, but the content was essentially unchanged. Each girl received a total of nine lessons, which, one observer noted, 'is the sum total of all that many of them are taught to prepare them for what will be to most of them the greatest responsibility of their life work!' Students made use of the Department of Public Health's booklet, *The Care of the Infant and Young Child*, and, following the successful completion of a final examination, each girl received a certificate and a badge. To insure that their mothers could also benefit from these lessons, the girls 'are encouraged to take their notes home for discussion with their mothers and are urged to put into practice what they have learned. They come back gleefully to report that they were allowed to bathe the baby, or dress the baby, and helping mother or the neighbours with baby seems often to take on a new meaning.'[69] Enrolment in the classes increased steadily during the 1920s. In 1922, 1,800 girls enrolled in a total of eighty classes successfully completed the course.[70] In 1923, 2,515 girls were enrolled; that number had risen to 3,289 by 1925.[71] Similar classes were held in Montreal, where the Victorian Order of Nurses established the first Little Mothers' League in 1922. Each meeting opened with the recitation of their pledge: 'I desire to become a member of the Little Mothers' League, and I promise to do all in my power to help reduce infant mortality in Montreal, and to make others well and happy.'[72]

Throughout this period, a small but significant number of middle- and upper-class mothers from Toronto participated in an experiment in child study and parent education. Under the auspices of the Canadian National Committee for Mental Hygiene, and supported by funds provided by the Laura Spellman Rockefeller Memorial Foundation and the Metropolitan Life Insurance Company, two nursery schools were established in Canada in the mid-1920s.[73] The Montreal school, McGill University's Day Nursery, closed its doors in 1930, but Toronto's St George's School for Child Study (later, the Institute of Child Study, University of Toronto) thrived under the directorship of Dr William E. Blatz. Although intended primarily as a laboratory school in which psychologists could investigate and test theories of child development, directors of the St George's School soon embraced parental instruction as part of their mandate. Parent education classes, attended primarily by mothers and complete with textbooks and homework, were held for parents of children at the nursery school.[74] In a 1928 *Chatelaine* article, Frances Lily Johnson, of the Parent Education Department, described the classes as follows:

The mothers are organized in a nursery school Parent Education Group, which meets regularly to discuss the problems that arise in connection with the nursery school children. The mothers keep records which are correlated with those kept at school. In addition, each mother must belong to a general Parent

Education Group ... These are discussion groups of interested parents in which a regular course in child management and training is given by qualified leaders. Here parents can discuss their problems with other parents and with the staff, and arrive at solutions.

In light of the fact that 'a complete course in parent education require[d] three years' to complete, participation in such a regimen clearly required a major commitment on the mother's part.[75] Classes were always restricted to a very small minority of the population, as the participants were drawn from the elite of Canadian society. The St George's School also established links with Toronto's Regal Road Public School and Windy Ridge, 'the Progressive School for Children.'[76] Staff from the St George's School conducted parent-education classes at both institutions, and, through their association at Windy Ridge, 'converted a great many upper-echelon Torontonians to the values of child study and the Blatzian philosophy.'[77] Furthermore, as students completed their Master of Arts degrees at the St George's School, they carried Blatz's methods to other parts of the country. In the late 1930s, Vi Ord established the first nursery school in the Maritimes in Halifax, Nova Scotia, and Gretta Brown traveled to Winnipeg, Manitoba, to carry on Dr Blatz's work.[78] Within Toronto, Blatz's work continued to expand throughout the 1940s and 1950s. When the Institute of Child Study moved to its present location on Walmer Road in 1953, the new building housed a nursery school, as well as a school-age program ranging from kindergarten to grade three, with a total enrolment of one hundred school children and some forty-five staff.

In addition to these direct educational endeavours, child-care advisers throughout the period employed a number of indirect educational methods. Plays appear to have been a popular method of reaching an audience beyond those women who might attend a well-baby clinic or child-health centre. In 1930, for example, the Local Council of Women in Hamilton, Ontario, found an entertaining way of transmitting the message of the importance of maternal health. The council's health committee staged 'The Pageant of Motherhood' in 1930, a musical drama written by Nora-Frances Henderson. The story was 'constructed along the lines of the morality play' with 'Humanity, Progress and Science' representing the forces of good and 'Selfishness, Apathy, Ignorance and Acceptivity' taking the part of evil. The following description of the play appeared in a review in the *Canadian Public Health Journal*:

One beautiful and pathetic scene shows the spirits of little unborn children awaiting entrance to life. Time stretches out loving, welcoming arms, but the sinister figure of Human Destiny counts them over and takes many away. They are to be deprived of the gift of life. Selfishness, Apathy, Ignorance and Acceptivity flaunt themselves laughing ... The last scene shows Progress, Science and Humanity, renewing their pledges to fight for mothers. The radiant, perfect mother of the future, who shall bear her children without danger, comes before them in a vision. Time stretches out his arms to them, he tells them he will ever be with them in their long, lonely, difficult journey into the future.

The play was so popular that 'nearly 500 were turned away the first night and the theatre was packed again for the second performance.' Attesting to the success of the effort, Dr Sarah McVean noted that 'the public library and its branches ran out of text books on maternal and child care after the presentation.'[79] During the interwar years, plays were also used by Toronto's Department of Public Health to publicize the need for prenatal care.[80]

Plays were also used by a number of different organizations during the 1950s, and, once again, large numbers of people were in attendance. In 1951, for example, seven Toronto Home and School Associations and the Canadian Mental Health Association co-sponsored the staging of a play entitled 'Scattered Showers.' According to a *Chatelaine* report by Ted Allen, nine hundred mothers 'and some fathers' attended the performance. Following the play, the parents were divided into discussion groups, led by forty psychologists, psychiatrists, social workers, and teachers. The play depicted the daily lives of three very different mothers: the 'strict' mother, and her frightened son; the 'confused' mother, and her excitable son; and the 'sensible' mother, and her well-adapted son.[81]

Radio was one of the earliest forms of the new media used to convey health and baby-care information. During the 1920s, the Canadian Social Hygiene Council prepared a series of fifteen-minute radio talks which were delivered on station CKCL in Toronto. The talks addressed such issues as 'parental responsibility,' 'child hygiene,' and 'a mother's duty to the state.' Transcripts of many of the broadcasts were reprinted in the *Public Health Journal*.[82] Beginning in October 1938, the Publicity and Health Education Division of the Department of Pensions and National Health initiated a series of health broadcasts 'designed to stimulate Canada's concern for public health.' By year's end, fifty-eight radio stations were providing this service to listeners in every province of the country, carrying an average of twenty messages each month.[83] The number of stations participating in the broadcast continued to grow during the Second World War, as stations across Canada carried the program 'Here's a National Health Note.'[84] The program consisted of a daily health fact and an announcement regarding free government health publications. Local radio broadcasts encouraged women to seek the services of public health nurses for assistance with prenatal and infant care.[85]

Films were also used as an educational tool. Film number 98 of the Canadian Government Film News Service was the first of its kind in Canada. Released on 13 June 1921, the film was made 'to show some pages and pictures of the "Canadian Mother's Book,"' and may have been prepared primarily as a promotion for that publication, which had been released the previous year.[86] The film was first screened at the Regent Theatre in Ottawa and was shown at additional theatres across the country. During the Second World War, an American film, 'The Birth of a Baby,' was distributed through Famous Players Canada and was shown in sixty-seven theatres across Canada. Over half a million people saw the film during its first four months; that number had increased to three-quarters of a million people after eight months.[87] Ernest Couture, chief of the Division of Child and Maternal Hygiene, justified the use of this film as follows: 'We need this picture to seize the imagination of the public because some twenty years of intensive and constant educational efforts have failed to impress parents with the value of prenatal care.'[88]

With rapid developments in film technology during the 1940s, production of Canadian visual material began in earnest following the Second World War. The film strips 'Nine to Get Ready' and 'Introducing Baby,' accompanied by commentary on disc, were made 'for use in connection with educational activities at prenatal and well-baby clinics and elsewhere.'[89] According to a 1952 report of the federal Department of Health's Child and Maternal Health Division, the film strips were 'used widely by the public health services and by voluntary agencies.'[90] In addition to film strips, a fifty-minute film, entitled 'Mother and Her Child,' was produced, and shown across the country by provincial departments of health. The Division of Child and Maternal Hygiene published a small folder highlighting facts about the care of mothers and infants for distribution at showings.[91] The National Film Board, established in 1939, accumulated over a hundred titles related to health in its health and medical films department, many of them concerned with infant and maternal health.[92] In addition, during the 1950s the National Film Board and the Department of National Health and Welfare commissioned a series of award-winning films on child development entitled the 'Ages and Stages' series.[93]

Still, printed literature remained the most convenient and popular means of spreading the message of modern motherhood to the nation's women. Virtually every newspaper and magazine in the country could boast a column on child care, frequently penned by prominent medical personnel from the developing government health apparatus. Helen MacMurchy, for example, wrote a monthly column entitled the 'Well-Baby Centre' for the *Canadian Home Journal* during the early 1930s, and John McCullough, former chief medical officer of health for Ontario, wrote 'The Baby Clinic' for *Chatelaine* from September 1930 until his death in February 1941. McCullough was replaced by Dr Elizabeth Chant Robertson, whose column appeared in *Chatelaine* from 1941 until 1960. On occasion, articles by Dr Marion Hilliard, prominent obstetrician at Toronto's Women's College Hospital, Dr William Blatz, director of the Institute of Child Study, and Dr Alton Goldbloom, author of the popular advice manual *The Care of the Child*, appeared in the pages of *Chatelaine*. Publications and information services were also provided by church groups, women's organizations, and a range of corporate enterprises including drug manufacturers and life insurance agencies. Metropolitan Life Insurance Company produced over forty pamphlets, including *The Baby*, a thirty-two page pamphlet 'prepared by experts,' and *Information for Expectant Mothers*. These publications were promoted in the pages of *Chatelaine* and other women's magazines.[94] Life insurance groups also contributed to the Canadian Council on Child and Family Welfare to assist them in the production of their literature. Advertisements for an astounding range of products including Eagle Brand Condensed Milk, Sidway Baby Carriages, Vicks VapoRub, and Mennen Borated Baby Talcum advised mothers to write for free booklets on the care of babies. Many companies offered free samples in addition to printed literature and, of course, all made claims about the amazing benefits their products could bring. Some included testimonials from mothers such as Mrs W.J.P., who wrote, 'I started using Eagle Brand for my five months old baby two months ago. Now she wakes up laughing and cooing and is more than satisfied.' Mrs W.J.P.'s baby also 'won third prize at a recent baby show' and the proud mother was certain that 'Eagle brand helped her to win.'[95]

Despite such initiatives from the private sector, however, the vast majority of the publications distributed during these decades were produced under the auspices of the various health departments of the federal, provincial, and municipal governments. The initial publication produced by the federal government's Division of Child Welfare was *The Canadian Mother's Book*. Received from the printer on 3 March 1921, it reached a distribution figure of 150,000 by the end of its first year. A publication that began at some fifty pages and eventually expanded to over two hundred pages, *The Canadian Mother's Book* went into six editions, and approximately 800,000 copies had been distributed to mothers across Canada by the time the division was disbanded in 1933. The most popular of all the federal government's publications, *The Canadian Mother's Book* was replaced by *The Canadian Mother and Child*, which first appeared in 1940 and is currently in its fifth edition.[96] Both books were well received by the medical profession. The *Canadian Medical Association Journal*, for example, offered a highly favourable review of the 1927 Diamond Jubilee edition of *The Canadian Mother's Book*, terming it a 'very practical volume, clearly written, and contain[ing] all the information which the expectant mother should know in reference to herself and her baby.' The reviewer continued: 'We congratulate the Government of Canada on its publication, and we can strongly recommend the book to every family in our Dominion.'[97]

In addition to *The Canadian Mother's Book*, the Division of Child Welfare produced a series of booklets which soon became known to the general public and government alike as the 'Little Blue Books,' a term first used by mothers in their letters to the Division of Child Welfare.[98] The Little Blue Books included the pamphlets *How to Take Care of the Baby*, *How to Take Care of the Mother*, *How to Take Care of the Children*, and *How to Take Care of the Father and the Family* in its 'Mother's Series' and a range of other information in its 'Home' and 'Household' series. By the end of its first full year of existence, the Division of Child Welfare had distributed a total of 365,503 copies of their advice publications.[99] These astounding figures were to continue throughout the interwar years. While the distribution figures were lower for *The Canadian Mother and Child*, the demand remained constant. For example, 30,000 copies of the first French edition were produced in July 1941 and the entire run had been exhausted within the month. A run of 90,000 copies of the first English edition lasted less than eleven months, and 38,000 copies of the second edition were sent out in less than four months.[100] In his 1943–4 report, Dr Ernest Couture noted that since 1940 over

470,000 copies of *The Canadian Mother and Child* in both French and English had been distributed 'upon request' and that the demand was 'ever-increasing.'[101] By the early 1950s, an average of 10,000 copies of *The Canadian Mother and Child* were being distributed to mothers each month.[102] In 1950 the Mental Health Division of the Department of Health and Welfare produced *Up the Years from One to Six*, a publication dealing with preschoolers; once again, demand for that publication greatly exceeded the number printed.[103] During the 1950s that division also produced a series of 'Child Training Pamphlets' on topics such as jealousy, sleeping habits, play and playmates, and the only child. Until 1955 all federal maternal and child-care publications were distributed free of charge upon request. In that year, the division began to charge for some copies of *The Canadian Mother and Child*.[104]

The federal Department of Health's Division of Child Welfare (later Child and Maternal Health Division) was only one of several branches of government producing advice literature during this period. Ontario's Provincial Board of Health issued its first publication on child welfare, *A Little Talk about the Baby*, in 1912.[105] This was soon replaced by the province's most popular publication, *The Baby*, the first edition of which appeared in March 1917. Within two years, nearly 25,000 copies of that pamphlet had been distributed to mothers across the province.[106] *The Baby* remained popular with mothers and medical practitioners alike, receiving the following review in the *Canadian Public Health Journal* in 1933: 'This book, with its bright cover and easily read contents, is a welcome relief from the usual government blue book publication. It is scientifically accurate and practical and contains a fund of information for expectant and young mothers.'[107] By 1943, when the final edition appeared, the booklet was seventy-two pages long. *The Baby* was replaced by another Ontario Department of Health pamphlet on prenatal and infant care, *The Early Years*, which was first published in 1954.

Municipal governments also produced advice literature for mothers within their jurisdiction. The initial publication of the Division of Public Health Nursing of Toronto's Department of Public Health was *Pre-Natal Care – Advice to the Expectant Mother*, which first appeared in 1922. The material was later expanded into two pamphlets termed 'The Red Books' because of their covers. The second of these, *The Care of the Infant and Young Child*, had been reprinted seventeen times by 1931.[108] Like the other advice literature of the period, these pamphlets were available at no cost, and could be obtained at well-baby clinics or from the visiting public health nurse. The Department of Public Health has continued to produce and distribute literature on prenatal and infant care up to the present day.[109]

A major source of advice pamphlets during the interwar years was the Canadian Council on Child and Family Welfare (CCCFW).[110] Established in 1920, the council operated under the powerful directorship of Charlotte Whitton until her reluctant retirement in 1941.[111] Initially a partner of the Division of Child Welfare, the CCCFW replaced the division upon MacMurchy's enforced retirement in 1933. The council assumed sole responsibility for the distribution of federal child and maternal health publications between 1933 and 1937, and continued producing and distributing health information until 1947, when the responsibilities of the Division on Maternal and Child Hygiene were transferred to the Department of National Health and Welfare.[112] The CCCFW produced several sets of letters addressed to mothers, including the *Prenatal Letters*, which appeared in March 1926, the *Post-Natal Letters* in August 1930, the *Pre-School Letters* in March 1934, and the School Age Letters in June 1938. The council sent a set of letters to individual homes upon request, and provided provincial health departments with bulk shipments for distribution through their own channels. In addition, the council produced a series of habit-training folders in cooperation with the Mental Hygiene Institute of Montreal. The council also produced a poster and rhyme booklet series, and a publication called *Child and Family Welfare News*. Finally, the CCCFW cooperated in the distribution of booklets on behalf of commercial organizations, including *Travels of a Rolled Oat* and *Around the World with Hob* for Quaker Oats[113] and *The Children's Booklet: Selected Poems and Adapted Nursery Rhymes* for the National Dairy Council.[114]

Commercial child-care manuals, both hardcover and softcover, represent the final significant source of child-care information available to Canadian mothers. Prominent medical men like Dr Alan Brown and Dr Frederick Tisdall of Toronto's Hospital for Sick Children and Dr Alton Goldbloom of Montreal's Children's Memorial Hospital wrote health-care manuals designed to supplement the advice available to women from their private physicians.[115] The manuals received highly favourable reviews in the medical journals of the day. A 1924 review of *The Normal Child*, for example, suggested that 'it should find a place in every Canadian home where there are children.' Noting that many child-care books sought to 'usurp the place of the family physician by emphasizing too strongly the treatment of disease,' the reviewer reassured his readers that Brown's book was safe on that score, since it contained little information on diseases.[116] A later edition of the *Canadian Medical Association Journal* praised Goldbloom's book, stating that the journal could 'strongly recommend it to physicians as one in every way suitable to place in the hands of young mothers and nurses who desire general advice on the management of growing children.'[117]

Regarding the impact of hardcover manuals, Norah Lewis has argued that 'although many books were recommended to parents, there is little evidence they were extensively used. Although the books may have been overly expensive for many parents, it is more likely that parents were looking for a more pragmatic type of manual on child care. The publications provided by the various health agencies were not only free, but also better suited to parents' needs.'[118] The volume of sales of these manuals and the number of editions which appeared would seem to belie such an interpretation. Goldbloom noted that his own book 'went through five editions in English, was translated into French and went through three French editions.'[119] Alan Brown's book enjoyed similar success. It is probable, however, that distribution of hardcover manuals *was* limited to middle-class mothers who could afford the two- or three-dollar investment.[120]

Following the Second World War, mass-market paperbacks transformed the child-care manual scene. By far the most popular of these was, and continues to be, *The Common Sense Book of Baby and Child Care* by Dr Benjamin Spock, a book which has sold over 30,000,000 copies since its initial appearance in 1946. Although exact sales figures are not available, the book has enjoyed significant distribution and success in Canada. For example, the initial test marketing of *The Pocket Book of Baby and Child Care* sold 3,000 copies in Canada within six weeks. Encouraged by these sales, the publisher, Pocket Books, proposed allotting 100,000 of the next run for sales in Canada.[121] Dr Goldbloom attributed the demise of his own book to the appearance of 'paper editions that sold for thirty-five cents [which] put an end, not only to my book, but to any others in hard covers that sold for two and three dollars.'[122]

Child-care publications were widely promoted throughout the interwar and post-war period. Copies of manuals were frequently mailed to editors of local papers with a request that the publication be reviewed and promoted in the newspaper.[123] *Chatelaine* carried advertisements for the publications of the CCCFW with its child-care columns, and articles often advised mothers to write for free publications. Many agencies, including the National Council of Women of Canada, the Federated Women's Institutes, and the United Farm Women of Ontario, cooperated in the distribution of literature. Women's organizations took a particular interest in assisting in the distribution of information on maternal health.[124] As well, infant- and child-care literature was distributed at fall fairs, and by public health nurses during the course of their work in well-baby clinics, child-welfare displays, and home visits.

Although new standards of child care were established and promoted in the advice manuals of the day, women were not passive 'victims' in this process that Veronica Strong-Boag has termed an 'assault by childcare experts upon women's competence.'[125] On the contrary, the historical evidence indicates that women actively sought assistance with the often difficult tasks of child rearing. In light of the breakdown of traditional support networks and the staggering rates of infant and child death, it is not surprising that women sought help. What they received, however, was rarely direct aid of any kind. Instead they received advice and information, as child-care experts adopted an almost exclusively educational approach. The question we must ask, then, is, what were mothers being taught? In the chapters that follow, I will address that question, focusing first on the issue of the medicalization of motherhood.

3

Medicalizing Motherhood: Pregnancy and Childbirth

This is not some strange thing which is going to happen to you. It is the right, natural and healthy thing for you, just as it was for your own mother when you were born. Too sacred to be spoken, the dearest wish of a true woman is to be a mother.
Helen MacMurchy, 1923[1]

As soon as I was visibly and clearly pregnant, I felt, for the first time in my adolescent and adult life, not-guilty. The atmosphere of approval in which I was bathed – even by strangers on the street, it seemed – was like an aura I carried with me, in which doubts, fears, misgivings, met with absolute denial. *This is what women have always done.*
Adrienne Rich, 1976[2]

Since time immemorial, women have been bearing children. As Adrienne Rich observes, pregnancy represents to a great extent the quintessential female state. Nonetheless, over the course of this century, pregnancy has become a site of increasing medical intervention, as doctors, nurses, and public-health officials have attempted to institute a regimen of routine prenatal care. Birth has also become an increasingly medicalized procedure, taking place almost without exception in hospital. In this chapter I will examine the ways in which the supremely female domains of pregnancy and birth have been transformed into scientific events, requiring specialized medical supervision.

By the 1920s the infant mortality rate in Canada had begun to decline.[3] The reasons remain hotly contested, but the decline was likely the result of a combination of factors including improvements in sanitation, refrigeration, and the care and handling of milk, as well as the increased medical supervision of infants and children, a rising standard of living, and changes in the gathering and recording of statistics.[4] While the rate of infant deaths declined, however, experts 'discovered' that the rate of maternal mortality in Canada remained staggeringly high, especially when compared with most other modern industrial countries.[5] Thus, medical personnel, officials in the newly formed health bureaucracies, and activists in the infant-welfare movement turned their attention increasingly to the issue of maternal health.

Like infant mortality, maternal mortality was an all-too-familiar fact of life for many Canadian families. As early as the 1890s, organized women's groups had begun to work towards a solution to what they perceived to be the joint problems of infant and maternal deaths. Through their efforts, the Victorian Order of Nurses was established in 1897, an organization that reflected a concern on the part of the National Council of Women of Canada for the fate of women in remote areas of Canada who were often forced to give birth without benefit of medical attention. Their efforts were hampered, however, by class and professional conflicts, and did nothing to provide much-needed midwives to the women of outlying areas.[6] These initiatives remained scattered until the 1920s, when the issue was finally placed on the agendas of various levels of government.

At the first meeting of the Dominion Council of Health in October 1919, Helen Reid, child-welfare representative on the council, asked the newly formed Department of Health to provide information on a number of topics including 'prenatal care, infant feeding and hospital and home treatment of maternity cases.'[7] In response to this and other requests for information, Helen MacMurchy, chief of the department's Division of Child Welfare, conducted investigations and presented her report to the Dominion Council of Health in June 1923.[8] A summary of her findings was also presented at the Canadian Medical Association's conference on medical services in Canada in December 1924, and at that time the Canadian Medical Association commissioned MacMurchy to conduct a more comprehensive study of the problem of maternal mortality. With the aid of some sixty members of the medical profession, and the approval of the deputy minister of health, members of the Dominion Council of Health, and provincial health authorities, MacMurchy designed the necessary research tools. Letters were sent to every doctor in Canada, then some 8,000 in number, 'asking for advice and help in the Enquiry.'[9] The 641 'letters of advice' MacMurchy received were one of the major resources upon which she drew in drafting her report, *Maternal Mortality*.[10] Special gender-specific editions for men and women were also prepared, written in language deemed to be more accessible to the lay person.[11] As with the issue of infant mortality, Helen MacMurchy's report effectively set the terms for much of the discussion of maternal mortality for the coming decades.[12]

The results of MacMurchy's study were startling. Of a total of 237,199 live births during the year under investigation, 1,532 maternal deaths were recorded, for a national maternal mortality rate of 6.4 maternal deaths per 1,000 live births, a rate higher than in any of the three previous years.[13] When compared with the other leading causes of death of women of childbearing age, maternal deaths ranked higher than any other single cause except tuberculosis. In a chart comparing Canada's maternal mortality rate with that of seventeen other Western industrialized countries, MacMurchy placed Canada fourteenth; she noted that Canada's 1922 rate was forty-five per cent higher than England's.[14]

The significance of these figures lay, to a large extent, in the links that the report established between infant and maternal mortality. Babies whose mothers died in childbirth stood a much greater chance of dying in infancy. MacMurchy cited Robert Morse Woodbury of the United States Children's Bureau as follows: 'Of the children whose mothers die within a year after the birth, the infant mortality is 450 per 1,000 living births. If the mother dies from one month to one year after the birth, the infant mortality is 367 per 1,000. If the mother dies within a month after the birth, infant mortality is 607 per 1,000.'[15] In Canada, 'the number of children left motherless was 4,305, an average of 4.5 children to each mother.'[16] When the 768 newborns who survived their mothers' deaths were added to that total, it meant that 5,073 children were left motherless between 1 July 1925 and 1 July 1926. In MacMurchy's view, many of those children could not be expected to survive.

Many observers outside of the Department of Health agreed with MacMurchy's assessment. Responding to the report in 1928 in the newly established women's magazine *Chatelaine*, Bertha Hall, assistant superintendent of the Victorian Order of Nurses, advised: 'If we are to further reduce our infant mortality rate, we must give the mother better care – "We must make Canada safe for the mother and she will make Canada safe for the baby."'[17]

There were other links between infant and maternal mortality as well. Improvements in sanitation and the quality of milk during the first two decades of this century had caused a decrease in the number of infant deaths due to gastrointestinal causes, thereby making prematurity and respiratory infections the chief causes of infant mortality. In light of the fact that respiratory infections were frequently associated with premature birth, itself often the result of maternal health factors, both of these conditions could, in fact, be linked to poor maternal health and inadequate prenatal care.

The report identified a number of causes of maternal deaths, chief among them puerperal septicaemia or sepsis (the cause of 418 deaths), haemorrhage (357 deaths), and toxaemia (344 deaths).[18] Poverty, and the attendant variables of overwork, malnutrition, and fatigue, were also cited as factors in a significant number of deaths. MacMurchy stated: 'In 68 cases the doctor stated that the patient was very poor. Poverty as a cause of maternal mortality was mentioned 24 times in letters of advice. In the above cases it is evident that, in the opinion of the physician, the mother's life might have been saved if she had not been so poor, destitute and uncared-for.'[19] Despite this connection, MacMurchy was unprepared to give *serious* consideration to socioeconomic causes; instead, she focused on strictly medical causes of maternal mortality. Of these, puerperal septicaemia accounted for the largest number of maternal deaths. Surmising that some of the 'unreturned histories' were probably due to sepsis (infection), MacMurchy concluded that sepsis was responsible for about thirty-three per cent of maternal deaths.[20] Sepsis was closely related to a number of other factors, including the use of forceps, Caesarean section, and other medical interventions during labour and delivery. In her study of maternal mortality in Ontario during the interwar years, Lesley Biggs has argued that 'prominent members of the profession identified meddlesome midwifery as the primary cause of sepsis,'[21] a term which referred to excessive intervention on the part of the birth attendant, whether it be a doctor or a female midwife. MacMurchy herself noted that 'fifty-six letters of advice mention hurry on the part of the physician as a cause of the use of forceps,' ending this section with the observation that '[it] is well known that traumatism from the use of forceps increases the danger of sepsis.'[22] Despite those comments, however, MacMurchy was not prepared to conclude that physicians' haste might have been at least partially to blame for the high rates of maternal mortality in Canada.

MacMurchy's report also included extracts from articles in medical journals which condemned doctors for their failure to combat maternal mortality. Writing in the journal, *Preventive Medicine and Obstetrics*, Dr W.G. Cosbie noted:

It appears ... that the defects in our present method of practising obstetrics are many and that improvement in the practice of obstetrics by the general profession has not kept pace with the progress in surgery and medicine ... At the present time there is a widespread feeling that this is largely due to the fact that the profession as a whole has been slow to adopt the routine study of the pregnant woman from the onset of her pregnancy ... Our failure to successfully combat the problem of maternal mortality and morbidity should weight [sic] heavily on our professional conscience.[23]

Although both MacMurchy and the medical experts she cited found evidence to suggest that physicians were at least partly responsible for high rates of maternal mortality, in the final analysis both Mac-Murchy and the profession chose instead to blame 'the problem on the ignorance of the mothers for not obtaining adequate prenatal care.'[24]

Maternal Mortality revealed that of the 1,532 women who died, fully 1,302 had received *no* prenatal care. Of the 230 women who had received prenatal care, it was reported that in forty cases 'the pre-natal care did not avail because the mother did not follow instructions, or because she came to see the doctor only once or twice at the beginning of the pregnancy and did not return.' While no direct causal connection could be established between the lack of prenatal care and maternal deaths, MacMurchy was fully prepared to infer such a correlation. In a chart detailing the causes and possible means of prevention of maternal deaths, MacMurchy included these 1,342 women as lives 'Lost Partly Because There Was No Pre-Natal Care.' In the opposite column, under the heading 'Can Be Saved By,' MacMurchy claimed these cases 'Can Almost Always Be Saved By Pre-Natal Care.' Ignoring the overwhelming evidence that both sepsis and poverty were major factors in maternal deaths, MacMurchy determined that the most effective solution to the joint problems of maternal and infant mortality would be to encourage women to obtain early and sustained prenatal care. As she stated unequivocally, 'pre-natal care safeguards the life of mother and child.'[25]

MacMurchy's report attributed the extremely low rates of prenatal care to two distinct factors: the failure of women to seek out prenatal care and the failure of the medical profession to take the provision of prenatal care seriously. Letters from both physicians and women's groups documented the nonchalant attitude many doctors adopted towards their maternity patients. MacMurchy herself employed a critical tone: 'Many doctors and nurses say they believe in pre-natal care, but their actions speak louder than their words and it is well known that some mothers who have been persuaded, often with difficulty, to consult a doctor for pre-natal care have been dismissed by the doctor without any directions about examination of the urine, and without any arrangement to see her again even for the estimation of blood pressure and pelvic measurements.' Elsewhere in her report, Mac-Murchy noted that 'nine times, in letters of advice, these words are repeated, almost word for word: "Doctors do not take these cases seriously enough."'[26] Articles in contemporary medical journals echoed this observation. In a 1924 article in the *Canadian Medical Association Journal*, Joseph Nathanson argued that most physicians placed too little value on prenatal care, noting that for this reason 'the average patient is given too little prenatal care.'[27]

The key recommendation to emerge in MacMurchy's report was the importance of regular medical care during pregnancy and of hospitalization at childbirth. Doctors were urged to place a higher priority on obstetrical care and to observe aseptic conditions at childbirth. For their part, women were encouraged to put themselves under the care of a doctor who would supervise the pregnancy and officiate at the birth of the baby.[28]

To convince women of the importance of prenatal care and of hospitalization for childbirth, reformers launched an educational campaign that closely paralleled the campaign against infant mortality. Women's groups, long anxious to see action on the issue of maternal mortality, embraced the solution of prenatal care, establishing or supporting local maternal-welfare committees, and attempting to link the celebration of Mother's Day with efforts to improve maternal care. Doctors and government officials also took up the cause of prenatal care, producing reams of literature detailing the proper conduct of pregnant women. Prenatal care effectively represented another aspect of maternal education, as experts set out to teach women the rules for ensuring a successful pregnancy and birth.

In an age when most women routinely present themselves for monthly and eventually biweekly and weekly medical check-ups during pregnancy, it is difficult to recognize that the provision of medical care for pregnant women is a very recent development in human history. One reason for the lack of medical supervision may have been the absence of any reliable method for the diagnosis of pregnancy. Prior to the development of laboratory tests in the 1920s, doctors were forced to rely largely on women's reported symptoms to enable them to make even a probable diagnosis of pregnancy. Victorian attitudes of female delicacy and propriety would likely have inhibited women from reporting such symptoms, even to a trusted physician.

Throughout the Victorian period, pregnancy was widely regarded as a private, almost secret matter. Such attitudes persisted until well into the twentieth century and represented one of the major stumbling blocks to the establishment of prenatal care. As Mrs A.M. Plumptre of the National Council of Women noted in 1928: 'pregnancy – especially in Anglo-Saxon communities – is wont to be regarded as a condition to be concealed – either as a sacred or a guilty secret – as long as possible.'[29] Articles in medical and nursing journals during the 1920s and 1930s decried the fact that 'the expectant mother hesitates to talk to others about her condition and absolutely revolts at the idea of attending a prenatal clinic where she may meet other women she knows.'[30]

The image of pregnancy as a 'natural' phenomenon may also have served to delay the implementation of prenatal care. While pregnancy itself was not a disease, it nonetheless caused pregnant women to suffer from a number of unpleasant symptoms, and it was to the relief of these symptoms that the authors of the growing body of maternal and obstetrical literature in the nineteenth century turned their attention. Women were advised on the importance of diet, fresh air, exercise, and rest, and the avoidance of excessive passions, entertainment, or 'conjugal enjoyments.'[31] These recommendations were largely for the woman's comfort, rather than for the well-being of the fetus. In that regard, the authors of advice literature and members of the medical profession adopted an attitude that amounted to letting nature take its course. Nineteenth-century faith in the naturalness of pregnancy underscored a belief that nature would ensure that all went well. Maternal and infant deaths were viewed as unfortunate but unavoidable, part of God's will and His mysterious ways.

A shift from this 'natural,' almost fatalistic approach to a more 'scientific' one could not occur before the recognition of the relationship between maternal care during pregnancy and the survival and future health of the new baby. The following extract from the 1924 edition of the Ontario government publication *The Baby* illustrates the radical shift that was required before prenatal care could become a medical priority: 'There is little doubt that the most critical period in one's life is the first ten months – the nine months before birth and the first month afterward – and that the care which is given during these months influences one's physical state, for good or ill, throughout all the rest of life.'[32]

While the concept of the need for routine medical supervision of pregnancy is decidedly a twentieth-century one, many of the earlier ideas about pregnancy remained in force. Throughout the advice literature, pregnancy continued to be portrayed as a natural phenomenon. Helen MacMurchy asserted that 'we can never teach too often that pregnancy is not a disease. It is a right and natural condition. All down through the ages that condition has fulfilled the highest hopes of humanity.'[33] This emphasis persisted in the 1940s, as Ernest Couture, MacMurchy's successor as director of the Division of Child and Maternal Health and author of *The Canadian Mother and Child*, maintained that pregnancy should be viewed as 'a perfectly normal physiological function, and not as an abnormal state or as a sickness.'[34]

Although pregnancy was deemed to be a natural condition, it nonetheless required certain changes in a woman's lifestyle. A 1927 Toronto publication explained: 'The woman who habitually carries out the simple practices of healthy living and is in good physical condition, needs to make little alteration in the routine of her daily life. She must not consider herself an invalid, but the physical changes that take place in her, together with the demands made upon her by the baby in the nine months before he is born, make certain adjustments of her health habits necessary. These adjustments we call the hygiene of pregnancy.'[35] One of the most inventive explanations for the necessity of these adjustments appeared in that publication. Taking up the question of why women experience such discomfort as the result of a supposedly natural process, the author responded: 'This is for the most part due to the fact that as a result of our modern methods of living, having departed so far from nature and nature's laws, we have developed such sensitive nerves that we cannot quickly accommodate ourselves to sudden changes.'[36] To cope with these discomforts, then, women were required to alter their 'modern' ways of living. Many of these adjustments concerned the importance of rest and sleep. Expectant mothers were urged to sleep from eight to ten hours per night and to rest for one to two hours during the day. Helen MacMurchy advised the pregnant woman to 'take off your clothes, put on your nightdress and lie down two hours every afternoon.'[37]

While women were supposed to take a daily nap, they were also reminded that they needed 'exercise and fresh air as much as ever.' Not surprisingly, perhaps, housework was said to provide just the right kind of exercise. MacMurchy noted: 'Most of us Canadians do our own housework, and you will be able to keep on with this. It is really the best kind of work for you.'[38] Only certain types of housework, however, were suitable. 'Do not lift anything heavy nor do the washing, except a few little things,' Helen MacMurchy admonished. 'Don't let me see you stretching up to hang out the clothes on the line. Somebody else must do that.'[39] MacMurchy did not suggest upon whom the mother might rely to perform such chores.

Work outside the home received sporadic attention in the publications. The final edition of The Canadian Mother's Book (1932) told mothers, 'If possible, do not work outside your own home for the last two or three months before the baby comes.'[40] The replacement volume, The Canadian Mother and Child, contained no reference to work outside the home, at least in the 1940 edition. That omission was reversed, however, in the 1953 revision, which advised the mother that she would need more rest, particularly if she were working 'outside the home as well as inside it.' This edition continued: 'If you work outside the home, there is no reason to stop during the first six or seven months, provided the work does not involve heavy lifting, pulling or pushing. You will, however, have to make some arrangements for your housework so that you can get extra rest at home.'[41]

Worry was one of the most frequently mentioned problems of pregnancy. Helen MacMurchy exhorted women to 'cheer up. We are all standing by you.'[42] Similar advice was offered in the first edition of The Canadian Mother and Child: 'Take cheerfulness as your motto for the coming months. Cheerfulness will work wonders for you, your baby, and your home. Keep in mind the overflowing happiness that a delightful, lively, rosy-cheeked baby will bring to you in a few months.'[43] In the event that a simple command to cheer up was insufficient, women were threatened with the dangers which worry presented to their home and family. Couture warned: 'Worry and anxiety may rob you of the happy anticipation to which you have a right, and may even affect your attitude to your family and to the child itself.'[44]

Sexual intercourse during pregnancy was a subject dealt with in veiled terms in Helen MacMurchy's pamphlets. Advising expectant mothers to 'sleep alone if possible,' she suggested: 'You will be well, but you will likely feel disinclined for exertion during the last three months. That is a good hint from nature to be still more careful.'[45] The 1940 edition of The Canadian Mother and Child was less restrictive regarding 'marital relations,' reassuring the expectant mother that 'no radical changes' were necessary 'unless there has been a previous miscarriage or unless the doctor has given contrary instructions.' In the final six weeks of pregnancy, however, the woman was reminded that it was her 'duty to abstain completely' to avoid the risk of infection.[46] A similar, though less strongly worded prohibition appeared in the 1953 edition.[47]

A number of activities were recommended to keep pregnant women busy and free from worry. The first edition of *The Canadian Mother and Child* suggested that the expectant mother keep her mind 'busy by reading light literature.' She was advised to avoid excessive reading, however, as this might keep her from getting her necessary exercise. Medical books were to be avoided, 'as such reading is easily subject to misinterpretation, and may cause undue worry over minor symptoms.' Radio and the movies were considered to be 'pleasant diversions,' but women were warned that 'there is danger if some restrictions are not imposed. Real harm may be done to the nervous system by the radio which is played too loudly and too continuously.' 'Prolonged and closely repeated sessions at the movies' were also deemed to hold some risk, 'particularly if the picture is of such a nature as to upset the emotions.'[48]

Shopping, that stereotypical female pastime, also came under fire in *The Canadian Mother and Child*. Noting that 'nothing is so tiring as going about crowded stores,' Couture commanded the expectant mother to 'forgo the pleasure of jostling at the bargain counter.' Sports events were also prohibited 'because of the excitement, and also at times on account of the prolonged exposure to cold.'[49] Those restrictions were omitted from the 1953 version, which generally adopted a less restrictive approach to the rules of prenatal care.[50]

The father had a special role to play in ensuring that his wife received the proper care during her pregnancy. A 1922 pamphlet reminded men that 'the father's responsibility does not end with conception, for the birth of a healthy baby depends upon the father as well as the mother.'[51] The father's role centred primarily on two themes: money and worry. Since most authors assumed that the father was the breadwinner, they urged him to spend the necessary money on prenatal care. In her special pamphlet for men, Helen MacMurchy appealed to the father-to-be's business sense, urging him to 'tell the Doctor you want your wife to have the best Pre-Natal Care.'[52] In the same vein, the first edition of *The Canadian Mother and Child* tried to disabuse men of the idea that regular medical care was a 'luxury rather than a necessity.'[53]

Fathers were also expected to cheer up their wives during the difficult months of pregnancy. MacMurchy assured her male readers that 'you will be able to please her when none of the rest of us can.' Warning the unsuspecting husband that his wife might be 'rather unreasonable and cross and hard to please,' MacMurchy explained that 'it is part of her condition.'[54] The first edition of *The Canadian Mother and Child* offered the following description of the ideal prospective father: 'His attitude should be patient, kind, and forebearing. He should take special care to avoid any remark or gesture which might increase his wife's irritability or bring about a collapse in her weakened condition.'[55]

Although pregnancy was still considered to be a natural condition, it nonetheless placed the expectant mother in a 'weakened condition.' In this way, experts were able to resolve the apparent contradiction between the concepts of pregnancy as both a natural and a medical phenomenon.[56] To insure that women did not fall prey to life-threatening problems during pregnancy, the major recommendation in the advice literature for pregnant women was the importance of early and sustained prenatal care. All of the publications insisted that the mother obtain the services of a physician as early during her pregnancy as possible. *The Baby* advised that 'the mother should, on the slightest suspicion of pregnancy, consult the best physician available, put herself under his direction and be guided by his advice.'[57] 'If there is anything wrong with you at all ... ask the Doctor about it at once,' MacMurchy reassured the mother, for 'there is always something the Doctor can do to make you better. That is what a Doctor is for.'[58]

Women were advised that it was best to see their own doctor – 'the trusted family physician.'[59] In the event that a woman did not already have a family doctor, MacMurchy suggested that she ask her friends – 'sensible, trustworthy people' – to recommend a physician. 'Consider this matter of choosing a doctor carefully,' she cautioned. 'Having found a good Doctor, you will then have good medical advice and supervision all through your pregnancy.'[60] Elsewhere, MacMurchy promised: 'With proper care from a good Doctor, you will do well. Doctors are now able, if you go in time, and if you follow their advice to keep the Mother-To-Be and her Baby safe and well and comfortable. There are very few exceptions to this rule.'[61]

Such a promise could be fulfilled, of course, only if the doctor's orders were strictly observed. Therefore, MacMurchy admonished women: '*Do what the doctor tells you.*'[62] The doctor would determine which activities were acceptable, and which were to be avoided. Writing in the *Canadian Medical Association Journal* in 1924, Joseph Nathanson explained the doctor's role in prenatal care as follows: 'At the very outset the patient should be instructed as to her personal hygiene, the type of housework which she may carry on, her mode of living, the recreations in which she may indulge, etc., and if on interrogation, any or all of these should be found to be faulty, then it is incumbent upon the physician to rectify them.'[63]

Throughout the section on prenatal care in *The Canadian Mother's Book*, MacMurchy repeated her command to 'Ask the Doctor' about problems ranging from morning sickness to bleeding. Mothers were cautioned against attempting to understand such symptoms themselves, because 'the Doctor is the only one who knows whether it is dangerous or not and so the Doctor must be had at once.'[64] An Ontario government publication also warned women about the importance of consulting the doctor regarding the 'danger signs' of pregnancy. 'Do not attempt to carry the responsibility yourself, and under no circumstances take the extreme risk of following the advice of a neighbour or friend.'[65]

One of the most powerful means of ensuring that women consulted and followed their doctors' advice was to attack the credibility of traditional sources of information. Although MacMurchy urged women to consult their friends regarding the choice of a suitable doctor, she and many other authors included explicit admonitions against taking the counsel of relatives or friends on any other issues. In 1927, under the heading 'Advice of Relatives and Neighbours,' a City of Toronto pamphlet contained the following warning: 'Neighbours and relatives may tell you much gossip in regard to the bearing of children which will tend to alarm or misguide you. While in most cases the intention is good, the advice is generally unsafe to follow, and the alarming story is very likely untrue.'[66]

Female friends and relatives were blamed for spreading 'old wives' tales' about a vast range of subjects. Markings or maternal impressions – the belief that a mother's shocking or upsetting experiences could maim or disfigure the fetus – caused authors of advice books and articles great concern and they took pains to dispel these beliefs. Stella Pines, writing in *Chatelaine* in 1928, informed her readers that 'the possibility of markings and impressions on the baby ... have, through scientific research, proven themselves fallacious.'[67] A nurse, writing in the *Canadian Public Health Journal* in 1934, indicated how widespread the beliefs were: 'The mental disturbances, the fear and anxiety, caused by the age-old superstitions of markings are met with daily.' Noting that 'the patient has for her belief the very excellent authority of mother, grandmother, and aunt,' she advised her readers 'to be very tactful in dealing with these strong personal opinions.' To combat such superstitions, 'the nurse must be armed with well built up scientific facts, an infinite amount of patience and tolerance for the mother's ideas, and an understanding of how she happens to be afflicted with the ideas.'[68]

Despite these efforts, however, the concept of markings appears to have been remarkably resilient. References to this 'old wives' tale' appear even in publications from the 1950s. *The Canadian Mother and Child* informed mothers: 'The appearance of the baby or its features cannot be influenced by accidentally encountering something terrifying or ugly, and there is no cause for concern if any such occurrence takes place. On the other hand, it is of no avail to go out of your way to gaze at beautiful people.'[69] Kate Aitken, a popular Canadian radio and magazine personality, offered equally reassuring advice for mothers in her book *It's Fun Raising a Baby*, serialized in *Chatelaine* in 1955. In response to the question 'Can accidents or fright mark your baby,' Aitken replied: 'Let's put that clear out of your mind once and for all. Mothers have worried for months lest an accident or a fright or a sudden scare would permanently mark the unborn child. The truth of the matter is the appearance of your baby or his features or his body cannot be influenced by your encountering something ugly or horrible.'[70]

While authors were virtually unanimous in dismissing such beliefs as 'old wives' tales,' Ann Oakley argues that, prior to the late nineteenth century, it was in fact *scientists* who stressed the significance of impressions. Citing evidence from popular obstetrical texts of the day, Oakley notes that 'until well into the nineteenth century, the question for most medical men ... was not *whether* maternal impressions could cause deformed features, but *how* they did so.'[71] It is indeed ironic that the twentieth-century counterparts of those medical men took such great pains to blame women – old wives – for these theories. Perhaps they feared admitting that their forefathers had been wrong, since such an admission might reflect on the fragility of their own 'scientific' knowledge.

Female friends and relations also came under attack for attempting to destroy a woman's confidence in her doctor. The following excerpt from the first edition of the *Canadian Mother and Child* contained an explicit attack on women's sharing information:

Gatherings such as bridges and teas, are often occasions of unwise discussions as to the relative merits of doctors. After careful consideration, you have chosen a doctor, therefore, do not let yourself be influenced by those who are not qualified to advise. There is nothing more disheartening than to hear your doctor criticized, or other doctors praised above him. To be happy you need to have complete confidence in your doctor. Anyone criticizing him to you ... lacks discernment to say the least, and should not be taken seriously.[72]

Sustaining a woman's confidence in her chosen physician was a key task of the public health nurse during these decades. Countless articles in the *Canadian Nurse* reminded nurses of the debt which they owed to the medical profession. A 1927 article for example, advised readers: 'In her relation to the physicians the nurse must be so convinced of the rightness of their procedures that she gives unquestioning loyalty and confidence, since her work is of necessity an interpretation of their ideas and wishes. She must appreciate the fact that every detail of maternity work originates in, and is guided by the medical profession.'[73]

So important was a patient's faith in her doctor deemed to be that the public health nurse was expected to support him even in the face of evidence indicating he might no longer be entitled to such faith. In 1930, Gordon Jackson, Toronto's medical officer of health at the time, stressed the point: 'Public interest demands confidence in the medical profession, and for that reason [the public health nurse] bends all her woman's skill to maintaining a family's faith in its chosen physician, *even though she herself may have lost faith in him.*'[74] Writing in the *Canadian Nurse* in the same period, Ethel Cryderman reminded her readers that 'regardless of the fact of whether he gives satisfactory antenatal supervision or not, every effort [must be] made to persuade the mother to go to her own doctor.'[75] Nurses were urged to remind women attending prenatal classes that the courses were 'not designed to take the place of your doctor's supervision ... but rather to round out his care of you – to fill in the little practical details which will help you now and after your baby comes.'[76]

Public health nurses were in the forefront of the provision of prenatal care. Through home visits and prenatal clinics, nurses ministered to thousands of Canadian women. At the same time, however, they took great pains to sustain and support the work of the medical profession, who remained firmly in control of the reins of power. In the midst of a struggle to professionalize the practice of nursing, nurses were 'reluctant to challenge doctors on such other issues as care of infants and mothers.'[77]

Like nurses, authors of advice literature took great pains to reinforce the importance of the doctor's role in the provision of prenatal care. This may have been to undercut any fears that doctors had that the proliferation of prenatal and child-rearing pamphlets would encroach on their domain. Such fears might well have been warranted, given the fact that most advice literature was provided free of charge, while doctors charged a fee for their services. The Canadian Council on Child Welfare's *Prenatal Letters* began with the disclaimer that 'the monthly letter offered to you will be of value in the way of general advice, but can in no way replace the personal service of your family doctor.' Their first piece of advice to an expectant mother was that she 'at once place [herself] under the care of [her] family physician.'[78]

As the records of the Canadian Council on Child Welfare reveal, the importance of regular consultations with the doctor was a concern frequently stressed by the health-care experts with whom Charlotte Whitton consulted. Responding to Dr G.A. MacIntosh, Nova Scotia's provincial officer of health, Charlotte Whitton pointed out that in the prenatal letters 'at each turn the mother is referred to her family physician.' She noted that 'in reference to all health questions in the postnatal letters reference will be made also to the desirability of consulting the local physician.'[79]

Throughout the interwar years, authors of advice literature were quick to reassure the medical profession that no conflict existed between their advice and the doctor's role. John Puddicombe, Staff Obstetrician for the Canadian Council on Child and Family Welfare, told the annual meeting of the council in 1934 that the prenatal and postnatal letters 'contain information on nearly every question that may enter the mind of an expectant mother. The seriousness of such symptoms as the mother erroneously may believe negligible are explained to her. On their appearance she is urged to report to her doctor immediately. In fact the necessity of seeing the doctor frequently is being kept constantly before her.' Puddicombe reassured doctors that they need not fear the competition provided by the pre- and post-natal letters. Rather than undermine the doctor's value, the letters were able to 'take up so much that the busy doctors cannot possibly go into.

In no way may they be used as a substitute for medical attention, yet in so many ways they supplement and are constant reminders of the doctor's advice.'[80]

To underscore the importance of direct medical supervision, pamphlets contained explicit instructions regarding the frequency of visits to the doctor. During pregnancy, women were advised to consult the doctor two or three times during the first six months and then once a month (or more frequently if the doctor requested it) until the time of confinement.[81] Later volumes recommended more frequent visits. Ernest Couture urged a mother-to-be to remain 'under the constant supervision of a medical man,' recommending that she have her urine examined 'once a month during the first five months, twice a month during the sixth and seventh months, and once a week from then on.'[82]

In recognition, perhaps, of the considerable expense involved in prenatal care for the vast majority of Canadian women who lacked any form of medical insurance,[83] alternative solutions were sometimes proposed. *The Baby* suggested that 'if you cannot afford a doctor, apply to a hospital or dispensary where experienced doctors and nurses will advise and care for you.'[84] Toronto's pamphlet, *The Expectant Mother*, noted in 1927 that 'the hospitals of the City and the Department of Public Health conduct clinics at which [prenatal care] is given to those who are unable to afford the services of a physician.'[85]

Given the prohibitive cost of regular medical visits, it seems likely that the Canadian public would have been reluctant to invest in prenatal care. Many people might have felt that such care was merely a clever way for physicians to line their pockets at the expense of expectant mothers and their husbands. Helen MacMurchy tackled this misconception head-on in her reports on maternal mortality. Acknowledging that 'there are black sheep in almost every flock,' she reassured Canadians that 'there are not many black sheep in the Medical flock. We don't keep them in the flock if we know it.'[86] To avoid unpleasant surprises when it came time to pay the medical bills, MacMurchy advised couples to arrange the doctor's fee at the first visit. 'It is a comfort to know what the Doctor's "inclusive fee" is,' MacMurchy reassured her readers, 'for then one can be prepared,' adding, 'It should be a moderate fee.'[87] Writing in *Chatelaine* in the 1940s Elizabeth Chant Robertson countered the views of what she termed 'uninformed people' who viewed regular check-ups as a 'racket.' Doctors, she argued, had more work than they needed, and provided prenatal care as a service to mothers and children.[88]

In 1946 Ontario's Public Health Act was amended to provide one free prenatal visit for each woman by the physician of her choice.[89] This measure, of course, fell far short of the 'constant' medical supervision recommended in the advice literature. Despite Couture's claim in the first edition of *The Canadian Mother and Child* that 'all Canadian mothers, without exception, can obtain the benefit of proper guidance during and after pregnancy, if they are willing to seek it,'[90] it is likely that prior to the implementation of a national system of medical insurance, such supervision, whether desired or not, would have been beyond the reach of many Canadian women.

Nonetheless, by the end of the Second World War, acceptance of the importance of prenatal care appeared to be growing among the community at large, and prenatal clinics in hospitals and community centres were becoming widespread. While the clinics themselves were not a new phenomenon, having been established in urban areas during the early decades of the century,[91] the clientele had changed considerably. In an article on Toronto's prenatal classes during the 1920s, Ethel Cryderman stated that over seventy per cent of the women who attended came 'from the more congested districts.' On balance, she noted sadly, 'the major part of ante-natal teaching is not with normal families.'[92] By the 1940s, perhaps as a result of the continued emphasis placed on prenatal care coupled with the growing number of pregnant women in the labour force because of the war effort, the situation had changed dramatically. Writing in *Canadian Nurse*, Constance Gray noted that 'the appeal of the prenatal classes has been to a group of young women who are intelligent, informed, of average economy, and who are receiving their medical care from private physicians and obstetricians ... Classes tried in the poorer areas of Toronto have had to close for lack of pupils in spite of the fact that clinic patients have been referred to them in various ways.'[93] In 1945 Toronto boasted sixteen prenatal and five post-natal clinics held in hospitals each week. In addition, city public health nurses visited an average of three hundred expectant and recently confined mothers in their homes each week.[94] For whatever reasons, however, many women remained unwilling to attend such a public forum 'in their condition.' Writing in the 1950s Dr Jean Webb, Couture's successor as chief of the Child and Maternal Health Division, noted that public health workers were still 'sometimes disappointed by the small numbers in attendance.'[95] While embarrassment may have been a factor,[96] Webb suggested that the attitude of local physicians may also have played a role: 'Frank opposition is rare, but condemnation by faint praise is as great a liability to public health workers ... There are those physicians who feel that the less the little woman knows about all this, the better.'[97]

That criticism notwithstanding, it appears that many doctors did begin to espouse the importance of ongoing medical care during pregnancy. Concern over the health and well-being of their patients, coupled with the growing recognition that prenatal screening might help to prevent maternal and infant deaths, led many doctors to take up the cause. Furthermore, while some physicians may have been reluctant to provide prenatal care, feeling that it was inadequately remunerated, doctors and their organizations increasingly realized that if they were to establish themselves as a family's main provider of health care, they would need a point of entry. Supervising care during the prenatal period reserved a place for the doctor at the childbed during labour and delivery. A successful outcome would insure that the family would return to the doctor for help with ongoing medical problems.[98] Over these four decades, doctors increasingly asserted their hegemony over the processes of labour and delivery, ensuring that birth took place under their watchful eyes in the safety of a hospital.

While the number of women in Canada who have obtained some form of prenatal care has increased steadily since the 1920s, a far more dramatic change has been the transition from home to hospital as the site of parturition. The percentage of births that took place in hospital rose from 17.8 in 1926, the first year for which national statistics are available, to 94.6 in 1960. Today, over 99 per cent of all births take place in a hospital.[99] Although those figures mask considerable regional variation, they reveal a major shift in the practice of childbirth in Canada.

As hospitalization for childbirth became increasingly routine, a number of other medical procedures, including the medical induction of labour, the isolation of labouring women, and the routine use of forceps, anaesthetics, and episiotomy gradually emerged as standard practice during 'normal' deliveries.[100] As well, accompanying the transition from home to hospital was a shift from midwife to doctor as the appropriate supervisor of labour and delivery. These developments have led Wendy Mitchinson to call childbirth 'the major area of medicalization for women' in the twentieth century.[101]

In the past two decades, a great deal of literature has been written documenting the changes that have taken place in the technology, supervision, and location of birth. While these works were initially British and American in origin,[102] a significant body of Canadian literature has appeared in the past ten years.[103] Although some debate exists within the literature as to the impact of medical changes on labouring women themselves, there can be little doubt that over the course of this century control over the process of birth shifted increasingly into the hands of the medical profession, as midwives and other non-professionals were progressively excluded from the birthing chamber.

Despite the wealth of advice on prenatal care, almost no direct references were made to the birth process itself. Since the major prenatal recommendation of both the public health nurses and the advice literature of the period was the importance of ongoing medical attention, it is likely that experts felt women did not *need* to know the details of labour or delivery, as their doctors could be expected to have matters well in hand. Virtually every publication of the period stressed the value of a doctor's care during labour and delivery. In *Mother – A Little Book for Women*, Helen MacMurchy suggested that labouring women required the services of both a nurse – 'a trained nurse if possible' – and a doctor. In addition, she advised the mother: 'Don't forget that sometimes it is better for you and the baby if the Doctor has another Doctor to help him' during the delivery.[104]

To ensure that it was a doctor who supervised labour and delivery, rather than a midwife or 'neighbour woman,' the literature contained explicit condemnations of such women. A 1924 article in *Canadian Nurse* warned: 'It is unfortunate that every community has more than its quota of so-called "practical nurses," and that these women, while well-meaning, though lacking in any training in asepsis, themselves become many times the innocent cause of maternal mortality, to say nothing of infant mortality.'[105] The 1922 edition of Toronto's *Pre-Natal Care* advised its readers, 'Do not engage a mid-wife, it is illegal.'[106]

While midwives were not, in fact, technically illegal, they did operate under severe legal constraints which limited their capacity to supervise and assist at births. By the 1920s in British Columbia, for example, 'only physicians registered with the College of Physicians and Surgeons were permitted to give medical or surgical assistance at births.' Norah Lewis notes that 'in British Columbia, as in other parts of Canada, only physicians were permitted by law to administer anaesthetics; therefore, if women were to escape the pains of childbirth they must have a physician in attendance.' Furthermore, in nursing schools, student nurses received no special training in birthing procedures, a provision which meant that nurses could be little more than helpmates in the birthing room. These restrictions ensured that doctors held both a legal and a professional monopoly on childbirth.[107]

The failure to license the practice of midwifery was by no means accidental. Doctors were anxious to secure their monopoly over childbirth, and they lobbied long and hard against the registration and training of midwives. Doctors and their organizations maintained that their superior skill, training, and education should guarantee them the exclusive rights of entry into the birthing chamber.[108] Despite early initiatives by women's groups to establish a system of midwifery in Canada, their efforts were always thwarted by interprofessional rivalries and the powerful lobby of the medical profession.[109]

When surveys on maternal mortality during the 1920s revealed the large numbers of women who were forced to give birth unattended, pressure mounted once again for the implementation of a system of licensed midwives, to serve at least the remote areas of the country. Once again, many doctors resisted this measure. Defending the value of prenatal care, Dr John W.S. McCullough, Ontario's former chief medical officer of health, argued in the pages of *Chatelaine* in 1931 that 'education of women in the urgent need of supervision during the pregnant period is of infinitely greater value than the substitution of the midwife for the doctor.'[110]

While doctors and their organizations consistently opposed the introduction of a national system of midwifery, public health officials like Dr Helen MacMurchy appear to have recognized that the issue was not one of the substitution of the midwife for the doctor but, more often, of the choice between a midwife and *no* medical attendant at birth. In a 1923 supplement to *The Canadian Mother's Book*, MacMurchy provided detailed information regarding proper medical procedures during childbirth. Designed to meet the urgent medical needs of women giving birth in outpost communities, the booklet was directed towards local 'neighbour women' who served as midwives, although the supplement was stamped 'FOR DISTRIBUTION BY DOCTORS AND NURSES ONLY' on its front cover. While MacMurchy would undoubtedly have preferred that only trained physicians deliver babies, she recognized that many women in outlying areas were suffering needlessly as a result of the absence of trained medical attention.[111] Only two editions of the supplement were produced, however, and the Department of Health's desire 'not to give this book out broadcast [*sic*]'[112] suggests 'a willingness to sacrifice the needs of women to the demands of physicians.'[113]

It is interesting to note that while much of the advice literature from the interwar years condemned the practice of midwifery, literature from the post–Second World War period seemed to reflect a reluctant acceptance of the need for midwives, especially in outlying regions. While the 1940 edition of *The Canadian Mother and Child* strongly urged mothers to obtain the services of a doctor, the book also contained a technical chapter on the details of birth, in recognition of the fact that 'some 16,000 mothers [were] without medical attendance for the birth of their babies.' In a surprisingly positive statement, Couture offered the following words of praise for the nurse/midwives who ministered to labouring women: 'One cannot but admire the sacrifice and devotion displayed by many of these women who try to fill the gap and lend a helping hand to the mothers who need such care.' Lest any reader take these words as support for midwifery, however, the author warned that '*no amount of practical experience or reading of instructions can take the place of the doctor with his long and intensive training, or equal the services of a fully qualified nurse.*'[114] Although a doctor was strongly preferred, then, Couture recommended that 'if you have to rely on the services of a neighbour, or so-called midwife, for your confinement or aftercare, make sure that no illness exists in her family, and that she is not connected with a febrile case elsewhere, and above all, see that she herself is healthy, clean and tidy.'[115]

The 1953 edition of *The Canadian Mother and Child* also contained detailed information on the birth process, this time headed 'A Chapter for the Midwife.' Lacking entirely the condemning tone of earlier editions, this revision stated simply: 'A number of babies are born every year without benefit of doctor or hospital. Sometimes it is planned that way; sometimes it is due to unforeseen circumstances – impassability of roads, an earlier birth than expected, or some other reason.'[116] In view of the fact that by 1953 the vast majority of births in Canada were attended by a physician, perhaps the authors felt that the need for strict condemnation of the practice of midwifery, such as those contained within many of the publications of the interwar years, had passed.[117]

Given that mothers were strongly urged to obtain the services of a doctor for both prenatal care and delivery, it is not surprising that most publications contained few details of the birth itself. Sections on childbirth routinely described the signs of the onset of labour, telling the mother to 'notify your doctor and nurse when labour begins.'[118] Many publications included detailed information regarding the items required for a home confinement, but advised the mother to hire a nurse to assist her with the sterilization of bed pads and other preparations.[119] Not seeing any need to include details of the baby's arrival, both the City of Toronto and the Ontario government's publications began the section 'When the Baby Comes' with the following suggestion: 'There should be a warm, soft blanket to receive the baby.'[120]

In marked contrast, nurse Kate McIlraith told her colleagues in 1950 that 'it is important that the expectant mother should understand *how* a baby is born.'[121] When women were equipped with this knowledge, they were able to see birth as an amazing experience and to approach it calmly and without fear. Among medical experts, however, McIlraith stood virtually alone in such a view.

Many authors may have felt reluctant to describe the details of labour and delivery for fear of frightening pregnant women. References in the literature advised the expectant mother not to listen to 'stories of difficult labour that some gossip' might want to tell her, reassuring her once again that having a baby was 'natural and normal.'[122] The first edition of *The Canadian Mother and Child* was even more critical of such stories: 'During the course of your pregnancy, do not listen to versions of their labours given to you by friends. They are likely to exaggerate the details of their experience, and give you a false impression and cause misgivings.'[123]

Once again, sharing of information between women was dismissed as the telling of 'old wives' tales.' Condemning such stories, Mrs A.M. Plumptre wrote in 1928: 'Almost every mother feels herself competent to give expert advice to her daughters based on her own experience of twenty or thirty years ago – regardless of the progress made in medical thought and practice in the last quarter of a century.'[124]

The actual pain of labour was in fact not mentioned in the literature until the first edition of *The Canadian Mother and Child* (1940) and then reference was made only to reassure women that doctors had the problem well in hand. Couture wrote: 'The problem of the relief of pain in labour has, for a number of years, been a matter of considerable interest for mothers as well as for physicians. Following intensive efforts on the part of the Medical Profession a number of treatments have been evolved producing results of variable character.' While he acknowledged that the perfect solution had not yet been reached, Couture assured women that 'a good many preparations exist which ... will give very appreciable relief without harm to either mother or child.'[125] Only doctors, of course, were legally entitled to offer such 'relief.'

The preferred location for childbirth received considerable attention in the literature, and, not surprisingly, the balance of favour shifted increasingly towards the hospital as the century progressed. Prior to 1920, 'only the unmarried or the very poor gave birth in hospitals, or lying-in homes, where infant mortality rates were shockingly high.'[126] That situation began to change following the First World War. Publications of neither the City of Toronto nor the Province of Ontario indicated any preference in location during the 1920s. In *Pre-Natal Care*, Toronto advised the expectant mother to notify her 'doctor and nurse when labor begins,'[127] giving no indication what would take place once they arrived. The 1920 edition of *The Baby* contained no information on the confinement, while the 1924 revision contained detailed instructions on the preparations necessary for a home birth.[128]

By the 1930s, however, both publications appeared to recognize the trend towards hospital births. Toronto placed responsibility for this decision squarely in the doctor's hands, advising the expectant mother to 'consult her doctor early in pregnancy about plans for her confinement.' At that time the doctor might 'advise her to remain at home or to go into hospital.'[129] In the same vein, the 1948 edition recommended that if the doctor 'has advised a confinement at home, you will want the assistance of a trained nurse or visiting nurse to help prepare the articles needed and to help the doctor.'[130] *The Baby*, in contrast, noted that it was 'becoming more common for women to have their confinement take place in hospital' during the 1930s, offering the following argument in favour of a hospital birth: 'It has many advantages, everything necessary in the way of equipment being at hand if any emergency should arise, and assuring the mother of satisfactory care and supervision following delivery, as well as relieving her of the cares of the home.' The same edition of *The Baby* also contained information on home confinement, suggesting that 'if the mother prefers to have her confinement at home, it is well to engage a competent nurse several weeks in advance.'[131]

In contrast to the authors of the Toronto and Ontario publications, Helen MacMurchy was an early advocate of hospital births. The 1923 edition of *The Canadian Mother's Book* offered the following advice regarding the preferred location of birth: 'At the time of the birth, you and the baby can usually be better taken care of in the hospital than anywhere else, whether you are paying your hospital fees yourself, or whether you are having your medical and nursing care free.'[132] MacMurchy did recognize that many women would continue to give birth at home. In this case, she urged: 'Engage your nurse in good time. The Doctor will advise you about this.'[133] It is interesting to note that cost was never mentioned as a factor in the decision regarding the location of parturition. It is likely that many Canadian women, particularly during the Depression, would have been unable to meet the combined costs of a physician and hospital care, costs which could amount to as much as $60 or more, depending on the level of complication the delivery entailed.[134]

By the 1940s giving birth in hospital was becoming increasingly common. In Canada's three largest provinces, more than half of all births took place in a hospital.[135] This shift was reflected in the literature, as the issue was increasingly framed in terms of the dual factors of safety and the doctor's preference. The first edition of *The Canadian Mother and Child* noted that the decision regarding the best location of birth 'depends on many things, but first of all, follow your doctor's advice. He is most assuredly interested in obtaining the best possible results in your case, and it is only fair that you should give him your full co-operation by allowing him to work under conditions of his choice. The doctor will usually be influenced in his decision by the state of your health, by the prospect of your labour, and by the choice of the most advantageous conditions for a happy issue.'[136]

A hospital birth was said to hold a number of advantages for the mother. Couture noted that 'the Maternity Department is isolated from the other services; the personnel is especially engaged to attend mothers and children; each individual mother has her own dressing and toilet equipment ... Furthermore, in a well-managed hospital you enjoy the benefits of well-planned attention and of conditions that make possible complete relaxation and freedom from worry about home affairs.'[137]

By 1953 it appeared that the transition was more or less complete. *The Canadian Mother and Child* noted that 'most babies are born in hospitals now,' adding that 'it certainly saves a lot of preparation.' The only preparation that the mother required was to 'pack an overnight case with everything you'll need at the hospital.'[138] Both editions of *The Canadian Mother and Child* also included information on home confinement, although by 1953 that section had been strategically placed *after* the section on hospital births. Furthermore, the photographs demonstrating how to prepare bed pads, newspaper bags, and other equipment required for a home birth had been omitted from the 1953 edition.

One final source of information on the hospital/home birth choice merits consideration. Although *Baby and Child Care* contained no information on prenatal care, Dr Spock did take up the issue of the location of parturition. In the first edition, published in 1946, Spock offered a remarkably even-handed approach to the question: 'Whether you have your baby at home or in a hospital depends mostly on where you and your doctor live. Doctors who are near hospitals and used to them usually prefer to deliver babies there for various practical reasons. But doctors who are used to home deliveries feel just as efficient there, as long as the case is not too complicated.' Spock then proceeded to describe what he considered to be the advantages in both places. A hospital, he noted, with its trained staff and 'magical equipment' was able to make 'the mother feel very safe and well cared for.' But, he added, a hospital had 'its mild drawbacks too, that [were] part and parcel of its virtues.' The mother might feel that it wasn't 'quite natural' to have her baby off in the nursery, being cared for 'so completely for a week or two by others.' It might leave the mother with a feeling of 'being somewhat ignorant and useless.'[139] A home birth, in contrast, offered the new mother the possibility of having her baby close by, giving her the feeling that 'he is really hers right from the beginning.' Such a mother 'has her family and possessions around her. She doesn't have to wait for the visiting hour. All of these are real compensations.'[140]

Foreshadowing the rooming-policies popular in hospitals today, Spock offered the following vision in his first edition: 'Someday perhaps it will be possible to discover ways to change the arrangements of maternity hospitals so that they will still be safe and restful, and yet give fathers and mothers a little more chance, right from the beginning, to feel close and useful to their babies.'[141] By the time the next edition appeared, some hospitals had implemented rooming-in and Spock included a description of such arrangements. Spock now spoke more decisively about the advantages of a hospital birth. Noting that 'nowadays most babies ... are born in a hospital,' he continued: 'There the doctor is closer at hand when needed, and he is assisted by interns, nurses, technicians and consultants. A hospital offers all the complicated equipment.' Spock still condoned a home birth for a normal delivery, adding that if the doctor 'foresees complications, he will advise hospitalization.'[142]

Expert advice concerning the immediate post-partum care of the mother changed dramatically over the course of the middle decades of this century. During the 1920s, a woman was expected to remain in bed for at least two weeks following the birth of a child. Toronto's *The Expectant Mother* explained the rationale for this practice as follows: 'After the birth of the baby the organs of the abdomen and pelvis gradually return to their usual size and position. In order to facilitate this the mother must remain at rest for some time. If there are no complications, her physician usually allows her to sit up about the tenth day and to rise at the end of the second week.'[143] By the 1930s the period of total bed rest had been reduced to ten days, although the mother was still advised to proceed very slowly with her resumption of regular activities. Helen MacMurchy recommended: 'On the tenth day, if the mother is doing well, she could get up out of bed for twenty minutes. On the eleventh or twelfth day she could get up after breakfast, but must take a good rest every afternoon and do no heavy washing or lifting or other heavy work for about six weeks.' To assist her in the home, MacMurchy suggested that she needed 'a Home Helper in the house till the baby [was] about six weeks old.'[144]

By the end of the Second World War, as doctors began to recognize the merits of exercise in hastening the new mother's recovery, the length of post-partum rest had been considerably reduced. *The Canadian Mother and Child* explained: 'It has been demonstrated in recent years that mothers need not stay in bed for the prolonged period which previously was considered essential.' Such a decision was not to be made without consultation with the doctor, however, as 'each case requires individual consideration.' In cases where no doctor was available, Couture recommended that the woman stay in bed for five days following the birth.[145] Once again, however, the mother was urged to be very cautious regarding the resumption of household chores. The literature continued to recommend that she wait at least six weeks before taking on the full load of the household. Nowhere did the authors suggest how she might be expected to postpone this eventuality.

During the course of this century, attitudes towards pregnancy and childbirth have changed dramatically. As concern over high rates of maternal and infant deaths became widespread, the importance of ongoing prenatal care gained wider public and medical acceptance, while the location of childbirth shifted increasingly from home to hospital. Concomitant with these developments, maternal mortality rates began to drop, beginning in 1938, and today, the risk women face of dying in childbirth is minimal.[146]

All of these statements, however, mask important regional, ethnic, and racial variations. Native women and children, for example, continue to die at much higher rates than non-Native Canadians.[147] Furthermore, many of these developments were purchased at a cost for all women. Although women were now offered prenatal care, they were told that it was their fault if they failed to seek out such care – even if they could not afford the cost involved in such care.[148] Prenatal care also contained a contradiction for mothers. While prenatal care may have given expectant mothers potentially useful information, it also delivered women into medical hands, for only doctors, and, in some instances, nurses, were deemed to be qualified to offer such care and only doctors could adequately interpret its findings. Authors of advice literature uniformly assumed that the doctor was a man, thus reinforcing the patriarchal relationship between practitioner and patient. Finally, although women were now *promised* safer, less painful births, women in outlying areas were forced to travel long distances to obtain this service,[149] and all women were required to leave their homes and families to submit to the regimen of hospitals. We must ask ourselves, then, at what cost these gains were achieved.

4

'Bringing Up Baby': The Care and Feeding of Infants and Young Children

If formerly it was believed that mother instinct or mother love was the simple and safe basis for the problems of [child] training, it is now known that a much more adequate guide is the kitchen timepiece.
William E. Blatz and Helen Bott, 1928[1]

Trust yourself. You know more than you think you do ... Bringing up your child won't be a complicated job if you take it easy, trust your own instincts, and follow the directions that your doctor gives you.
Benjamin Spock, 1946[2]

During the course of this century, ideas about the best ways to care for infants and young children have changed dramatically. In an effort to reduce high rates of infant and child mortality by rendering child rearing more scientific, advice literature written during the interwar years sought to transform the rearing of infants and young children from a largely affective, tradition-based relationship into something that more closely resembled a carefully controlled and managed experiment. Every activity was to be closely monitored and tightly scheduled, as child-care experts promoted a style of child rearing based on the notions of scientific management and behaviourism. By 1945, as statistics on infant and child health improved, a shift in both the content and the tone of child-rearing advice took place, and the rigid dictates of scientific child rearing made way for the more flexible, child-centred approach of the post–Second World War era.

Underlying the changing dictates were markedly different views of children and the way in which they learn and develop. The strict approach to child rearing of the early decades of the twentieth century was initiated and sustained by the work of two key figures. The publication of *The Care and Feeding of Children* by Dr L. Emmett Holt in 1894 marked a turning point in the transition to scientific child rearing. The book went through twenty editions between its initial publication and 1943, and, in its day, was described as a 'Bible for young mothers.'[3] Dr Holt, professor of diseases of children at New York's Polyclinic, attending physician to the Babies' Hospital and the Nursery and Child's Hospital, and paediatrician to the family of John D. Rockefeller, Jr, was a major force in the development of a scientific approach to infant feeding.[4] Holt trained many of North America's prominent paediatricians, including Toronto's Dr Alan Brown and Montreal's Dr Alton Goldbloom, and his influence is unmistakable in the writings and teachings of his students.[5] Equally significant was the work of the American psychologist Dr John Watson, author of *Psychological Care of the Infant and Child* (1928) and the 'father' of behaviorism.[6] Moving beyond the realm of the physical, Watson advocated the extension of the dictates of scientific child rearing into the child's psychological development. While neither author was mentioned by name in the Canadian advice literature, the influence of their approaches was apparent in virtually every publication produced during the interwar years.

At the core of scientific child rearing was the concept of habit training – a term which embraced virtually every facet of human learning. In the parlance of the day, the word habit referred not merely to 'bad' habits, but to 'all the customary reactions exhibited by individuals in the round of daily life.'[7] In many regards an extension of Frederick Taylor's ideas of scientific management into the home, habit training promised to elevate child rearing to the level of efficiency of the industrial sector.[8] In this manner, the training of workers suited to the regimen of the industrial workplace could begin at birth, thereby saving employers precious time and money. Even the literature of habit training was framed in terms of time and cost effectiveness. Writing in 1928, Frances Lily Johnson, of the parent education department of the St George's School of Child Study, and a staunch advocate of habit training, compared the role of the habit to 'electrical appliances in the home. As a time and labor-saver, it is invaluable.'[9]

To facilitate habit training, authors of child-care literature advocated regularity and regimentation in all dimensions of a child's development.[10] The key to scientific child rearing was the establishment of fixed times for every activity. From the minute the baby arrived home from the hospital (and indeed from the moment he or she was born) a rigid timetable was to be established. Detailed charts indicating the correct time for feeding, sleeping, elimination, bathing, and even sun-bathing were included in almost every pamphlet. To help women adhere to the assigned times, the Canadian Council on Child and Family Welfare's *Post-Natal Letters* noted that 'many mothers find it helpful to print the baby's schedule on a card or paper and tack it up by the baby's bed.'[11]

Each activity was to take place 'by the clock.'[12] Only then would the baby learn what was expected. Mothers were urged to awaken the baby 'if necessary ... to feed him, or carry out other parts of his routine.' To insure that the mother kept on schedule, the *Post-Natal Letters* noted that the mother would 'find a clock in the room in which the baby sleeps almost indispensable.'[13] In keeping with the reverence for science during the late nineteenth and early twentieth centuries,[14] references to clock-like regularity[15] and machine-like children appeared frequently in the advice literature of the interwar years. Dr Alan Brown went so far as to promise his readers that 'as a result of a careful regime regarding feeding, sleep, bathing, and airing, and the performance of its various functions at stated times every day, the baby will soon develop into a "little machine", as one mother called her babe.'[16] Lest the reader fail to see the benefit of this mechanical behaviour, Brown reassured mothers that 'such a child causes no trouble and thrives far better than one who is fed every time he cries, day or night.'[17]

Training in habit formation was to begin early, as the following publication of the City of Toronto explained: 'It is in the first few days that the baby's habits are formed. He is born without habits, and it is just as easy to form good ones as bad ones.'[18] Authors repeatedly castigated parents who felt that they could begin habit training at any point in a child's life. In an article in the *Public Health Journal* in 1927, Adelaide Plumptre relayed the following fictitious interchange between a doctor and a mother, to stress the importance of early habit training:

'Why have you not trained the baby to lie in his cot?' asked a doctor of a young mother who was walking the floor with her infant.

'O! doctor, he is only three weeks old,' replied the mother.

'Then you are three weeks late in beginning his education,' said the doctor.[19]

Experts believed that the early habits of eating, sleeping, and elimination formed the building blocks for the later development of social and emotional habits. Frances Lily Johnson explained: 'all habits are built up on the basic habits which have their foundation in the fundamental needs of the body.'[20] The 'simple beginnings' of habit training in eating, sleeping, and toileting, were critical because 'at no other period are habits and mental characteristics so rapidly taking shape, and the sort of habits and attitudes your baby learns during this first twelve months, and *how* he learns them, will exert a lasting influence upon his whole life.'[21] The rewards of habit training were great, then, as mothers were assured that 'regularity from the day a child is born makes a better baby and a better mother.'[22]

By the post–Second World War period, many of the principles of rigid habit training had been rejected, as the maturational-developmental approach came to dominate the field of child study. First advocated by Arnold Gesell at the Yale Clinic of Child Development, these views did not come to widespread public attention until the publication of Dr Benjamin Spock's *Baby and Child Care* in 1946.[23] Throughout Canada, the United States, and much of Europe, citizens weary of the deprivation and hardship of the Depression and of the loss and suffering of the Second World War appeared eager to adopt a more flexible approach to child rearing. During the Depression, life for all but the most privileged Canadians had been harsh: few families could afford record players, nursery furniture, and other indulgences recommended in the pages of *Chatelaine*. In the period of economic boom that followed the Second World War, even working-class families were able to purchase at least some of the trappings of permissive child rearing. Higher wages meant that many families in both the middle and working classes could afford to embrace full-time motherhood. Electrical appliances, including refrigerators, automatic washers and dryers, although available to a limited population since the 1920s, were now within the reach of the majority of Canadians, as consumer credit reached into the working class. Large- and small-scale appliances, frozen and canned goods, ready-made clothes, and a myriad of other 'conveniences' eased some of the burden of domestic labour, leaving women with more time to devote to child-rearing tasks. In addition, scientific developments such as the discovery of a number of vaccines and drugs, coupled with a dramatic improvement in nutrition following the Depression, had led to better infant and child health. Thus, for the first time in history, physical health could give way to psychological well-being as the primary concern of advice givers and mothers alike.

By the 1950s 'common-sense' had become the watchword in child rearing, as parents were urged to take their cues from their children, rather than from rigid rules established in advice manuals. The author of the federal government's 1950 publication *Up the Years from One to Six* told readers: 'To raise a family successfully parents do need to know what children are like, what they can and what they can't do at each stage of their development ... Parents need to use a lot of imagination and understanding in order to try to see the world – and themselves – from the child's point of view.'[24]

Underlying this changing philosophy was a markedly different view of infants in the post-war period. While parents during the interwar years had been warned that 'the average baby of a week old is as artful as a wagon load of monkeys,'[25] Dr Benjamin Spock reassured his readers that they could safely enjoy their babies, secure in the knowledge that 'he isn't a schemer. He needs loving.' Spock continued: 'You'd think from all you hear about babies demanding attention that they come into the world determined to get their parents under their thumbs by hook or by crook. This is not true at all. Your baby is born to be a reasonable, friendly human being. If you treat him nicely, he won't take advantage of you. Don't be afraid to love him or respond to his needs.'[26] In 1954 Elizabeth Chant Robertson reassured readers of *Chatelaine* that their children '*Want* to be Good.'[27] Not surprisingly, then, authors of the post-war era disagreed vehemently with the principle of a rigid program of child training. Spock argued that 'in the first place, you can't get a baby regulated beyond a certain point, no matter how hard you try. In the second place, you are apt, in the long run, to make him more balky and disagreeable when you go at his training too hard.'[28]

Despite the more flexible approach to child rearing, references to the importance of a schedule of activities persisted in the literature throughout the 1950s. While *The Early Years*, for example, advocated a primarily child-centred philosophy, the advice on habit training echoed the words of earlier writers: 'Schedules should be arranged during infancy so that the child will come to expect a certain degree of conformity throughout his life.' The following passage contains an interesting combination of the philosophies of the interwar and post-war periods: 'These schedules should not, at any time, be rigid and should be subject to reasonable and gradual change as the child grows. Most children find a regular schedule comforting; it gives them the security of knowing 'what is coming next' and parents find it convenient.'[29]

While schedules were still acceptable, they should be adapted to meet the child's needs, rather than the reverse. No longer desirable was

Alan Brown's 'little machine.' Instead, parents were warned that a child who was never permitted to assert his will would become, 'a robot, a mechanical man. You wouldn't be able to resist the temptation to boss him all the time, and he'd stop learning and developing. When he was old enough to go out into the world, to school and later to work, everybody else would take advantage of him, too. He'd never be good for anything.'[30] Elizabeth Chant Robertson reminded parents that 'your ultimate aim is to socialize your youngsters without repressing their good qualities of curiosity and initiative or making them rebellious to all authority.'[31] Parents were urged to see children as individuals, developing at different rates on the basis of their own strengths and skills. 'Every baby's face is different from every other's,' Spock explained. 'In the same way every baby's pattern of development is different.'[32]

Finally, advice manuals in the 1950s told parents that their children needed love. The 1953 edition of *The Canadian Mother and Child* assured its readers that 'generally speaking,' the 'good books' on child rearing 'all say the same thing': 'Let him know you love him and think he's the finest baby ever; be easy-going; accept the child as he is; never waver in being kind to him; try to provide him with the things he needs to grow, physically, intellectually and emotionally; and really enjoy your baby and make him a welcome member of your family circle.'[33]

In a recommendation that stands in sharp contrast to the austere prohibitions of the followers of Watson during the 1920s, Elizabeth Chant Robertson reassured mothers: 'Babies do better both physically and emotionally when they are petted and hugged. So don't be afraid to pick your baby up, talk to him, carry him around and cuddle him ... Enjoy him quietly and he'll be all the better for it.'[34]

Advice on virtually every dimension of child behaviour reflected these underlying philosophies. During the interwar years, parents were told that in all endeavours, 'the first principle to bear in mind ... [was] regularity.'[35] The 1931 edition of Toronto's *The Expectant Mother* explained that a newborn baby 'should be fed regularly, should be made comfortable and left in his bed to sleep. He should not be handled any more than is absolutely necessary.'[36] Such a regimen was important because sleep was considered to be 'one of the prime requisites for health of an infant or child.'[37] A child who did not get enough sleep could become irritable, restless, and ill. To avoid such problems, authors stressed that 'regularity of sleeping habits [was] essential.'[38] In practice, regularity meant that the hour of the child's naps and bedtime should be the same *every day*. The *Post-Natal Letters* warned: 'Regular habits can be formed only if your baby learns by experience that he is to do the same thing every day at the same time. If you make exceptions to the schedule, if you keep the baby up an hour later in order to "show him off" to a visitor, if you take him out for a trip to the store at his usual nap time, you are building up the habit of "irregularity."'[39] Regularity was as important for naptime as bedtime. Frances Lily Johnson noted in 1928, 'If the afternoon nap is to be successfully accomplished, the hour it begins and the hour it ends should be immutable.'[40] If a mother adhered strictly to the proper schedule, she would be rewarded with a 'well trained baby' who would 'go to sleep when put in bed.'[41]

The use of soothing syrups, pacifiers, and comforts was strictly prohibited. Similarly, walking or rocking a baby to sleep was deemed to be 'harmful as well as useless.' In the 1942 edition of his child-care manual, Frederick Tisdall explained: 'If there is anything really wrong with the baby, rocking will not help. In addition the baby soon learns to demand this and other attentions. The habit is hard to break and causes a great deal of unnecessary trouble for the other members of the household.' Indeed, such sleeping aids were deemed to be unnecessary for a child who had been properly trained. Tisdall told mothers that 'a normal baby will frequently cry for a few minutes after he is put in bed.'[42] Rather than checking on the baby every few minutes to make sure he was all right, experts exhorted women to '*leave the baby alone.*'[43] Tisdall advised anxious mothers to wait a half-hour before looking in on a crying infant. At that point, she might pick him up, but only for the purposes of assisting him to 'bring up any uncomfortable gas.'[44]

Virtually every bedtime problem was said to be the result of faulty habit training. The fear of going to bed in the dark, for example, was not considered to be a common stage of childhood but 'the result of bad training.' Mothers were advised that 'this habit should be corrected at the earliest possible moment,' lest the child develop more serious sleeping problems.[45] Fresh air, exercise, and, above all, strict adherence to the child's schedule would ensure that sleep presented no problems for the mother of the well-trained baby.

Advice on nap and sleep times in the post–Second World War period reflected the general trend towards a more flexible approach to child rearing. While the 1940 edition of *The Canadian Mother and Child* still stressed the importance of sleeping at definite hours,[46] and included information about the number of hours of sleep required at each age level, the 1953 edition suggested that the mother let the baby develop his own sleeping pattern. In contrast to detailed sleep charts provided in earlier advice pamphlets, women were now told that babies need different amounts of sleep. A mother need not worry about how much sleep her baby got during its first year, for 'if his sleeping conditions are good, he will take as much sleep as he needs.'[47] Dr Spock suggested that 'the baby [was] the only one' who could tell the mother how much he should sleep. 'As long as a baby is satisfied with his feedings, comfortable, gets plenty of fresh air, and sleeps in a quiet, cool place, you can leave it to him to take the amount of sleep he needs,' Spock advised.[48]

Despite the more flexible approach prescribed in the post-war literature, regular hours for bedtime and training in proper bedtime routines were still stressed. The 1953 edition of *The Canadian Mother and Child* reminded readers: 'Regularity in his eating, sleeping and playing habits is most important. The baby who is fed his meals at the same hours each day is more likely to fall asleep at the same times than the baby whose routine is interrupted for one reason or another.'[49] The federal Department of Health and Welfare's 1950 book, *Up the Years from One to Six*, blamed 'faulty training on the parents' part' for 'such bedtime antics as refusing to go to bed without a light or without a parent lying down by his side.'[50] Parents were warned against giving the child the impression that they were 'in a hurry to get him out of the way,' for this would make the child 'thoroughly upset' and would result in resistance to going to sleep. Bedtime should be a 'relaxing,' 'pleasant' experience for mother and child alike.[51] Spock advised mothers to 'keep bedtime agreeable and happy ... Have an air of cheerful certainty about it.'[52] In such an environment, a child 'just naturally welcomes being tucked in his own little bed.'[53]

A mother's approach to naptime should be equally relaxed. Even if the child did not need an actual sleep, mothers were urged to put him down for an afternoon rest. Once again, problems at naptime were mother's fault: 'If his mother doesn't get herself all worked up when naps are missed, the child won't get a lot of wrong attitudes about sleeping ... Because he isn't worried – no one has made him feel guilty about *not* sleeping – he will play contentedly by himself. If his body needs sleep, he'll drop off. If not, perhaps he will rest for close to an hour before becoming restless and anxious to be up.'[54]

Rest, then, and how the child *felt* about sleep replaced the concern over the exact number of hours of sleep the child had clocked.

Of all the areas of child rearing, nowhere is the change in advice more dramatic than in the area of toilet training. In keeping with the philosophy of early toilet training adopted in the nineteenth century, authors of child-care literature written during the 1920s told mothers to begin toilet training as early as the second week of the baby's life in order to establish 'regularity.'[55] The correct method for early training was detailed in the 1920 edition of *The Baby*: 'Hold a small (warmed) basin or mug firmly in the lap. Place the baby above this with feet extended in the hands, back resting against the mother's breast. This should e done at regular times for stools, morning and afternoon. Place the baby on the basin at regular intervals when awake or before feeding for urination. Such a procedure will reduce the number of diapers.'[56] Later editions of *The Baby* postponed the onset of toilet training to three months. Nonetheless, that publication and many others recommended that the mother insert a soap-stick or suppository into the rectum for the first two or three days of toilet training to 'help him learn for what reason he is placed on the chamber.' 'After ten days or two weeks,' the author noted, 'the habit should be established.'[57]

As with other habits, regularity was the key to successful toilet training. Toronto's pamphlet, *The Care of the Infant and Young Child*, stressed that training 'should be done every day at the same hour and in the same place.'[58] 'If the time and place are always the same and the mother shows her approval for the first successes, the baby will soon learn what is expected of him,' the author promised.[59] While young babies obviously had to be held on the chamber pot, once the child was able to sit unsupported, he could be left on a toilet chair unattended. The length of time considered appropriate for the baby to spend on the chamber pot varied from five to twenty minutes. The *Post-Natal Letters* warned against leaving the child on the toilet chair for more than ten minutes, because leaving 'him for longer periods encourages habits of dawdling and offers opportunities for the development of the undesirable habit of handling the genital organs.'[60]

Bladder training presented a greater challenge for the mother, since young children tend to urinate at random times throughout the day and night. The *Post-Natal Letters* suggested to the mother of the five-month-old baby that if she had not already started to train her baby in bladder control, she ought to begin. 'The longer the "wet" habit continues,' the author noted, 'the more difficult it will be to acquire the "dry" habit.'[61] By six months, the mother should be able to place the child on a toilet chair for both bladder and bowel training and by twelve months, 'you will find ... that it is a good plan to discard your baby's diapers and put drawers on him instead.'[62] Many authors postponed the onset of bladder training until after the first birthday, when the child could be expected to have greater control over his functionings. The age at which a mother might expect her child to be fully toilet trained ranged from fifteen months to two years. The 1943 edition of *The Baby* contained the following explanation for such variations: 'Some parents are better teachers than others. Some children learn more rapidly than others.'[63]

Publications included elaborate schemes designed to teach the child 'the dry habit' at night. The 1940 edition of *The Canadian Mother and Child* recommended lifting the baby and putting him on the pot at 1 a.m. for several nights in a row. The time of lifting should then be moved forward to 2 a.m., then 3 a.m., and so on, until night dryness was achieved. The author warned: 'This routine must be followed closely and regularly to be effective. (An alarm clock is useful to indicate the time to lift the baby.) Eventually you will find that the baby can be made to go through the whole night without mishap.' 'This training is exacting,' the author warned, 'but is well worth the trouble, as much washing will be saved, and what is more important, is the beneficial effect on the child's mental attitude.'[64]

In addition to regularity, another key factor in successful toilet training was deemed to be the mother's attitude. A 1944 publication noted that 'she should be confident that with patience and regularity of time the child will achieve good bowel habits.'[65] In their 1928 book Blatz and Bott observed: 'One cannot say too emphatically that the mother's attitude is the most important factor in training. If she is quiet and calm and follows a consistent routine, being firm without forcing and using judgment in the measures she adopts, all should go well.'[66] Mothers were urged to 'approve successes and ignore failures' in order to achieve satisfactory results in toilet training.[67] Mothers were cautioned against scolding or punishing the child for accidents in toilet training, as these might result in resistance to the entire process of training.

Following the Second World War, a virtual revolution in toilet training began to take place. Beginning with Dr Spock's popular *Baby and Child Care* in the United States, and with the 1953 edition of *The Canadian Mother and Child*, experts began to express serious reservations about the value and impact of early toilet training. Reflecting developments in the rapidly growing field of paediatrics, authors noted that 'conscious bowel and bladder control is not well developed until well into the second or even third year.' The authors of *The Canadian Mother and Child* thus informed mothers that 'it is impossible to "train" a child under a year in the use of the toilet. The best you can hope for is to observe your child, notice the rhythm which he will himself establish, and try to put him on the pot or toilet at the time when you expect a bowel movement.'[68] In his 1946 manual, Dr Spock pointed out that such efforts at early training were not 'exactly training, because the baby really doesn't know what he is doing. It's the mother who's trained.'[69]

Many authors expressed the view that efforts at early training might in fact result in later behavioural difficulties. Stressing that a child is unable to control his bowel movements before the age of nine or ten months, the authors of *The Early Years*, an Ontario Department of Health publication which first appeared in 1954, observed: 'Of course there are mothers who say their babies were trained much earlier than this, but it was the mothers who were trained – not the babies. Many of these "early-trained" babies are the ones who later have bowel problems during childhood.'[70] The authors of *Up the Years from One to Six* warned that 'many doctors believe training so early may have harmful effects.'[71] In a section headed 'Don't Ask the Impossible,' the authors observed: 'A mother can be too demanding in her standards of cleanliness. A child who isn't yet developed enough to measure up to these standards is in a pretty tough spot. He can't help but slip. To him that means he's somehow failing to do what his parents expect of him. Don't ask the impossible. Feelings of inferiority can start very young and be a handicap throughout life.' 'In some cases,' the authors continued, 'because of his mother's disapproval,' a child might develop a loathing for dirt, becoming 'one of those over-fussy persons who just can't stand a speck of dirt.'[72] Dr Spock also expressed concern about the danger of fights over toilet training: 'When a baby gets into a real battle with his mother, it is not just the training which suffers, but also his personality. First of all, he becomes too obstinate, gets in a mood to say "no" to everything, whether he means it or not ... He becomes too hostile and "fighty."' In addition, the mother might cause the child to develop 'overguiltiness.' If the mother made the child 'feel naughty about soiling himself with the movement,' the child might come 'to dread *all* kinds of dirtiness.' 'If this worrisomeness is deeply implanted at an early age, it's apt to turn him into a fussy, finicky person – the kind who's afraid to enjoy himself or try anything new, the kind who is unhappy unless everything is "just so."'[73]

Authors of books and pamphlets produced during the post-war period seemed reluctant to offer a specific age at which the mother should begin to toilet train her child. Ontario's publication, *The Early Years*, suggested that 'the time to begin training is during the *second year* of life.' In sharp contrast to *The Baby*, Ontario's interwar pamphlet, *The Early Years* ordered mothers not to use *'suppositories, enemas or soapsticks in an attempt to establish a bowel habit*. These often hurt his rectum and frighten him so badly that toilet time is dreaded.' Mothers were advised that they should not expect their babies to be 'perfectly trained much before two years of age.'[74] Dr Spock suggested that 'the best method of all is to leave bowel training almost entirely up to your baby.' At some point during 'the latter half of the second year, he will be aware of when his movement is coming and be able to control it.'[75] *The Early Years* offered similar advice, noting that 'in most cases it is the baby who decides when he is going to be trained and your part is usually one of friendly guidance to get him started along the right path.'[76]

Mothers were urged to adopt a 'casual, friendly' approach to toilet training. 'Never make an issue of the toilet or shame the baby when he fails or has an accident,' Spock advised.[77] In remarkably similar language, the 1953 edition of *The Canadian Mother and Child* told mothers: 'The most important thing about toilet training is to be casual and friendly about it. Never make an issue over it, for many long-standing problems start with difficulty over toilet training.'[78] Spock advised mothers that they would not 'have much trouble with training,' if they realized that the baby would 'mostly "train" himself.' Mothers were urged to assume the role of 'guide' rather than trainer. 'Remember that a child will completely train himself sooner or later if no struggle has taken place. *Practically all the children who regularly go on soiling after 2 are those whose mothers have made a big issue about it and those who have become frightened by painful movements.'*[79]

The Early Years also reminded parents that 'very few children over the age of two years are not well bowel-trained,' and suggested that they should stop taking 'the matter so seriously.'[80] It is likely that the widespread use of automatic washing machines following the Second World War might have made it easier for mothers to accept such advice.

An equally relaxed approach was adopted towards bladder training. *Up the Years from One to Six* observed that 'most babies won't stay dry for as long as two hours until they are around 15 months; boys are usually slower than girls.' Before this milestone had been reached, efforts at bladder training were doomed to failure. Even this statement was qualified by the following words: 'Here as in every phase of growing up, wide variation can be expected in normal children.'[81] *The Early Years* observed that parents could not expect bladder training to be complete before the child's third birthday. 'Although day-time control is usually established sometime between the second and third birthday,' the author noted, night training could be expected to take longer, probably until the child reached three years of age.[82] Spock suggested that the mother leave bladder training largely up to the child: 'Go at it easily, when he's ready. It really isn't you who trains your child's bladder. The most you can do is show the baby where you want him to urinate.' Once again, faulty training could have disastrous results for the child. Spock continued: 'The worst you can do is to go at his training so hard that you get him to hate the idea of going to the bathroom.'[83] If she avoided such problems, Spock suggested that a mother could expect her child to become dry between one and a half and two and a half, a far cry from the six weeks promised in the literature of the interwar years. Elizabeth Chant Robertson extended the deadline even further, suggesting that a mother could expect her child to be dry during the day between the ages of two and three and at night between the ages of three and four.[84]

In contrast to the major shift in advice on toilet training, attitudes towards many aspects of infant feeding remained largely unchanged. Throughout these years, authors of advice literature consistently recommended breast-feeding, concurring with Helen MacMurchy's assessment that 'mother's milk is the only safe food for baby.'[85] Authors promised women that as well as ensuring safety, nursing 'develops maternal instinct.'[86] Writing in *Chatelaine* in 1928, Stella Pines noted that '"satisfied maternity is the happiest condition of woman", and it is only the mother who is a whole mother by giving her baby his birthright in natural feeding, who can experience satisfied maternity.'[87] More than a decade later, Ernest Couture made a similar claim regarding the emotional rewards of maternal nursing: 'It is said that mothers who nurse their babies develop a greater affection for their children. Whatever be the truth of this opinion, one has only to look at the picture of a mother nursing her child to feel that here exists a more complete realization of motherhood for there is established a most precious relationship between the infant and the parent, and a sweet memory for the mother to carry through the years.'[88]

Many authors railed against mothers who failed to breast-feed their infants. The following quotation from an article by paediatrician, Dr Urban Gareau, is indicative of the extent of mother-blaming in which experts were prepared to engage to 'encourage' breast-feeding: 'The mother should feed her child naturally because the best citizens and the greatest nations have been breast fed. The Roman Empire began to decline only when the Roman mothers began to refuse to feed their young at the breast.'[89] Dr Alan Brown, of Toronto's Hospital for Sick Children, was a staunch advocate of breast-feeding throughout his career. 'Breast milk is for babies, cow's milk is for calves,' he frequently declared. 'Breast milk is best,' he argued, 'because it doesn't have to be warmed, you can take it on picnics, the cat can't get at it and it comes in such cute containers.'[90] In an article in the *Toronto Star* following Brown's death, the author noted that Brown 'often lashed out at "modern mothers who sublet their duty to a cow".'[91]

An equally committed advocate of maternal nursing was Dr John McCullough, former chief medical officer of health for the Province of Ontario and author of 'The Baby Clinic,' an advice column which appeared in *Chatelaine* from September 1930 until his death in 1941. 'Of all mammals – animals which suckle their young,' McCullough noted, 'the human is the only one which is disposed to shirk the duty of nursing its own young.' The failure to nurse, which McCullough deemed to be synonymous with a 'lack of maternal care,' was 'the greatest cause of the deaths of babies.'[92] Numerous articles throughout his tenure as a columnist stressed the importance of maternal nursing. In a 1933 article McCullough argued that 'when for any reason a mother cannot nurse her own baby, a wet nurse should be provided.' Defending this practice, McCullough noted: 'The children of the well-to-do of many countries have generally been brought up on the milk of wet nurses. This was a common custom in the slavery days of the Southern States where the coloured mammies were so employed and so well fulfilled this duty.'[93] Elsewhere, McCullough attributed the survival of the Dionne Quintuplets to the breast milk provided by nursing mothers through Toronto's Hospital for Sick Children. 'It is doubtful if any sort of artificial feeding would have kept them alive,' he maintained, warning, 'think of this, you mothers, and hesitate before you abandon the use of the breast for a bottle!'[94] Indeed, McCullough, like virtually every author throughout the period under examination, maintained that declining rates of maternal nursing could be blamed almost entirely on mothers, rather than on a range of factors including the wide-scale promotion of commercial infant formula and the effect of faulty advice on proper breast-feeding procedures.[95] In his final column, published shortly after his death in February 1941, McCullough once again blamed mothers for shirking their duty: 'In most cases where the mother fails to nurse her baby, she is lazy or indifferent. She will say: "Oh! I just can't be bothered." Nursing her baby interferes with bridge parties or other pleasures. Some women take refuge in one or another excuse. Such do not deserve to have a baby.'[96]

As I have argued earlier, in a period before the widespread availability of refrigeration and sterilized infant formula, breast-feeding undoubtedly was the safest method of infant feeding. Scientific and medical research throughout this century has supported the merits of breast-feeding.[97] The problem with the way in which breast-feeding was recommended in the advice literature of the interwar years was two-fold. First, rather than offering scientific or medical evidence to support their recommendations, authors frequently resorted to the type of mother-blaming cited above. It is unlikely that being told that women's failure to breast-feed caused the decline of the Roman Empire would have helped many mothers to nurse their infants! Second, as I will argue later in this chapter, much of the specific advice on how to breast-feed would have rendered successful breast-feeding virtually impossible.

Throughout the 1940s and 1950s, authors continued to stress the importance and value of maternal nursing. Dr Elizabeth Chant Robertson, Dr McCullough's replacement at *Chatelaine*, urged that 'every healthy mother should nurse her own baby!' While acknowledging that in a limited number of cases women might be unable to breast-feed, Robertson maintained that 'for the rest of us who are strong and well, breast feeding should be a duty as well as a pleasure.' 'It's quite an accomplishment to have a baby,' Robertson told women, so 'why not top it off properly by nursing him too?'[98] In two articles which appeared in *Chatelaine* in 1955, Robertson attempted to counter the 'old wives' tales,' misconceptions, and fears that she believed were preventing growing numbers of women from breast-feeding. 'Now there isn't a doubt in the world that any child gets a better start in life – not only physically but probably emotionally too – if breast-fed for at least the first four to six months,' Robertson claimed.[99]

In the first edition of *Baby and Child Care*, Dr Spock also recommended breast-feeding because 'it's safer to do things the natural way unless you are absolutely sure you have a better way.' Noting that breast-feeding helped the mother's uterus to contract, and enabled a mother to feel close to her baby, Spock stated that a 'big advantage of breast feeding is that the milk is always pure.' Despite his praise for breast-feeding, however, Spock's treatment of the subject might be seen to contain a subtle if unintentional recommendation for bottle-feeding. For example, the heading 'The Value of Breast Feeding' was immediately followed by the subheading 'Are there disadvantages to breast feeding?' and the following observations: 'Fewer babies have been breast fed in recent years, especially in cities. The chief reason is that bottle feeding has gotten to be safe and easy.' 'Is bottle feeding easier?' Spock asked. 'It is in two ways. The mother isn't held down. And she doesn't have to worry about whether the baby is getting enough.' While Spock later reassured mothers that a breast-feeding woman could 'lead a normal life,'[100] such reassurances might have rung somewhat hollow in the face of the alleged advantages of bottle-feeding.

It is worth noting that, despite the fact that *every* author stressed the value of breast-feeding, child-rearing manuals paid increasing attention to the proper methods of bottle-feeding as the century wore on.[101] Helen MacMurchy's pamphlets and books, written during the 1920s and early 1930s, contained *no* information on the preparation of formula or sterilization of nursing bottles. MacMurchy was adamant that maternal nursing represented 'the One Best Way' to feed a baby from birth until nine months of age. MacMurchy reassured women that 'every Mother can nurse her baby. It is true.'[102] Elsewhere she wrote, 'you will be able to nurse the baby. Never think of anything else ... You can nurse the baby, and you will do it for you know it is better for the baby, better for you and better for Canada. It saves the baby's life.'[103] Refusing to include information on 'artificial feeding,' as bottle-feeding was termed, MacMurchy claimed: 'Nursing the baby is the easiest way. No formula with bottles and rubber nipples, and measuring spoons and milk-sugar and sterilizing, and no one knows what else, for the Canadian Mother. These things will get dirty, and dirt in milk is death to the baby.'[104]

Other publications during the interwar years also discouraged artificial feeding, including a small section on substitutes for breast milk, if the mother had not been entirely successful in her efforts at breast-feeding. In such instances, however, women were urged to consult their physician for detailed information on the preparation of formula and bottles.[105] One exception to this approach was Ontario's *The Baby*, which included detailed instructions for bottle-feeding, in a section headed 'The Bottle Fed Baby.' Mothers who resorted to bottle-feeding were urged to 'hold the baby on the arm in the same position as for breast feeding. *The bottle should be held by the nurse or mother throughout the feeding.*'[106] Women were told to 'ask your doctor to make out a proper formula ... do not let any one persuade you to use any of the patent foods, many of which are of very little value.'[107] The 1933 edition of *The Baby* included four pages of instructions on the preparation of bottles, utensils, and feedings. Similar instructions appeared in Toronto's *The Care of the Infant and Young Child*. Once again, mothers were told that 'every bottle-fed baby must have its own individual feeding formula ordered by a physician.'[108]

Advice literature from the post-war period continued to recommend breast-feeding whenever possible. Ontario's publication, *The Early Years*, left the choice of breast or bottle up to the woman's doctor, for he, 'in the final analysis, is the only one who can decide the proper procedure.' Regarding the alternatives of breast- or bottle-feeding, the author observed that: 'During the last half-century or more, the thinking of the medical profession as a whole has changed from one to the other, perhaps on several occasions. However, in recent years the trend of the thinking of most members of the medical profession has been towards breast feeding.'[109] The author nonetheless provided ten pages of detailed instructions on the preparation of artificial feedings, undoubtedly sufficient information to enable the reader to prepare her own infant formula. The federal Department of Health's publication, *The Canadian Mother and Child*, included a method for calculating the caloric requirements of babies to assist in the preparation of artificial feedings. No caveat regarding the importance of consulting the physician before beginning bottle-feeding appeared in that edition. Instead, the section on bottle-feeding concluded with the words: 'Remember to ask the doctor what to do when you don't know,' a decided shift from earlier publications which took maternal ignorance on the subject as a given.[110] The 1953 edition of that publication had amended its advice as follows: 'The formula is so important to a bottle-fed baby, that you should have your doctor's advice on your baby's needs. If no doctor is available, here is the way you can figure out the formula yourself.'[111] Many women, having obtained a satisfactory formula through an advice manual, may well have decided to avoid the additional expense of visiting a physician to obtain an alternative feeding.

Despite their proclamations on the value of breast-feeding, manuals increasingly included sufficient information to enable women to select the option of bottle-feeding. In light of the prevailing reverence for science, it seems likely that mothers could have viewed the detailed photographs and instructions as a silent endorsement of the more 'scientific' method of bottle-feeding and might well have opted for that method in preference to the 'natural' approach of breast-feeding. Apart from the scientific aspects of measuring, sterilizing, and the like, bottle-feeding had the added advantage of being more precise than breast-feeding. Mothers could readily determine the exact amount of formula the baby consumed at each feeding, thereby calculating any changes in the regimen that might be required. A breast-feeding mother, in contrast, had to weigh her baby before and after each feeding throughout the day in order to determine how much milk the baby had consumed. Such an approach was arguably more trouble and appeared, at least, to be less accurate, given the possibility of lost fluid through elimination and the necessity of leaving soiled diapers on until after each weighing.

Hospital procedures also contributed to the appeal of bottle-feeding. While staff in hospital nurseries praised the value of maternal nursing, they frequently encouraged women to provide supplementary bottles of formula to prevent weight loss before the mother's milk supply had come in. Supplementary bottles were also recommended when the baby failed to gain in accordance with weight charts. Night-time feedings of formula or 'sugar-water' enabled mothers to 'get their rest,' while keeping babies satisfied. And finally, commercial manufacturers of infant formula provided free samples to mothers and babies upon discharge from the hospital. Incentives such as discounts on future purchases and free baby booklets encouraged women to keep up the bottle habit once they reached home.[112]

In the post-war years, authors began to point out that bottle-feeding had the added advantage of enabling the new father to assume responsibility for feeding the baby. While *The Canadian Mother and Child* suggested that such an event would occur only 'occasionally,' nonetheless it would help 'develop a happy relationship between father and baby.' The same volume reassured mothers who were unable to breast-feed that they could still develop a close, loving relationship with their infants. Mothers were urged to 'give him the same attention he would have if he were nursing.' 'Always take time to spend twenty minutes five times a day to give your baby the comfort and companionship he needs,' the author advised.[113] If bottle-feeding proceeded in this manner, then even the promised emotional advantage of breast-feeding could be overcome.

While virtually every author stressed the value of breast-feeding, advice concerning the proper procedure to establish and maintain an adequate supply of milk shifted from an emphasis on strict regularity during the interwar years to a less rigid, 'self-demand feeding' in the post-war era. In keeping with the emphasis on scheduling that characterized the interwar years, publications during the 1920s and 1930s stressed the importance of 'regularity of nursing.' Frederick Tisdall warned mothers that 'the infant should always be fed exactly at the stated hour and never at irregular intervals, as this upsets the baby's routine and soon leads to stomach trouble.' If the child had not yet adapted to his schedule and woke before the appointed feeding time, Tisdall recommended that the mother simply change the child if he was wet, and offer him 'some plain boiled water.' If the child was still asleep when his feeding hour arrived, 'he should be awakened.' Treated in this manner, Tisdall promised, the baby would soon 'learn to wake up at or shortly before the appointed time.'[114] Similar advice was contained in all the publications of the period.

While most authors did not explain the rationale behind strict scheduling of feeding times, William Blatz and Helen Bott offered the following justification for the shift from demand feedings characteristic of earlier centuries to the four-hour routine of the interwar years. Noting that babies would naturally eat but 'not in a regular way,' the authors stated that in earlier times 'mothers used to allow a child to nurse at will, and even doctors subscribed to the old rule of "little and often."' The authors then proceeded to explain the way in which 'modern pediatric practice' had amended this approach: 'The intelligent mother does not now leave this matter to chance. On her doctor's advice she adopts a certain schedule of feeding – every four hours, let us say. The baby is fed at that interval for a given length of time. Then he is put down, and no protests on his part will avail until the time for the next feeding arrives. This means that the child learns to be hungry not so much by his sensations as by the clock. In other words, he is becoming conditioned to a part of experience originally quite foreign to the hunger sensation.'[115]

Most authors advised the mother to adopt a four-hour feeding schedule, unless the baby weighed under six pounds. In that event, the infant was to be placed on a three-hour schedule until he gained sufficient weight to justify the longer interval between feedings. Once again, studies by experts were cited to justify the four-hour schedule. Tisdall noted that 'careful investigation ... has shown that less trouble is encountered if infants are fed every four hours.' Such a routine contained an added advantage for the mother in that 'it is much less tiresome and the mother is not tied down so much.' Books contained sample schedules for appropriate feeding times. Tisdall, for example, recommended that the feedings be given at '6 and 10 a.m. and 2, 6 and 10 p.m. with a night feeding at 2 a.m.' Weary mothers were reassured that 'the night feeding is only necessary for the first two or three weeks of life.'[116]

Ironically, despite the tremendous faith that most authors had in maternal nursing, much of the interwar advice on breast-feeding would likely have posed problems for the nursing mother. Believing, for example, that the infant required additional nutrition until the mother began lactating, some authors advised mothers to provide a supplementary bottle of sugar water or formula for the first few days.[117] Present-day medical wisdom indicates that infants receive adequate nutrition from the colostrum present in the mother's breasts and do not require additional feedings. Indeed, recent studies have suggested that the provision of supplementary feedings may discourage the infant from sucking hard enough at the mother's breasts to establish successful nursing. Furthermore, a rigid four-hour schedule may also have made breast-feeding difficult, as insufficient emptying of the breasts led to painful engorgement and the possible complication of mastitis.[118]

To insure successful breast-feeding, mothers were urged to obtain sufficient rest and exercise. Tisdall recommended that the mother sleep at least eight hours during the night and an additional hour each afternoon. 'Insufficient rest through the demands of household duties, the care of other children and social engagements interfere with the secretion of milk,' Tisdall warned. 'If possible the mother should have someone to help her in the home.' Exercise was equally important. Tisdall advised the mother to 'spend at least 1 hour a day walking in the open air.' This had the combined advantages of providing her with 'exercise and fresh air and at the same time a change of scene which helps to relieve any monotony of her life.'[119] Tisdall's colleague, Dr Alan Brown, advised the mother to obtain 'regular out-of-door exercise, preferably walking or driving – at least a one-hour walk morning and afternoon – as soon as her condition will permit.'[120]

Brown praised the women of his day who 'take more outdoor exercise, and consequently are not so neurotic as their ancestors.' Observing that 'the neurasthenic woman makes the poorest possible milk-producer,' Brown continued: 'It is fortunate for the future of the human race that young women are transferring their allegiance from crochet and embroidery-needles to golf, and to other outdoor exercises equally as good. Imitation is one of the strongest characteristics of the human race, and the tendency to outdoor life pervades among the rich and poor.'[121]

Worry presented a special concern for authors of advice literature during the interwar years. While Frederick Tisdall noted that 'the regular and complete emptying of the breasts' was 'the most important factor in maintaining or increasing the milk supply,' 'the next most important factor ... is the mental attitude of the mother. Worry, anxiety, grief, fright, excitement and anger all diminish, and may even completely stop, the secretion of milk,' Tidsall warned.[122]

Many authors believed that anxiety could actually 'spoil' the breast milk, causing the baby to develop digestive difficulties. Brown warned that 'uncontrolled emotion, grief, excitement, fright, passion, may cause the milk to disagree with the child,' and should therefore be strictly avoided.[123] Writing in 1923, Helen MacMurchy warned that 'passion or temper or any other bad feeling should never enter the mother's room. Great emotion spoils the nursing milk and the milk secreted under such conditions makes the child ill.'[124] Reports of such incidents found their way into the pages of the *Canadian Medical Association Journal*, official journal of the Canadian Medical Association. Writing in 1923, R.R. MacGregor described a syndrome which was characterized by the appearance of eight to ten green frothy stools. According to the author, the problem sometimes developed 'in breast fed infants with neurotic mothers. This is believed to be due to some temporary changes in the breast milk and is not an uncommon thing in this high tensioned age. It is further aggravated when the symptoms appear to be induced by the fear that she is not going to be able to nurse her infant.'[125] How were mothers to avoid such fears, particularly in the face of strict condemnations of mothers who failed to 'do their duty'? For the most part, authors simply exhorted mothers to 'cheer up.' One article, however, offered physicians advice on dealing with the case of the 'anaemic, undernourished, nervous mother.' Writing in the *Canadian Medical Association Journal* in 1921, Arthur B. Chandler noted: 'These cases require study on the physician's part. Frequently every detail of their lives has to be gone into before the underlying cause can be discovered and removed ... These nervous women must be kept from worry and excitement and taught to live rational lives.' The author warned that 'if the physician does not dominate the situation the ever present neighbour, who has seen similar cases do well on a bottle, will prevail, and weaning will be instituted.' Before such interference could take place, the physician was urged to intervene, encouraging the woman to continue with her efforts to breast-feed.[126]

While diet and rest were considered to be important factors in successful nursing, authors stressed that 'anger and excitement are more apt to affect your milk and upset your child than any change in your diet.'[127] Publications from the post-war period also emphasized the dangers of worry in preventing successful nursing. *The Early Years* noted that 'worry and unhappiness will dry up the breast supply more quickly than anything else. The mother should avoid getting over tired and should rest as much as possible.'[128] Ernest Couture concurred: 'The state of your mind is important. Keep cheerful; do not meddle with problems which may cause a mental strain; do not over-exert yourself by too much work or exercise.'[129]

Although many aspects of advice concerning breast-feeding remained constant throughout these decades, it is perhaps not surprising that a major change took place on the issue of scheduling. While publications of the interwar years uniformly recommended strict adherence to a four-hour schedule, authors in the post-war period began to advocate a less structured approach to breast-feeding. Whereas earlier editions of Toronto's *The Care of the Infant and Young Child*, for example, had ordered the mother to 'feed regularly even if the baby must be wakened,' the 1948 edition recommended that the mother 'work gradually towards a regular schedule. Be guided by the baby's individual needs and rhythm.'[130] The 1940 edition of *The Canadian Mother and Child* prefigured the transition to 'demand feeding' in the following passage: 'In many instances doctors are recommending that the baby be allowed to establish its own feeding schedule. This method has proved to be very satisfactory, but in this case one cannot, of course, predict the hours which the baby will adopt or the spacing between feedings. However, eventually the child will establish its own regular feeding times and then its programme should be adhered to.'[131] Mothers were urged to consult their doctors for guidance on 'the self-demand method,' and, when the doctor was unavailable, to follow the four-hour schedule included in the manual.

By 1953 *The Canadian Mother and Child* had adopted self-demand feeding as the preferred method of breast-feeding. The author noted: 'Self-demand feeding or letting the baby establish his own feeding schedule has been widely accepted as the best way to start feeding a baby. The object is always to establish a regular schedule, but for the first few weeks the idea is to nurse the baby when he wakes and cries from hunger at a reasonable interval from his last feeding. This is regarded as the natural method of finding out when a baby needs food.' While the author termed the method 'self-demand feeding,' it amounted to what is now called 'modified demand feeding,' since the object was in fact to help the baby to establish a four-hour schedule. Such a schedule, mothers were told, 'is best for you ... for it means only five nursings a day and will give you more time for your other duties and for resting. It is better for baby, too, as it leaves a longer time between feedings and makes him hungry, which, in turn, stimulates the flow of milk.'[132]

To alleviate fears that an infant might never establish a feeding routine, authors reassured mothers that infants on a self-demand schedule were more flexible than babies fed according to a rigid four-hour routine. One author observed that such flexibility would enable 'the modern mother ... to attend a six-thirty cocktail party,' by waking the baby prior to his usual feeding time. As well, 'the infant so handled very early develops the characteristic of not demanding food the moment he wakens but is content to lie in his crib quite happily when the mother is late in arriving home from her semi-weekly shopping tour.'[133] Finally, experts suggested that self-demand feeding might also provide emotional rewards as well. Writing in a 1955 volume of the *Canadian Nurse*, Ethel Cooke claimed that 'good parent-child relationships are the mother's reward for watching the baby instead of the clock.'[134]

Perhaps the most famous advocate of demand feeding was Dr Spock, who challenged many of the interwar ideas about the importance and value of feeding schedules. In an effort to counteract the mythology that had developed concerning schedules, Spock provided a brief discussion of the historical roots of scheduling: 'Up to sixty years ago, before there was much knowledge of infant feeding, babies were fed when they seemed to be hungry, even in the most careful homes ... When medical scientists began to study the feeding of babies at the end of the last century, they had to make some order out of chaos. They discovered how much milk babies of different weights and ages needed on the average.'[135] Doctors found that the average baby was satisfied for about four hours, if he had obtained sufficient milk at a feeding. They also found that mothers frequently interpreted a baby's cries from indigestion as hunger cries and offered the baby more milk. This merely exacerbated the digestive difficulties. To prevent such errors, doctors developed the system of four-hour feedings and spread their message through advice books and their individual practices. While he was critical of the fetishization of schedules which he believed had occurred, Spock was careful not to blame doctors. The problem, he argued, lay not in the schedules themselves, but in applying the figures for an average baby to *all* babies.

A careful reading of the section on schedules in Spock's first edition suggests that the culprit may well have been mothers. Spock explained: 'Mothers have sometimes been so scared of the schedule that they did not dare feed a hungry baby one minute early. They have even accepted the idea that a baby would be spoiled if he were fed when he was hungry.' Mocking such an idea, Spock argued that a baby cries 'not to get the better of his mother' but because 'he wants some milk.' In turn, he sleeps for the next four hours 'not because he has learned that his mother is stern,' but 'because the meal satisfies his system for that long.'[136]

To demonstrate how a flexible schedule might work, Spock offered the example of a mother,

far away in an 'uncivilized' land, who has never heard of a schedule, or a pediatrician, or a cow. Her baby starts to cry with hunger. This attracts her attention and makes her feel like putting him to breast. He nurses until he is satisfied, then falls asleep ... She puts him down and goes about her work. He sleeps for several hours until his hunger pains wake him up. As soon as he starts crying again his mother nurses him. The rhythm of the baby's digestive system is what sets the schedule. He never stays unhappy for long. The mother follows her instinct without any hesitation. She doesn't have to bite her nails, waiting for the clock to say it's feeding time.[137]

This lengthy discussion of the mother in an 'uncivilized' land was dropped from the 1957 edition of *Baby and Child Care*. Although Spock still advocated self-demand feeding, he felt the need to include a section on 'misunderstandings about self-demand' to counter charges of permissiveness that had been hurled his way.[138] Once again it was parents, and in particular mothers, who came under fire. Acknowledging that there had been 'a certain amount of misunderstanding' about demand feeding, Spock explained that: 'Some young parents, eager to be progressive, have assumed that if they wanted to get away from the rigid scheduling of the past they must go all the way in the opposite direction, feed their baby *any* time he woke and *never* wake him for a feeding, just as if *they* were conducting a scientific experiment, or as if there were a fundamental superiority in irregularity.'[139] While such an approach might work for 'peaceful' children of mothers who did not have to worry about their own schedules, Spock warned that it might encourage the child to continue night feedings right to the end of the first year.

In concluding the section, Spock castigated mothers who followed 'self-demand to inconvenient extremes.' 'It makes other mothers shy away from [self-demand feeding] like the plague,' he observed. In a classic example of the interchangeable usage of the terms 'parent' and 'mother,' Spock described a 'group of mothers talking about schedules' as follows: 'one will say in a superior tone, "*My* baby is on self-demand," and another will answer rather indignantly, "Well, mine *isn't!*" When parents act as if the schedule is a matter of belief, like a religious or political conversion, it seems to me that the real point has been lost.'[140]

Spock was anxious to reassure readers that self-demand feeding had a scientific basis. In the 1957 edition of *Baby and Child Care*, Spock explained that 'the first experiments were carried out by Dr Preston McLendon and Mrs Frances P. Simsarian, a psychologist and new mother, with Mrs Simsarian's new baby.' By allowing the baby to breast-feed whenever he was hungry, they hoped to see what sort of schedule he might adopt. Spock noted: 'The baby waked rather infrequently the first few days. Then, from just about the time the milk began to come in, he waked surprisingly often – about 10 times a day – in the second half of the first week. But by the age of 2 weeks he had settled down to 6 or 7 feedings a day, at rather irregular intervals. By 10 weeks he had arrived at approximately a 4-hour schedule.' McLendon and Simsarian termed the approach 'self-demand' feeding, a term Spock himself disliked 'because it suggests the picture of a demanding baby, which isn't correct.' The success of the experiment, coupled with the discovery that contrary to former wisdom 'flexibility did *not* lead to diarrhea or indigestion,' resulted in 'a general relaxation in infant feeding schedules.'[141]

Advice on weaning and feeding the older infant and child underwent a similar shift from a rigid to a more flexible schedule. During the interwar years, most authors recommended exclusive breast-feeding for about nine months.[142] Alan Brown observed that 'under normal conditions it is never necessary for a mother to wean her child before it is nine or ten months of age.' 'Unfortunately,' he continued, 'there are not very many women who at the present age are able to nurse their infants so long. I consider a woman doing very well if she can nurse her baby entirely for seven months. Of course, if she can nurse it longer, so much the better.'[143]

Because of the high incidence of bacterial digestive infections during the summer months, mothers were urged to avoid weaning during the hot weather, weaning the child 'a month or two earlier than usual,' if necessary.[144] Mothers were admonished not to make the decision to wean on their own; weaning was always to be carried out under the direction of the family physician.[145] Tisdall explained that 'as it is a strain on the baby's intestinal tract to change from mother's milk to cow's milk, weaning should be done under a physician's care and advice.'[146]

Despite the often detailed instructions on the feeding of solid foods included in child-care manuals, mothers were advised to use such information only to supplement their doctor's orders. Infant feeding, Tisdall explained, was too complicated a matter to be left up to the mother's discretion.[147] The 1931 edition of Toronto's *Care of the Infant and Young Child* also stressed that its 'directions are not intended to take the place of the advice of the family physician. Always consult your doctor in regard to the feeding of your child.'[148]

The importance of obtaining instructions on infant feeding from a physician was stressed throughout the post-war literature as well. While *The Canadian Mother and Child* advised mothers to begin weaning at six months, Couture warned: '*Do not wean your baby, whatever the reason, without consulting your doctor.*'[149] *The Early Years* explained that 'your doctor knows your baby better than anyone else and is in the best position to decide when new foods should be added.'[150] In both editions of *Baby and Child Care*, Spock urged parents to consult their doctors regarding the details of infant feeding, and to rely upon his instructions only 'if you cannot consult a doctor.'

Attitudes towards other aspects of infant feeding changed markedly between the interwar and post-war years. Regularity and a code of 'strict rules regarding what it may and may not eat' characterized much of the advice on feeding during the interwar years. *The Baby* noted that 'these rules should never be broken, for only by unswerving adherence to such rules will children learn to eat what is put before them without begging or whining for those things which adults indulge in.'[151] To avoid such episodes, many authors advised that young children dine separately from the rest of the family. In a 1928 *Chatelaine* column, Frances Lily Johnson of the St George's School explained: 'Since children eat different food and at a different time from adults, a low table and chairs should be provided and their meals should not conflict. This is an advantage to the child as well as to the adult as both can talk freely, parents are not bored by having mealtime made a lesson in deportment, and the children can have the undivided attention of an adult, without being tempted by foods which they are better without.'[152] Lest a reader conclude that such a procedure meant that the child would eat his meals without supervision, Blatz insisted that 'the mother or a suitable substitute should always be present to preside over the meal.' No doubt addressing his remarks to the clientele of the Institute for Child Study, Blatz warned that 'to leave the child to eat off the kitchen table in the tutelage of an untrained maid is the worst possible procedure for forming good eating habits.'[153] Blatz recommended that children eat at a table by themselves until at least the age of five or six. At that time, parents might begin to introduce them slowly to the family meal, beginning with breakfast or lunch.

During the interwar years, the most commonly recommended procedure for dealing with a child's refusal to eat a particular food was to withdraw all food. The *Pre-School Letters* noted that: 'It may be necessary to allow him to get really hungry before he learns better. Missing a meal under such circumstances will not harm any child. Nothing but water should be given until the next regular meal time.'[154] In the same vein, Blatz suggested that a child who refused to eat should be allowed to 'starve' for a brief period of time. 'The difficulty in this connection,' Blatz noted, 'is to persuade the parent that the child will not be harmed thereby. The mother almost always weakens before the treatment has had a chance to work.'[155] Mothers represented the main obstacle to the success of Alan Brown's program for dealing with a child who refused to eat, a plan which sounds Draconian to the modern ear: 'The child is undressed and placed in bed and put under the care of one person, as though he were very ill ... He is allowed water to drink in plenty. For the first day he is given four ounces of plain chicken- or mutton-broth every three hours. The second day he receives six to eight ounces of the broth at three-hour intervals. On the third day he is usually ravenously hungry, and is then given three or four good meals. If he has any special dislike for any article of food, that is included in the first meal.' Brown noted with considerable disapproval that 'some mothers will not be party to such a heartless treatment, as they are inclined to call it.' 'This is a wrong view to take of it,' Brown explained, for 'a complete change of diet for a day or two would often be of benefit to all of us.'[156]

While feeding problems were generally seen to be the result of faulty habit training, ultimate responsibility for such problems rested with the mother. All too often, experts found mothers coaxing their children to eat. 'Over-anxiety on the mother's part generally defeats its own purpose,' Blatz argued, for 'it sets up a resistance in the child, or, worse still, suggests to the child a means of coercing the parent.' 'If the mother cannot control herself,' Blatz continued, 'it is better that she should go away.' In many instances, 'the mere withdrawal of the mother may lower the emotional tension so much that the child will finish his meal without further difficulty.'[157]

Similar blame was placed on mothers in the literature of the post-war period. In an article entitled 'Feeding Difficulties,' Elizabeth Chant Robertson noted that the most common cause of feeding problems was mothers trying to force their children to eat. 'If she could have kept calm and composed, instead of becoming agitated and concerned, these episodes would have passed by with little effect,' Robertson maintained.[158] In an article entitled 'Don't Fight to Make Him Eat,' which appeared in the same magazine thirteen years later, Robertson reiterated her view that almost all feeding problems were the result of parents placing unnecessary pressure on their children to eat. 'Many mothers are much too concerned about the amounts their children eat,' Robertson observed.[159] Such concern was often passed on to the child, causing him to develop feeding problems. The first edition of *Up the Years from One to Six* (1950) explained: 'Once the mother becomes worried, urges the child to eat larger servings, tries to force rejected items, the child becomes more stubborn and The Battle is on. The more she frets and coaxes, the less he eats. The less he eats, the more frenzied the mother becomes. Mealtime becomes an unpleasant thing, and with it the danger of an unhappy relationship between the mother and child.'[160]

In marked contrast to the advice of Alan Brown and other authors of the interwar period, the post-war literature urged mothers to *relax* about their children's eating habits. Mothers were exhorted never to force a child to eat a particular food. If the child rejected an item, mothers were told to remove it without comment. 'Never scold or force him if he keeps spitting out the food he doesn't want,' *The Ca-nadian Mother and Child* urged.[161] 'A mother who insists upon certain foods is very likely to build up in the child a resistance to these which will cause grief later on,' another author warned.[162] Indeed, the struggles that developed over food had far-reaching implications, as authors warned that 'such conflicts will lead to other behavior problems.'[163] Spock urged mothers to 'let [the child] go on thinking of food as something he wants.' Otherwise, feeding problems would develop that could last for years.[164]

By the post-war era, the focus on feeding problems had shifted almost entirely from the child to the mother herself. One of the most fascinating explorations of this theme was a film made in 1947 by Crawley Films for the National Film Board of Canada. The film was an exploration of the reasons why Tommy, a formerly happy, breast-fed baby, had become a skinny, sulky little boy. A number of causes of feeding difficulties were suggested, including over-adherence to routines, and parental fighting at mealtimes. Mothers were warned that mealtimes should be peaceful and quiet, with mother nearby to lend a hand. 'The wrong attitude on mother's part,' the narrator threatened, could turn a temporary dislike into a 'permanent battle over food.' In Tommy's case, viewers were told that Tommy had 'unconsciously [been] using the most powerful weapon known to a child,' his refusal to eat. When Mrs Smith and Tommy finally visited the doctor, he informed Mrs Smith that 'you are the problem, not the boy.' Shocked at the news, Mrs Smith returned home to mend her ways: 'Mrs Smith does a lot of thinking. She realizes that she has been tense since he was a baby. She has forced him to eat what she thinks he should eat and has been unresponsive to his feelings.' She realized that Tommy's refusal to eat had been his way of asserting his individuality. To prevent him from using food as a weapon, she would have to make clear to Tommy that 'she loves him and respects him.' 'Above all,' the narrator informed viewers, 'she must learn to know Tommy.'[165]

The emphasis on individual difference characterizes virtually every aspect of child-rearing advice in the post-war period. In direct contrast to the rigid prescriptions and strict guidelines of the interwar years, the 1953 edition of *The Canadian Mother and Child* told mothers: 'It can't be too often repeated that each child has his own personality and temperament. No two babies behave the same way.' Mothers were urged to relax, as they learned to read and interpret the particular needs of their children. 'Mealtime should always be a happy, peaceful, leisurely time,' mothers were told.[166]

Such a leisurely approach to feeding was often accompanied by the contradictory message that the early introduction of solid foods would produce the best results. Magazines and child-care manuals were filled with pictures of roly-poly, smiling babies. Both images and text suggested that rapid weight gain was best for baby, as the following excerpt from a 1957 advertisement for Farmer's Wife formula indicates. Entitled 'Stork Club Conversation,' the advertisement contains the following comments of two new mothers: 'My, I wish *our* baby would gain weight like your Jimmy. Are you ever lucky!' The second mother replies, 'It's not just luck – Doctor put Jimmy on this Farmer's Wife Partly Skimmed Milk Formula right from the start.'[167] Advertisements for Heinz, Swifts, and other baby food products suggested that meat could safely be introduced in the first month of life. 'Babies thrive on real meat,' Swifts promised: 'Here's meat they can eat at 3 weeks!'[168] Another ad showed a mother planting a red-lipped kiss on her baby's head, as she declared, 'Meat is a MUST for my darling!'[169]

The message of advertisements such as these prompted an author writing in a 1959 volume of the *Canadian Medical Association Journal* to complain: 'Today mothers are being constantly bombarded with advertising suggesting that bigger babies are better babies. Paediatricians are not altogether free from blame, for many encourage the feeding of solid foods almost before the umbilical cord has been tied.' 'The effect on the mother of all this,' he continued, was that 'if the infant [had] not gained at least 1 to 2 lb. a month she [was] upset' and suspected that her child had poor weight gain.[170] Cochrane's comments notwithstanding, advertisers in popular magazines continued to promote the advantages of rapid development and growth, sustained, of course, by the early use of their products. Such messages may well have contributed to the steady decline in the rate of breast-feeding, since babies fed on infant formula and introduced to solid food at an early age gained weight more rapidly than those who were breast-fed exclusively for the first six to eight months of life.

Despite a dramatic shift in the approach to child rearing between the interwar years and the post–Second World War period, many of the prevailing ideas about maternal ignorance and the necessity for maternal education remained firmly in place, as mothers were urged to consult child-care manuals, nursery school teachers, nurses, and doctors concerning the best ways to rear their children. Consistent with the medicalization of motherhood established during the earliest days of pregnancy, the doctor's role in the provision of advice about child care was deemed to be of particular importance.[171] Like pregnancy and childbirth, childhood itself was increasingly portrayed as a condition requiring specialized medical supervision. From the moment a child was born and throughout the infant, preschool, and school-age years, his or her care was deemed to require the careful supervision of a trained medical practitioner. With such care, 'the promise was held out, and for the first time could be kept, that babies could be successfully reared, *provided* that medical advice was faithfully followed.'[172] The doctor could offer the best advice and care on the many dimensions of child rearing, from proper feeding and bathing, to toilet training and sleeping. The emphasis on giving advice represented a major shift in the primary preoccupation of physicians. Concerned primarily with the treatment of disease in the nineteenth century, over the course of this century doctors increasingly turned their attention to the care of the 'normal child.' Dr Alan Brown, author of the popular child-care manual entitled *The Normal Child: Its Care and Feeding*, noted in 1931 that approximately fifty per cent of the paediatrician's practice pertained to such matters as play, rest, diet, and other activities of childhood.[173]

For paediatricians and general practitioners alike, prevention, rather than treatment, became the watchword. Writing in 1942, Frederick Tisdall, a colleague of Alan Brown at Toronto's Hospital for Sick Children for many years, noted that 'the practical application of the fundamental principles of health is the best means to prevent disease.'[174] Virtually every piece of advice literature stressed the importance of regular visits to a paediatrician or family doctor. Failure to take a child to the doctor on a regular basis could have dire consequences. Dr Tisdall warned: 'Periodic medical examinations are a most important factor in the prevention of disease. By this means minor disturbances are recognized and corrected before they develop into serious ailments. When one sees tragic heart and other conditions, which could have been avoided, one realizes the importance of regular medical examinations.'[175] While child-health centres were recommended in cases of financial need,[176] these remained the option of last resort. Far preferable were regular visits to a paediatrician or family physician. Once again, Tisdall warned: 'Your doctor alone can determine whether your child has or has not a healthy body. Infants or children who appear in the best of health may have defects which will produce serious results if they are allowed to persist. Every child should be examined at least every six months, and infants, because of the more rapid changes, should be seen more frequently.'[177]

Authors of child-care literature repeatedly stressed the importance of regular medical examinations, reminding their readers that 'these directions are not intended to take the place of the family physician.'[178] The Canadian Council on Child and Family Welfare's *Post-Natal Letters* advised: 'The monthly letters offered to you will be of value in the way of general advice, but can in no way replace the personal service of your family doctor. So our first and most important instruction to you as a mother is that you will continue to keep yourself and your child under the care of your family physician for regular advice and supervision.'[179] The *Post-Natal Letters* concluded with a reminder that 'if you have any problems in connection with your baby's physical or mental development, consult your doctor.'[180]

Such references continued throughout the post-war period as well. Dr Spock, for example, prefaced many sections of his popular handbook, *Baby and Child Care*, with the words 'if you cannot consult a doctor.'[181] Throughout her articles in *Chatelaine* during the 1940s and 1950s, Elizabeth Chant Robertson stressed the importance of regular check-ups. 'Your doctor alone can tell if all is well,' she informed mothers.[182] Indeed, by the post-war years many authors appear to have found it necessary to discourage women from using child-care manuals as a replacement for doctors. The federal Department of Health and Welfare's publication *Up the Years from One to Six*, for example, castigated parents for relying too heavily on advice literature in matters of sickness. 'Too many parents,' the author noted, 'consult a "book of rules" or frantically scan their "home book of medicine" and then assume the role of doctor in treating their sick child.' Such an approach would only make matters worse, as parents tried to carry out diagnosis and treatment, matters far too complicated for parents to undertake themselves. The author reminded parents that 'doctors and nurses must spend many years of hard study and training and practice before they become qualified to take over the management of disease.'[183] In the same vein, Dr Spock cautioned: 'This book is not meant to be used for diagnosis or treatment; it's only meant to give you a general understanding of children, their troubles and their needs. It is true that in certain sections there is emergency advice for those very few parents who are out of reach of a doctor. It's better for them to have book advice than no advice at all. But book advice is never so helpful or so safe as real medical assistance.'[184] While advice literature had an important role to play in the proper rearing of children, it was to be used only in combination with regular visits to the family physician or paediatrician.

Although doctors were deemed to be best qualified to offer advice on all aspects of child rearing, mothers maintained responsibility for carrying out their dictates. Authors stressed that the task of ensuring the development of good habits rested 'largely with the mother or attendant.'[185] In a later edition of *The Baby*, the authors delineated the lines of responsibility more sharply: 'The responsibility for the formation of habits of conduct in the child of normal mentality rests entirely with the parents, both parents sharing equally in this responsibility. Neither the primary school, the playground, nor the Sunday school can be anything but contributing factors.'[186] This reference to the equal participation of men and women in the tasks of child rearing was uncharacteristic of the literature of the period. For the most part, responsibility for insuring the proper formation of habits rested firmly with the mother. Alan Brown, for example, noted that 'it is from the mother, most especially, that this guidance will come.'[187] The *Post-Natal Letters* pointed out that 'the mental environment of the child is created by the mother. This is her responsibility and her opportunity.'[188] On occasion, references to the responsibilities of parents appeared in the literature, but often that term implied the mother alone.[189] Helen MacMurchy described the appropriate gender division of labour as follows: 'If you take care of the Mother then she can take care of the Baby. The Father is the only one who can really take care of the Mother and the Mother is the only one who can really take care of the Baby.'[190]

Such a division of labour continued virtually unchanged throughout these decades. Thus, a partnership was formed between doctors, who retained ultimate authority over how children should be reared, and mothers, who retained responsibility for the day-to-day care of their children. In the final chapter of this book, I turn my attention to the impact which this alliance had on the lives of mothers.

5

Thoroughly Modern Mother

The duty of bringing up children does not belong to the state, but rather to the mothers, and whatever we do we must not be too ready to relieve them of their responsibility. The state can, however, do much to see that the rights of the children are not ignored and that the mothers have the opportunity given them of learning how best to rear their children.
Charles A. Hodgetts, 1921[1]

We can spread our propaganda to the four winds and let it blow where it listeth, but until we educate parents as to their responsibility in controlling the mental, moral, social and physical development of their offspring, our sowing falls on barren wastes.
Dr Gordon P. Jackson, 1929[2]

The image of the family as a private realm, a refuge from the cruel world of the market-place, has persisted ever since the Industrial Revolution led to a separation of the public and private spheres in the late eighteenth and early nineteenth centuries. Yet, over the course of the twentieth century, the home has been increasingly 'invaded' as doctors, nurses, and other child-rearing experts attempted to create and enforce new standards of child rearing. As Veronica Strong-Boag has noted, 'After World War I, as the media and bureaucracies dealing with youngsters steadily extended their influence, it became increasingly difficult to bear or rear children in isolation.'[3] Bombarded by advice from a wide range of sources, mothers found themselves subject to 'heightened public scrutiny.'[4] New standards of mothering, based largely on an Anglo-Saxon, middle-class family model, attempted to dictate a way of life for modern mothers and their children. Measured against such standards, many mothers found themselves wanting.

As the quotations which open this chapter suggest, child-care experts were well aware of the importance of ensuring that their advice reached Canadian homes. Reports from each division of child welfare were replete with charts indicating the number of pieces of literature that had been distributed during the preceding year. The volume of that literature was truly staggering. Between March 1921 and March 1922, for example, a total of 365,503 child-welfare publications were distributed by the federal Division of Child Welfare.[5] When compared with the total female population of child-bearing age of 2,142,000, that represents more than one piece of literature for every six women in Canada.[6]

During its twelve-year lifespan, 800,000 copies of *The Canadian Mother's Book* were distributed, a figure that represents nearly one copy for every four live births in Canada between 1921 and 1932.[7] Equally dramatic figures were reported by the Canadian Council on Child and Family Welfare and various provincial and municipal divisions of child welfare.[8] The demand for literature continued virtually unabated throughout the period under consideration in this book. During the Second World War, the federal Division of Publicity and Health, the division of the Department of Health responsible for the production and distribution of child-care information, reported that they received as many as 500 requests for literature a day. The author of the report claimed that there had been a 'noticeable increase in public interest in health literature compared with the pre-war years.'[9] Demands for *The Canadian Mother and Child*, the replacement volume of *The Canadian Mother's Book*, outstripped available resources throughout the war years, and the division was forced to maintain a lengthy waiting list.[10] The 1943–4 report of the Division of Child and Maternal Hygiene noted that, since its appearance in the fall of 1940, over 470,000 copies of *The Canadian Mother and Child* had been distributed in French and English 'upon request,' and that the demand for that publication was 'ever-increasing.'[11] The Publicity and Health Education Service reported that these demands continued *despite* cutbacks in government expenditure and in publicity as a result of the costs of the war effort. 'This great demand for information regarding health furnishes conclusive proof that people are more than ever conscious and desirous of preventing disease and knowing more about health,' the author noted.[12]

Circulation figures may, in fact, underestimate the readership of child-rearing literature. Nancy Pottishman Weiss has suggested that the widespread practices of sharing information, techniques, and even the manuals themselves, mean that we 'must necessarily go beyond raw sales figures.' Weiss cites a letter from a mother in Bellingham, Washington, who requested a second copy of the U.S. Children's Bureau's *Infant Care*: 'Unless I learn it by heart, it will do me little good, for, as was the case with the first monograph, I am so constantly lending it, that I never have it on hand for quick reference.'[13] My interviews indicate that such sharing of literature was a common practice among Canadian mothers as well.[14]

Much of the demand for literature came in the form of personal letters. Charlotte Whitton defended the accuracy of the Canadian Council on Child and Family Welfare's distribution figures by noting that 'there was no promiscuous distribution [of literature] at exhibits, etc. They must be requested.'[15] Helen MacMurchy also took heart from the large number of personal inquiries she received: 'No one will ever convince the Canadian Department of Health that mothers do not want to learn. Thousands of mothers' letters are on the departmental files to prove the contrary. Some of them are such sweet and simple letters that you look at them twice, with tears in your eyes.'[16] While thousands of requests came in the form of postcards distributed to new mothers through district registrars, many thousands of others were in the form of personal handwritten letters.[17] Many mothers learned of *The Canadian Mother's Book* through articles and advertisements in newspapers, and pinned the newspaper clippings to their requests for 'That Little Blue Book.' Some, however, were not pinned: 'They were sewed on the left hand upper corner of the piece of paper with a white cotton thread. There is something touching in the thought of the mother sitting down tired to read the newspaper, cutting out the extract, no pin to be found, threading her needle, putting on her thimble, sewing the cutting to her letter – with the baby in her arms perhaps, and the ex-baby at her knee.'[18]

Mothers wrote not only to government officials but to newspapers and women's magazines as well. In 1929, for example, *Chatelaine* announced the beginning of its 'personal service in child training': 'Have you any particular problem with your children that you would like to discuss in confidence with an authority? Does it seem impossible to break Mary of her habit of dawdling? Or will Peter insist on telling little lies? Mrs. Johnson, who conducts this monthly department, "What of your child?" is a noted authority on child psychology. Letters asking for advice, addressed to this department will receive her attention.'[19] Selected letters were reprinted in future columns of 'What of Your Child?' A similar service was provided in *Chatelaine* by Dr John McCullough during the 1930s and by Dr Elizabeth Chant Robertson in the 1940s and 1950s. Countless other women's magazines and newspapers offered women the opportunity to write for information and personal advice on a range of infant-care and child-rearing problems.[20]

Individual authors of child-care manuals also received large numbers of personal letters from readers. Dr Alton Goldbloom, Montreal paediatrician and author of the best-selling *Care of the Child*, reported that he was flooded with 'correspondence from across Canada, much of it in the form of fan mail,' after chapters of his book were read over the radio. 'Letters would come from remote settlements, from the far North, from the Island of Anticosti, all telling me how isolated they were, how many miles from a doctor and how helpful the book had been to them.'[21] While individual authors might have been inclined to exaggerate the volume of such requests, the fact that virtually every successful author reported a similar experience suggests that women did seek additional personal information and advice from authors of child-care manuals.[22]

Oral testimony also supports the notion that women were aware of and sought out child-rearing literature and advice. Almost all of the twelve mothers I interviewed indicated that they had made use of at least one manual during their child-rearing days. While one working-class woman noted that 'wages were so poor then, you just didn't have the money to buy books,' even she indicated that she had 'a good Baby Book.'[23] Winnie Weatherstone, whose first child was born in 1934, relied on Dr Goldbloom's *The Care of the Child*. 'Oh, Dr Goldbloom is so sensible,' she recalled, more than fifty years after she first purchased his book.[24] Kay Herrington received 'quite a big book from the public health [nurse]' when her first child was born in 1935. 'That was my Bible,' she recalled. 'They were brought up by that book.' In addition, she read articles on child rearing in various women's magazines. 'Any article that had to do with child rearing I read,' she told me. 'I always figured, well you can't know too much.'[25]

Mothers from the post-war era indicated that they owned a copy of Dr Spock's *Baby and Child Care*, first published in 1946. 'I think everyone had it around our lot,' testified one mother who also read various articles from women's magazines that circulated among her network of friends.[26] One mother, whose children were born in England prior to the family's emigration to Canada in the 1950s, used the *Good Housekeeping* baby book. 'That was sort of my Bible,' she remembered.[27] Another mother, who purchased Dr Spock's *Baby and Child Care* after the birth of her second child in 1946, recalled: 'I don't know whether I ever read it straight through. I probably read fair amounts of it and then sort of looked up things ... to know whether something is normal or whether it's something I should take the child to the doctor with. That's ... how I used it.' When I asked whether she had a subscription to any women's magazines, she laughed: 'Sounds silly, but I didn't get a lot of time to read.'[28]

Attendance at prenatal and well-baby clinics and at child-welfare lectures and displays may also indicate women's desire to learn about infant and child care. In the summer of 1914, for example, Toronto's Department of Public Health carried out an experiment in infant welfare. From 9 July to 21 August, the Toronto Ferry Company lent the department one of its boats three afternoons a week in order to conduct outings for mothers with children under the age of two. A spokesman for the department stated that 'it is hoped to counteract by this means the unhealthy atmosphere of the congested districts from which these children are taken, thereby lowering the death rate.' The trips were extremely popular – a total of 1,963 mothers and 2,318 babies participated in the nineteen trips, and Dr Charles Hastings, Toronto's medical officer of health at the time, reported that 'many mothers walked quite long distances, some two or three miles, often carrying their babies in their arms rather than miss the sail.'[29] Each voyage was supervised by a public health nurse, who provided health-care information, and assisted in the preparation of feedings for bottle-fed babies. At the end of the summer, the experiment was discontinued because of the cost and the heavy work load of the public health nurses.

When examining such data, we are presented with a problem of interpretation. It could be argued that mothers went on the ferry-boat rides primarily because of the opportunity for an outing that it provided. It is also conceivable that women accepted the information and advice as a necessary, but largely unwelcome by-product of the trips. Attendance figures at well-baby clinics may also be interpreted as an indication of women's desire for services rather than information and advice. Regardless of their reasons for attending such clinics, however, mothers were exposed to the latest ideas in infant and child care, receiving literature and advice from the public health nurses.

Attendance figures for infant-care lectures offer an opportunity to assess the degree of interest in an explicitly educational enterprise. At the prenatal and infant care talks held at Eaton's, for example, between twenty and thirty-nine women were in attendance. The author of the report describing the effort noted that most of the women 'had come not because they happened to be in the store, but because they wanted to hear the talks. At least one came three times; once for the talk on the Expectant Mother and twice for the talk on the Care of the Baby.'[30] Following the lecture, women left their names and addresses in order that baby-care literature could be sent to their homes. Sessions held by various departments of health enjoyed similar success, a fact which suggests a desire on the part of expectant mothers to learn about infant and child care.

Over the past four decades experts in child development have conducted numerous studies to assess the degree to which parents seek out and attend to information on child rearing. Since a complete examination of this literature is beyond the scope of this book, I will briefly review the findings of five key studies.[31] While the vast majority of these studies have been conducted in the United States, their findings are corroborated by the interview data and letters which I will introduce later in this chapter. In an article which appeared in 1961, Nathan Maccoby examined what he termed 'information-seeking behavior.' Employing the concept of a 'critical-period' group to denote those people directly affected by a particular subject, Maccoby and his colleagues found that 'critical-period mothers were more likely to seek out information relevant to their needs; and, once exposed to such overt information, to attend to it.'[32] Studies which attempted to distinguish other variables that might affect information-seeking behaviour were less conclusive. Melvin Brooks, Douglas Rennie, and Roger Sondag, for example, found a correlation between education and the reading of child-rearing information sent to mothers in Jackson County, Illinois. No correlation was found between any of the other factors examined, including social class, social mobility, and urban or rural location.[33]

In a 1978 article based on three separate studies, Alison Clarke-Stewart noted that 'a remarkably high proportion [of parents surveyed] reported that they had read child-care materials while their children were young.' Of the random sample of Chicago parents, 'ninety-four percent claimed to have read at least one child-care article or book; 38% said they had read more than 10 articles; and 25% reported reading more than five books. Seventy-one percent had read Dr Spock.' Clarke-Stewart also distributed questionnaires to people borrowing child-care books from the Chicago Public Library. Once again, respondents reported a high degree of familiarity with advice literature. The author reported that 'on the average, each mother had read two books before; one had read – and reviewed for us – 31 such popular child-raising books!' While these respondents were clearly drawn from a literate population, Clarke-Stewart noted that 'the parents were not of professional or executive social status, but represented about equal proportions from the working class (bus driver, steel worker), lower middle class (salesman), and middle class (teacher, engineer); 10% could be classified as lower class.' In contrast to 'the common stereotype of the kind of mother who reads this literature,' Clarke-Stewart found that 'these readers of child-care books ... were not the highly educated, affluent, stay-at-home mothers in suburban splendor ... That is not to say that the latter mothers do not also read child-care books; most likely they not only read them but buy them, rather than using a library copy. The point is that upper-middle-class moms are not the only people who read the popular "expert" literature; less affluent mothers with full-time jobs do, too.' On the basis of her studies, Clarke-Stewart concluded that parents from diverse backgrounds 'are eager for information about children and child rearing and are actively seeking it out.'[34]

Similar findings were reported by Michael Geboy in a 1981 article. In a study conducted in Tyler, Texas, Geboy found that 'nearly all of the parents contacted said that they did at least some child care reading when their children were young (96.9%).' The author continued: 'Nearly three-fourths of the respondents had read at least two books, and over one-third of the sample said they read four or more books. Magazine articles were also a common source of information about child care. Nearly three-fourths of the parents said they read at least five articles and approximately one-third said they read more than ten.'[35] In addition, nearly forty per cent of parents reported that they had attended a class or course on child care.

It can be argued that such a high proportion of parents reported that they had consulted child-care literature because they wanted to present themselves to the interviewers as responsible, concerned parents. Jay Mechling maintains that 'while there is evidence that official advice in childrearing literature affects parents' *recall* of childrearing behavior as it is reported to a social scientist, there is no persuasive evidence that the official advice affects the parents' *actual behavior*.'[36] However, the mere fact that parents stated that they had read the literature indicates a degree of familiarity with the genre as a social norm.

Furthermore, parents in several of the studies were able to recall many specific details of the child-rearing advice contained in the manuals, a fact which suggests that the literature had not simply remained unread on their bookshelves. A British study conducted by Cathy Urwin indicates that the significance of the literature extends beyond the level of general awareness. In a study involving forty mothers, Urwin found that 'most of the first-time mothers had one or more books which at some time they had consulted regularly, and sometimes read several times over.' One mother reported: 'I found even the pamphlet they gave you at the hospital helpful. I was reading it again and again. It helps just to put your mind at rest. I think you just need something to reassure yourself.'[37] Not only did the women in Urwin's study report that they had consulted child-care authorities and manuals, but they frequently presented concepts such as maternal deprivation as 'statements of what the mothers believed themselves,' rather than as 'pieces of dogma which could be evaluated and accepted or rejected.' She argues that her interviews demonstrate that developmental psychology had an impact 'not only on how these women saw their children's development but also on how they thought they should spend their time with their babies,'[38] a finding which indicates a high degree of internalization of expert advice.

Why did women turn to experts for advice on prenatal and infant care? As traditional female support networks broke down with the exodus from the family farm, new mothers found themselves alone on what must have often appeared to be alien terrain. The decline in family size also meant that women lacked the experience in caring for young children that had traditionally accompanied life in a large family. As Sheila Kitzinger has observed, 'the expectant mother in contemporary industrialized Western society may never have touched, or even seen, a newborn baby before. The appearance and needs of a tiny baby may be as much a mystery to her as the breeding of giant pandas.'[39] As a result, twentieth-century mothers increasingly found themselves in the position that one author has termed 'double jeopardy – they have no one to teach them and no previous experience.'[40]

Oral and written testimony by Canadian mothers attests to the impact of declining family size. One mother observed: 'My own experience, as the youngest of two, was never to have contact with any babies or young children until my sister produced some – and even then the contact was minimal.'[41] Another mother confessed, 'I was so dumb when it came to children.' She felt that she 'couldn't have navigated' without her advice manual. 'Everything the book said, I would do,' she explained: 'Of course, you wouldn't do it like that today, but I mean, I wasn't used to small children. I was rather scared, you know, that I wouldn't be doing things right so I thought, well, this book, whatever it says has to be right. You can't go wrong.'[42] Another woman, who had had little contact with younger siblings, described her feelings when her first child was born as follows: 'It was certainly mind boggling. I mean, what are you doing with this piece of animal life? And totally responsible for it!'[43]

While fertility rates declined first among the urban middle classes in English Canada, that trend gradually spread throughout the rest of the Canadian population. Furthermore, women in both urban and rural areas faced the issues of infant mortality and morbidity, and the fears engendered by those harsh realities, coupled with an acute shortage of medical care for rural and poor women, led many women to seek help from child-rearing experts.

Rapid changes in ideas about child rearing may also have led many women to seek expert help. Information about the latest scientific discoveries, ranging from immunization to the importance of vitamins, was available only from a doctor, public health nurse, or other childcare expert. Not surprisingly, then, many women turned to their family physician or well-baby clinic for information on the most up-to-date views on child care.

At least one expert expressed concern about mothers' growing dependence upon their doctors. In a passage about the preparation of infant feedings, Dr Alton Goldbloom, of Montreal's Children's Hospital, complained: 'Young mothers are still bewildered by what is in reality a ridiculously simple discipline, and it is their utter and needless dependency that keeps many a pediatrician across the country busy and causes him to waste needless hours on the telephone allaying groundless fears and advising on that which should no longer need advice.' Goldbloom blamed 'this employment of a busy doctor as a vicarious thinker and unquestioned arbiter of the obvious' on what he termed 'the almost total lack of motherhood training,'[44] ignoring the role that the medical profession itself played in encouraging frequent consultation with the doctor.

Dramatic changes in medical wisdom also meant that few women could turn to their own mothers for help – even if their mothers were geographically accessible. As Beatrice Whiting points out, 'The mother who was told by her physician to wean early and put the child on a formula so that she could tell to the ounce how much food her infant was getting is not in possession of either experience or folk wisdom when her daughter needs advice on breast feeding.'[45] This problem was greatly compounded by the systematic attack on traditional methods of child rearing that began in the early decades of this century and has continued to the present day. Authors of advice literature repeatedly urged mothers not to 'try out fancy theories learned over the back fence.'[46] While Dr Goldbloom might have been disturbed by what he termed 'the incessant telephone calls over trivialities,'[47] caveats like the following surely encouraged just such a religious adherence to the doctor's advice. In a passage headed 'The Periodical Visit to Your Physician,' the author of the *Pre-School Letters* warned readers: 'Be sure to tell him all that you have observed and follow his instructions minutely. Avoid the advice of neighbours or relatives and accept that which you pay for getting.'[48] Mothers were warned that 'superstitious, needless fears, [and] half-truths ... handed down for generations by word of mouth ... [were] not the best source of information for modern mothers.'[49]

New mothers were frequently warned of the dangers of seeking advice and assistance from their own mothers. As a 1923 nursing bulletin reminded its readers, 'A "Holt" in the hand is worth more than two grandmothers in the bush.'[50] Thirty years later, author June Callwood referred to grandmothers as 'a species doctors feel are the natural enemies of modern science,'[51] an assessment based on interviews which she had conducted with doctors. Another *Chatelaine* columnist adopted a slightly more sympathetic stance, acknowledging that 'an expectant mother's mother can be one of her greatest comforts, provided she has a sensible outlook.' She felt duty bound to add, however, that 'grandparents can do a great deal of harm through failing to recognize that "things are different" from their young days.'[52] The message in the advice literature, the magazines, and the advertisements was straightforward: modern mothers consulted the experts, not their hopelessly old-fashioned mothers. Such counsel would have contributed to the physical isolation many mothers were already experiencing.

The shift in the location of parturition from home to hospital may also have contributed to women's reliance on expert advice. In marked contrast to a home birth, where a woman made the transition to motherhood surrounded by family and friends in a familiar setting, a hospital birth offered the new mother efficient baby nurses who took command of the care and feeding of the baby. While the quality of care the baby received may have been above reproach, many women found that the combination of hospital procedures in a foreign environment left them feeling alienated from their newborns. Ina May Gaskin, an American midwife who gave birth to her first child in the mid-1960s, reported: 'I remember being shocked when five days [after the birth] they were going to turn me loose with her, and they hadn't even given me a class on how to take care of her. Here I was only allowed to touch her when they said I could, and then they took her away. And I really got the feeling that she was theirs and that I was some dirty, ignorant person.'[53] In 1982, when I gave birth to my first child, hospital rules dictated that new mothers could not carry their babies in their arms, but only in the portable bed the hospital provided. The result of such procedures was that I felt completely incapable of caring for my baby, and was disabused of the notion of hiring a private duty nurse only by the promise of daily help from friends once I returned home. As Ina May Gaskin explained, 'I had the feeling I had to go to some expert to find out what to do and then follow their instructions, but there was nothing within me that knew what to do.'[54]

The combination of demographic changes, the shift from home to hospital for childbirth, and the assault by child-care experts on traditional methods of child rearing, created the potential for a powerful dependence on new sources of child-care information and advice. In the face of high rates of infant and child mortality, mothers feared for their children's well-being. Child-rearing experts warned mothers that failure to adhere religiously to their prescriptions could result in serious illness or even death, an outcome that would be blamed almost entirely on the mother.

How did mothers feel about the advice they received? Did they appreciate the efforts of child-rearing experts? To assess the maternal response, I have turned to three sources: the records of the health-care professionals, letters written to child-rearing experts, and interviews with mothers. One sector which considered the question of compliance was the nursing profession, and its observations are recorded in the *Canadian Nurse* and in materials deposited in the City of Toronto and Province of Ontario Archives. In contrast to doctors, who rarely commented on this issue, assuming, perhaps, that their dictates would be followed without question, nurses did attempt to assess mothers' response to their advice. It appears that among most sectors of the population nurses found their advice increasingly welcomed as the century progressed. The author of the following article, which appeared in *Canadian Nurse* in 1923, described women's ready acceptance of the nurses' counsel: 'The effect of this constant teaching has been well seen during the past summer. The rate of mortality from summer diarrhoea among these babies this year has been only one-fourth the rate from the disease in the city on a whole. Many mothers have said, "Yes, baby began to get sick last week, but I did just what the nurse said and he got all right by the next day."'[55]

Surveys of participants in prenatal classes in Toronto during the 1940s indicated an equally positive response to the teachings of public health nurses. In a report based on one such survey, the author noted that 'with very few exceptions, the comments on the value of the classes, educationally and practically, were enthusiastic.' One mother was quoted as saying that 'classes helped more than all baby books could do.' Another indicated that she had 'enjoyed motherhood so much more because of knowledge given in classes.'[56] A second report, based on 363 surveys of participants in prenatal classes, offered similar evidence. One mother remembered: 'I came home from hospital with my new baby feeling confident and not in the least nervous about having to handle such a tiny creature.' Another confirmed that 'classes gave me confidence. I am far more at ease with the baby and she in turn is contented and happy.'[57]

Evidence from the Second World War also indicates that many women appreciated the services offered them by public health nurses and sought to implement the advice they received. An article in the *Canadian Nurse* used excerpts from a mother's clinic diary to show her response to the Royal Canadian Naval Well Baby Health Service. The diary detailed the clinic visits of the mother and her two children, showing how the entire family came to look forward to these occasions, despite the inoculations! Following her first visit, for example, the mother recorded the experience: 'After filling out the children's history sheets, the doctor sent us out to see Nursing Sister Amberry. She gave Bobby a cookie, and gave me two very helpful booklets put out by the Welfare Council, and also samples of cod-liver oil which the children must take every day. She was very kind and such a big help to me. I'm sure Sandra and Bobby will be the finest children in the world if I follow her good advice.'[58] Another mother described the home visit of a public health nurse in a letter to her husband serving overseas during the Second World War. The nurse offered advice on

problems ranging from tonsillitis to temper tantrums. The mother concluded: 'I really feel much better about things since I've got to know
that nurse. I'm going to go back to the clinic every week for a while
to have the baby weighed – and the nurse said I could talk over any
problems I had about the baby or the other children any time I wanted
to.'[59]

Non-English-speaking immigrant mothers represented a special challenge for public health nurses. In an effort to reach the growing population of immigrants in the city, Toronto's Department of Public
Health appointed Matilda Simone, an Italian-speaking nurse, in 1914.
The following year, Zara Price, a Russian-born nurse who also spoke
German, Ukrainian, Polish, and Latvian, was hired. The appointment
of Pareska Stamenova in 1920 to work with Macedonian immigrants
completed the roster of 'language nurses.'[60] In addition, the Department of Public Health began translating its prenatal- and infant-care
literature into Italian and Yiddish. When Nurse Simone resigned in
1921, however, the department chose not to replace her. Janet Neilson,
author of a 1945 history of public health nursing in Toronto, explained
the decision as follows: 'It was beginning to be realized ... that the
appointment of nurses to serve our non-English-speaking population
was not altogether wise and that, instead, every effort should be made
to have these people use the language of the Country.'[61]

Whether they could speak the language of immigrant mothers or
not, public health nurses faced other barriers in their efforts to persuade immigrant mothers to adopt the methods of scientific child rearing.[62] As Marion Royce explains in her biography of Eunice Dyke,
director of the Public Health Nursing Division of Toronto's Department of Public Health from 1911 to 1932: 'Language was not the only
barrier ... Equally formidable were the fears and forebodings of the
immigrant mothers. Far from their native soil, they were baffled by
the nurses' unfamiliar ways of infant care. They insisted, for instance,
that a child should not be bundled into layers of clothing that the
mothers thought essential to its comfort.' While Royce notes that the
nurses' 'new-fangled' methods were unfamiliar to Canadian-born
mothers as well, she suggests that those women more readily accepted
the nurses' advice. 'So radical a departure from traditional ways was
less acceptable to perplexed immigrant mothers who misunderstood
and often resented the nurse's interference even if the infant might
be more comfortable.' Royce concludes, however, that while the nurses

were 'outsiders in an immigrant community', nonetheless 'they were there, calling and to be called in case of need, and over the years mutual respect often blossomed in friendship.'[63]

During the 1950s, as high rates of immigration following the Second World War transformed the ethnic composition of Toronto's population, Italian, Portuguese, and Greek mothers attended child health clinics in large numbers. Lacking medical practitioners within their own communities, and, perhaps more important, often lacking any form of health insurance, immigrant women readily embraced the services provided free of charge by the city's Department of Public Health.[64]

The only reference I found that contradicted this overwhelmingly positive image presented in the literature between 1920 and 1960 was an article published in *Canadian Nurse* in 1930. Lamenting expectant mothers' unwillingness to attend prenatal clinics, the author complained: 'The older and more experienced prenatal case has consistently been found to develop a still more *independent* attitude towards offers of clinical help or advice during this very important period, and in many cases the result of her *indifference* works to the detriment of both mother and child.'[65] Elsewhere, public health nurses commented on the receptiveness of first-time mothers, finding them subject to neither the 'independent attitude' nor the 'indifference' exhibited by mothers who already had older children. Writing in *Canadian Nurse*, for example, B.E. Harris noted that 'the young wife, especially the primipara [first-time mother], is usually eager to be sold knowledge of maternity and care of offspring.' Harris reported that 'the greatest joy' of prenatal nursing was 'found in the interest exhibited by the primipara. Education is usually easy with this prenatal case, which is eager to know all things.'[66]

To assess the almost uniformly positive response, two additional factors must be considered. First, the evidence cited is based primarily on official reports of public health nurses, directed to supervisors or to other members of the profession. Such reports, it could be argued, might tend to present a positive image of the programs, in order to secure future funding. We must question whether, perhaps, negative comments were either screened or actively discouraged. Second, it is possible that the mothers cited in the nursing reports were expressing gratitude primarily for the services and assistance rather than the advice they received.[67]

To assess women's response to printed materials and advice, we must turn to the testimony of the mothers themselves. Virtually all of the mothers I interviewed talked about the help they had received from advice literature.[68] One mother, who used Dr Goldbloom's book throughout the 1930s, referred to his book as 'a tower of strength.'[69] Another mother, the wife of an obstetrician, used Dr Spock's *Baby and Child Care* throughout her child-rearing years. 'He was a great comfort in those days,' she recalled. When other child-rearing experts were lecturing her with 'all the "you shoulds",' Dr Spock reassured her that 'it's O.K. to ... follow your instincts.'[70]

Letters written by mothers to authors of child-rearing literature also expressed tremendous gratitude for the help they received. Almost without exception, mothers indicated that they followed the advice, and that the result was better health for their children. The following excerpts from mothers' letters were among those included in the 1942–3 report of the Maternal and Child Hygiene Division of the Canadian Welfare Council:

The letters you sent to me helped wonderfully – my baby is 8 months old now and a perfect child according to her doctor here in Montreal ... My first baby died due I think to ignorance of prenatal care resulting in Toxaemia. The second baby now is a credit to your help and guidance.

I would like you to know the postnatal series of letters were indeed a great help to me in raising my little baby to one year old. He is healthy and a very happy, contented baby and I'm depending on the next series to be just as helpful.

I found the last book a great help in raising my baby. She is a fine healthy girl today thanks to you.

When my baby was born the Victorian Nurse gave me your first book covering the first year of a child's life which I found so valuable. I went by it as for change of food, sleeping habits, etc. and I really don't know just what I'd have done without it.[71]

Mothers frequently attributed the successful outcome of their pregnancies to the prenatal advice they received in booklets and other publications. Mrs Fernando Plourde, for example, wrote the Canadian Council on Child and Family Welfare to 'express all my gratitude, for it is thanks to your kind advice that my confinement has been such a normal one, and that my baby is so well.'[72] Mrs Romeo Payne, of

Hull, Quebec, reported, that 'thanks to [the prenatal letters] and the advice contained therein, which I carefully followed, I had the satisfaction of giving birth to a healthy baby boy on June 4th.'[73] A Kapuskasing mother wrote: 'I would like to take this opportunity of thanking you very much for [the] series of pre-natal and post-natal letters which helped us very much. I had a very comfortable pregnancy and confinement and was rewarded with twin daughters, five and one-half and six pounds.' The proud mother enclosed a picture of the twins on their first birthday.[74]

Many letters expressed a feeling of closeness with the authors of advice manuals. A Quebec mother, writing to the United States Children's Bureau in 1921, told Miss Rude: 'Much I would like to know you, as your [sic] just like a mother to me, as I'm an orphan.' 'Words can not express what I feel for you in my heart,' she continued. 'I can only write that I thank you infinitely for your kindness towards helping me with my baby.'[75] Another woman, living on an Alberta homestead, 'miles from a telephone and many more miles from a doctor or any dependable person of whom I could ask advice,' expressed her gratitude for the pre-natal and post-natal letters. 'They have been just like letters from a very dear and trusted friend and I miss looking forward to their arrival,' Mrs W.E. Corbett wrote.[76] As Nancy Pottishman Weiss has observed, for women living in isolated regions or far from family, advice manuals seem to have served 'not only as expert tutors or informed curricula, but also as substitutes for friends and relations.'[77]

Radio broadcasts, such as the ones conducted by Dr Allan Roy Dafoe, doctor of the famous Dionne Quintuplets, appear to have played a similar role for women living far from friends and family. One listener, who lived in the mountains near Boulder, Colorado, told Dr Dafoe: 'I have no one to advise me on the care of my three babies, and surely do appreciate your help.'[78] Another mother confessed, 'I never miss your broadcasts and believe I've learned more from them than from all the advice given by friends and relatives.'[79]

In examining both written and oral sources, I was able to uncover virtually *no* evidence of resistance to child-rearing advice. One of the few mothers who recorded her scepticism about the experts was Phyllis Knight. 'Although I grew up in a big family,' Knight recalled in her life story, 'I didn't really know anything about child rearing – except the basics. But then, who does? Certainly not the people who write those silly psychological books on child care.'[80] A poet writing in

Chatelaine in 1932 may have expressed the private feelings of many mothers during the interwar years. Entitled 'Modern Mother,' the poem attacked the canons of scientific child rearing:

I have tried philosophy,
And applied psychology –
But when Johnnie bumps his knee
I forget – and kiss it!

'Never sing them lullabies –
Fairy tales are silly lies' –
But when drowsy baby cries
I forget – and rock him!

I should like to ask to tea
Little mothers who would be
Deaf to child psychology.
Quaint, perhaps, but modern surely
Mothers who could find delight
In that ancient ceremony –
'Tucking children in,' at night![81]

If those were the feelings of other Canadian mothers, however, they remained deeply buried.

How are we to interpret the letters mothers wrote to child-rearing experts? On the face of it, at least, they would appear to indicate that women welcomed child-rearing advice, finding it helpful in dealing with the tasks of motherhood. I would question, however, whether the official records of the Canadian Council on Child and Family Welfare or the federal Division of Child Welfare provide us with the complete picture. First, the vast majority of letters received by the Division of Child Welfare were destroyed.[82] While a much larger number of letters to the CCCFW remain intact, they nonetheless represent only a portion of the total volume of mail received by the council. Letters which were retained, and, in particular, those which were forwarded to other agencies, such as funding bodies, were undoubtedly selected to create a positive effect. Charlotte Whitton, for example, often sent forward appreciative letters from mothers to the life insurance companies, a major funding source for the council. One such packet of letters was sent to the managing director of the London Life Insurance

Company, accompanied by the following note from Charlotte Whitton: 'In going through some of our correspondence the other day I asked Mme Chasse to pick out some typical letters in which I thought you might be interested.'[83] In the years between 1934, when the council took over responsibility for federal distribution of child-care literature from the federal Division of Child Welfare, and 1937, when the division was re-established, Whitton sent similar packets to Dr R.E. Wodehouse, then deputy minister of pensions and national health.[84] Whether such glowing letters were indeed 'typical' is impossible to determine, since we do not have the entire volume of correspondence upon which to draw. The possibility that Whitton chose to present a positive face to her major funding bodies cannot, however, be ignored.

Finally, I would suggest that mothers who did not have a successful outcome to their pregnancies, or whose children died early in life, would have been unlikely to bring such information to the attention of child-rearing experts. Advice literature laid responsibility for children's health and well-being squarely in mothers' laps. If something went wrong, the literature stressed, mothers had only themselves to blame. It would seem unlikely that such mothers would voluntarily come forward to admit their failure.

Despite the concerns that I have raised, I believe that the letters represent eloquent testimony of the isolation of new motherhood and the desperate need many mothers felt for information and help. The few negative letters that remain on file decry the lack of medical services available to Canadian women during the interwar years, particularly in Northern and rural areas. Mrs Leonard Renaud of Wawbewawa, Ontario, for example, wrote to the Department of Health to complain that neither of the two doctors in the nearest town would attend her confinement without first being assured that they would receive their $25 fee. Since the Renauds were able to pay only $5, Mrs Renaud was forced to give birth without medical attention.[85] A similar complaint was made by Mrs Doris Denman of Sudbury in a letter to the minister of health. She stated: 'We have no baby clinic in Sudbury ... We pay forty dollars to have a baby and then another five dollars if we want an examination afterwards. It is not at all unusual for women to have to undergo a later operation because her doctor wouldn't take the trouble to see if the uterus had returned to its normal place.' In an appeal to the government, she asked: 'Do the doctors boss you or do you boss the doctors? Isn't it possible for you to pass a law saying that every doctor must examine every maternity patient before they are paid by them?'[86] In a letter requesting copies of the prenatal and post-natal letters for his wife, Emile Dupuis noted, matter-of-factly, 'We have no doctor in our municipality and if you can render this service to my wife, I'll be very glad.'[87] Living on homesteads, far from neighbours and family, without medical attention or help, many Canadian women undoubtedly appreciated the information and even companionship that the advice pamphlets provided. As one rural mother told Helen MacMurchy, 'I intend letting other farm women like myself know about these books so full of valuable information to lonely farm folks.'[88] Given the isolation and poverty of many Canadian mothers, particularly during the interwar years, the following praise for MacMurchy's publications might well apply to all advice literature. Writing in the *Toronto Star* on the occasion of the unveiling of MacMurchy's portrait by the Federation of Medical Women, the author noted, 'The Little Blue Books brought valuable information to mothers living far from medical care or in such poverty that medical care was almost as far removed.'[89]

Even after the Second World War, as electrification, telephones, and improved roads began to break down rural isolation, motherhood remained a lonely experience. The breakdown of extended family networks, the geographic mobility of nuclear families, and the physical isolation of nuclear family units within suburban developments meant that mothers continued to spend long periods of time alone with their children. That trend towards the isolation of women and young children – a condition Adrienne Rich refers to as the 'solitary confinement of "full-time motherhood,"'[90] – has continued virtually unabated to the present day.

Not only did women appreciate the companionship that advice literature provided, but many women attributed the successful outcome of their pregnancies and the health and well-being of their children to the advice they had received from child-rearing experts. Does the historical evidence support their view? Statistics of infant and maternal mortality and morbidity rates clearly indicate that, over the course of this century, *all* of these rates declined significantly. By mid-century, the risks associated with childbirth had been dramatically reduced and mothers and children were enjoying longer, healthier lives. Ernest Couture, chief of the federal Division of Child and Maternal Health, attributed improvements to the campaign of maternal education: 'Education – by radio, press, magazines and through government and municipal publications distributed to the public – is paying dividends. More interest is being shown by mothers in breast feeding; the care of the premature infant has been given increasing emphasis in recent years; the public is now convinced of the value of early and regular pre-natal medical supervision.'[91] A similar claim appeared in a 1958 article in *Canadian Nurse*. Esther Robertson, nursing consultant for the federal Division of Child and Maternal Health, claimed: 'Today more people recognize the need for health knowledge to prepare them for the demands of daily living. More printed health education materials are available through departments of health and more articles on health matters are appearing in popular publications ... Certainly through reading, listening to the radio and watching television, individuals have become more aware of the relationship of health to success and happiness.'[92]

Optimistic as such reports were, the issue of whether we can attribute improvements in maternal and child health to changes in health-care services and the widespread availability of prenatal- and child-care advice remains hotly debated by historians. On the positive side of the debate stand such scholars as Norah Lewis and Neil Sutherland of the University of British Columbia. In an article on maternal mortality, Lewis argues that 'although the decline in maternal mortality cannot be directly attributed to any one specific cause, evidence indicates that three distinct but interrelated educational influences tried to affect the change.' The influences which Lewis identifies are the increase in physician-attended births, the increase in hospitalized births, and the wider availability of prenatal and post-natal information. As a result, 'from 1920 onwards British Columbian women had access to better health care, better medical attention, and were better informed about self care than their mothers had been.'[93] Although Lewis is careful to note that 'it is impossible to draw a direct cause and effect relationship between the decline in maternal mortality and the increase of births in medical establishments,' she states unequivocally that 'women who gave birth in a hospital setting certainly had the advantage of superior care and treatment in a more sterile environment than those who gave birth at home.'[94] 'Within hospital settings,' she continues, 'maternity cases were treated as surgical cases, and as a direct result, fewer women developed puerperal septicaemia (childbed fever).'[95]

Such claims regarding the safety of hospital births have been disputed by a number of historians. In her Master's thesis on maternal mortality in Ontario, Lesley Biggs maintains that 'maternal mortality rates were much higher in hospitals than in homes until the early 1940's.'[96] The eventual decline in maternal mortality rates 'can be attributed to the introduction of sulfa drugs and to improved socioeconomic conditions,' rather than to the efforts of the educational campaign.[97] While acknowledging that 'prenatal care is useful in the early detection of problems of pregnancy,' Biggs points out that 'considering the chief causes of maternal mortality (i.e. sepsis and toxemia) it is apparent ... that prenatal care failed to address the issues of meddlesome midwifery, poverty, and malnutrition – the main factors associated with sepsis and toxemia.'[98] A similar assessment is offered by Jo Oppenheimer. In her article on the transition from home to hospital for childbirth in Ontario, Oppenheimer notes that, prior to the Second World War, rates of infection were 'substantially higher among women whose babies were born in hospital,' and that 'maternal deaths were consistently lower among rural mothers who tended not to go into hospital.' Only after the widespread introduction following the Second World War of sulfa drugs and antibiotics to treat infection did death rates among urban mothers begin to drop below rural rates.[99]

In a recent article on the decline in maternal mortality rates, Suzann Buckley argues that improved prenatal nutrition played a significant role in the decline in maternal deaths following the Depression. Buckley cites a wartime study conducted by noted paediatrician, Harry Ebbs, and his colleagues at the University of Toronto. By supplementing the prenatal diet of a group of low-income women and comparing the outcome of their pregnancies with a control group of women whose diet was inadequate, researchers concluded that 'pregnant women on an inadequate diet had poorer health and more complications than those on adequate diets. These women were also worse obstetrical risks and were more likely to experience miscarriage, stillbirth, or premature labour.'[100] In a subsequent study focusing on the effects of improved nutrition on infant well-being, researchers found once again that 'the addition of certain simple foods to the diets of the low income group of women ... resulted in a very much better record throughout their pregnancy when compared with another group of women' who remained on an inadequate diet. In addition, the authors noted that 'the effect upon infant mortality and morbidity was striking.'[101] Women in the group with a supplemented diet were better able to breast-feed and their babies were found to be much healthier than the offspring of the control group. Such studies suggest that the ability to obtain adequate nutrition *may* be a crucial factor in improving infant and maternal health.[102]

A 1944 article by Dr Ernest Couture, director of the Division of Maternal and Child Hygiene, supports the notion of the effect of improved nutrition. Citing declining maternal mortality rates during the Second World War, Couture suggested that 'we have good reason to believe that better nutrition is playing an important role in enhancing the results in maternity.' Improved economic conditions since the Depression, rationing, and food controls, which had resulted in food being 'more evenly distributed and more easily accessible,' and 'the very active campaign favouring good nutrition,' had combined to ensure that Canadian mothers were enjoying better prenatal diets.[103]

A number of historians have also attributed improvements in infant mortality rates and in child health to the changing practices recommended in advice literature. As Norah Lewis notes, 'Developments in medical science, advances in disease prevention and control, and increased knowledge of both child nature and development between the 1880s and the 1920s' focused attention increasingly on the physical care of children. As a result, Lewis continues, 'for the first time in history, infants had a good chance of surviving to adulthood if parents adopted the new scientific approach to child care.'[104] In his chapter on the campaign against infant mortality in Canada, Neil Sutherland also attributes at least some of the improvements in the mortality rates during the first two decades of this century to what he terms 'the climate of opinion generated to improve the life chances of the newly born.' Sutherland maintains that the 'climate' influenced the 'infant and child care practices' of 'thousands of mothers who had not studied domestic science at school, who had never visited a pure-milk depot or baby welfare station, who had not read a copy of *The Canadian Mother's Book* or a Metropolitan Life pamphlet.'[105] Sutherland himself notes, however, that improved sanitation and pure milk and water supplies were key factors in accounting for improvements in infant mortality rates throughout the Western world.

While elements of the child-rearing advice available to mothers may have had a positive effect on the health of their children, we cannot view the impact of advice literature as entirely salutary. Much of the advice mothers were offered has since been partially and, in some cases, entirely disproven. In the area of childbirth, for example, during the interwar years mothers were ordered to remain in bed for ten to fourteen days following delivery. While some women may have welcomed the rest such an order provided,[106] others found themselves extremely weak as a result of the inactivity. By the time they were finally permitted to rise from their beds, their muscles had weakened to such an extent that they required special exercises to regain proper muscle tone. One mother described her experience after the birth of her first child in 1943 as follows: 'They made me, that was in the old days, I stayed in bed, right in bed, for at least ten days, because I can remember the day that they said I could get up and I put my feet on the ground and just went "oop." And I had been having some physiotherapy in bed because Ruth [a friend] was a physio and she used to come in and give me exercises to do, but even at that I just had to collapse, my legs wouldn't hold me up after all that time.' While she was fortunate enough to have the assistance of a physiotherapist friend during her lying-in period, she was still required to remain in hospital for a number of days 'learning how to walk again.'[107] Another mother, whose first child was born in 1946, was also ordered to remain in bed for 'ten or twelve days.' She recalled that 'when I got up I was so weak I was perspiring all over, it was silly, from not having walked or done anything around.'[108] While the length of time women were required to remain in bed following childbirth declined steadily over the course of the century, that does not alter the negative effect such practices had upon the thousands upon thousands of mothers subjected to them.

Many other practices associated with childbirth in hospital had an equally detrimental effect upon labouring women. The introduction of 'twilight sleep,' or hyoscine, as an anaesthetic for childbirth was heralded by women's groups of the first wave of feminism.[109] Despite the claims that twilight sleep could render childbirth painless, it actually 'functioned as an amnesiac, removing not the pain of childbirth, but the memory of it.' Furthermore, while hyoscine generally 'obliterated any subsequent memory of pain, it frequently intensified the actual experience of it during labour. The result was often wild and uncontrolled behaviour by labouring women.'[110] To avoid injury to the patient, doctors placed labouring women in a 'specially designed crib-bed.'[111] Dr Van Hoosen, an early advocate of twilight sleep, explained: 'As the pains increase in frequency and strength, the patient tosses or throws herself about, but without injury to herself, and may be left without fear that she will roll onto the floor or be found wandering aimlessly in the corridors. In rare cases, where the patient is very excitable and insists on getting out of bed ... I prefer to fasten a canvas cover over the tops of the screens, thereby shutting out light, noise and possibility of leaving the bed.'[112] For some women, even the memory was not obliterated. Eleanor Enkin, who was given the drug for the birth of her first child in Saskatchewan in 1950, describes her experience as follows:

As the labour got harder, they gave me a drug called hyoscine, and I absolutely lost control. They told me this drug would make me forget – it's an amnesiac. It didn't. All I remember is being completely out of control. It was a very demoralizing feeling. First of all, I kept saying to myself, this is the most excruciating pain I've ever felt. And nurses came in, and I had the feeling they were yelling at me. Then, the next memory I have of that is about five people standing around my bed in the labour room yelling at me, 'push, push, push,' and I felt I had absolutely no control. I had no way I could push, and I was told later on I was making a lot of noise, and it was just a real horror.

Mrs Enkin was eventually given a general anaesthetic, a common practice in the 1950s, and her baby was delivered by forceps. 'I don't know that I was deprived of any feelings for her,' she recalled, 'but I did look back on that experience as a horror.'[113]

Other standard hospital practices made the transition to new motherhood difficult. For example, rigid scheduling, coupled with the routine use of supplementary feedings until the mother's milk came in, may, in fact, have rendered breast-feeding almost impossible. While most doctors officially recommended breast-feeding as the safest, most effective method of infant feeding, many of the specific details of their infant feeding advice would have rendered breast-feeding difficult, if not impossible. Failing, for example, to recognize the value of colostrum, many hospitals concluded that it was not useful to make a newborn 'struggle on an empty breast,' and as a result, they delayed the start of breast-feeding until as late as the fourth day. One mother, who developed mastitis during her hospital stay, explained: 'I think the reason was that they didn't bring the baby in fast enough, right after he was born. They seemed to think they had to give the mother rest ... In the mean time, [indicating her breasts] "whoo", like this, it just got so hard that he couldn't feed, he couldn't nurse properly.' She did eventually succeed at nursing after receiving sulfa drugs and employing a breast pump, which, she recalled, 'nearly killed me, after it was inflamed.'[114] Another mother reported a similar experience. 'I hate to seem critical,' she began tentatively, 'but I feel they didn't bring me the child early enough, so by the time she was brought to me, I was bigger than Mae West and my nipples had almost disappeared from view. And it was very painful. To be able to manipulate to try and give the child an opportunity of a nipple to suck was difficult and painful.'[115] While Mrs Weatherstone persevered, leaving the hospital a nursing mother, not all women were as determined or as fortunate. All too often hospitals were quick to recommend formula as the solution to the mother's feeding difficulties.[116]

The number of women who breast-fed their babies during this period is impossible to determine as detailed records of maternal nursing practices were not kept. A 1950 article by a Montreal physician, Dr Hilary Bourne, claimed that 'it is a well-known fact that the worst place in the world as regards breast feeding is the United States; Canada runs a close second.'[117] The author provided no data, however, to corroborate her 'well-known fact.' One of the few pieces of evidence I encountered was a survey conducted in 1951 among women who had attended prenatal classes held by Toronto's Department of Public Health. The results indicated that of the 297 women who completed the questionnaires, 172 of the respondents were breast-feeding at the time of the questionnaire, while 125 mothers were not. Of those who reported that they were not breast-feeding, only 19 stated that they had never attempted it; the remaining women had breast-fed their infants for periods ranging from a few days to three months. Their reasons for not breast-feeding included the following: insufficient milk (63); cracked, small, or inverted nipples (10); breast infection (6); milk unsatisfactory (6); doctor's orders (3); worry (2); and other reasons (13). A number of the women surveyed expressed a desire for more information on breast-feeding, 'specifically prenatal care of nipples, nursing techniques, use of breast pump, how to maintain breast milk supply.' In addition, the report noted that 'several mothers were critical of hospital staff because they gave no help or encouragement to breast feed.'[118] A similar survey conducted by the Department of Public Health the preceding year produced similar results. Although the reasons for not breast-feeding were not solicited in the earlier survey, 'several [of the mothers] asked for more practical information on breast feeding, especially on preparation of breasts for breast feeding, techniques of nursing, with more emphasis on encouraging mothers to persist in breast feeding.'[119]

The reasons for women's failure to breast-feed are complex. Changing fashions and 'fads,' the availability and widespread promotion of infant formula through advertisements and hospital nurseries, and the difficulties of combining participation in the paid labour force with breast-feeding are among the many factors that might affect rates of maternal nursing. As the results of the survey cited above suggest, lack of information about and encouragement for breast-feeding were among the factors that affected the respondents' decision not to nurse their infants. In addition, it should be noted that while 'insufficient' milk was the largest single reason for failure to nurse, that condition often results from improper nursing techniques – e.g., rigid scheduling and the provision of supplementary bottles of infant formula, practices routinely recommended during the middle decades of this century.

Many of the other regimens of child care imposed similar hardships on the lives of infants and young children. The use of soapsticks and anal suppositories, advocated during the interwar years to encourage 'regularity,' had fallen into disfavour by the post-war period, as experts began to recognize the dangers of such procedures. *The Early Years* warned that suppositories, enemas, or soapsticks 'often hurt [the baby's] rectum and frighten him so badly that toilet time is dreaded.'[120] Spock and other post-war authors also criticized the practice of early toilet training recommended in the literature of the interwar years. Spock noted that 'many times the baby rebels against these efforts [at early training] when he is old enough to realize what is happening to him.' Mothers might never realize the full extent of the damage such practices had caused, as Spock warned that 'some psychologists think that early training is harmful, in certain cases at least, whether the baby rebels later or not.'[121] Virtually every publication of the post-war era warned of the serious, long-term psychological effects of attempts at early toilet training, attempts that had been recommended throughout the advice literature of the interwar years.

Strict schedules and the practice of letting the baby 'cry it out' had also fallen into disfavour by the post-war years. Nonetheless, countless babies suffered through such harsh regimes, as their mothers ignored their inclinations to comfort a crying baby in the interests of establishing and maintaining the all-important routine. As John and Elizabeth Newson have noted, 'Innumerable women made valiant efforts to stifle their natural desire to cuddle their babies and to feed them when they were hungry, or were wracked with guilt and shame when they "mawkishly" rocked the child or sentimentally eased his stomach pangs in the small hours with a contraband couple of ounces.' The

Newsons offer evidence from letters and interviews with British women to demonstrate the effect that such a regime had on mothers. 'What stands out in such accounts,' they note, 'is the emotion which is still generated in the mother by her own memories' – the feelings of guilt and sorrow for having adhered to the rigid dictates of scientific child rearing.[122]

A number of the mothers I interviewed recalled their attempts to follow a four-hour feeding schedule, particularly with their first baby. One woman, whose first child was born in 1943, quickly found herself at odds with her paediatrician. According to the doctor's weight charts, the baby was gaining adequately on a four-hour schedule of breast-feeding. But the baby cried between every feeding. 'Looking back on it,' the mother recalled, 'I know that she was hungry and that's why she cried so much. And of course the rules were you don't feed them unless it's four hours.'[123] Eventually, when the baby reached three months of age, she was able to persuade her paediatrician to allow her to transfer the baby to a formula and to begin supplementing the diet with solid foods.

Another mother, who gave birth to twins in 1929, reported that she had no problem with breast-feeding the babies, despite the fact that she had been separated from them for nearly a week following the difficult birth. Nonetheless, she still expressed reservations about the value of schedules: 'At that time they were very strict about feeding. You were supposed to feed them every four hours, even if they were asleep, you know, in the four hours, you woke them up. It was ridiculous. And so, that complicated, disrupted your rest quite a bit. However, it never occurred to me that it wasn't the best thing to do.'[124] The evidence suggests that even if it did occur to women to question the efficacy of such routines, it would have required considerable self-confidence to challenge the canons of medical science.

In the preceding chapter, I documented the changes which took place in a number of aspects of child-rearing advice over the course of this century. What did this mean for mothers who found themselves in the middle of their child-rearing years when the shift from scientific child rearing to permissiveness took place? One American mother described her experience this way: 'I was serving a new vegetable to the boys. Suddenly I realized that I expected Peter, the oldest, to clean his plate. Daniel, the middle one, didn't have to eat it but he had to taste it. And little Billy, as far as I was concerned, could do whatever he wanted.'[125] While she was able to view her dilemma with humour, many women found it difficult to make sense of the conflicting messages contained in the advice literature. Even within periods, women were apt to encounter contradictory advice. Spock, for example, made a shift from a permissive approach in the 1946 edition of *Baby and Child Care* to a stress on 'parental rights' and the importance of setting guidelines in the 1957 edition.[126] Women whose child-rearing years often stretched out over twenty years or more undoubtedly found themselves struggling to keep pace with the changes in methodology and philosophy advocated by child-care experts.

Indeed, by the 1950s, articles in professional journals began to consider the dilemma such shifts posed for mothers. A 1954 article in the *Canadian Nurse* noted: 'The underlying uncertainty of conflicting philosophies of child care is one of the difficulties with which our modern mother has to contend. Indeed, mothers are exposed to so many different sets of ideas regarding child care that they are apt to become confused or indecisive.'[127] In another article in the same issue, the authors observed that many mothers 'have heard and read so much about "scientific" methods of child rearing, that they have come to mistrust their own instincts and feelings.'[128] In marked contrast to the tone of articles from the interwar years, public health nurses were urged to avoid 'overteaching,' which could 'curb a mother's self-confidence.' Another author reminded nurses: 'We aim to be *guides, not dictators*. The mother's co-operation and self-confidence are two of our major concerns.'[129] While such an approach would undoubtedly have represented a welcome change for many mothers, it is impossible to determine the extent to which such cautions actually served to change nurses' behaviour.

Such confusion may, in fact, be a logical consequence of expert advice itself. As I have argued throughout this book, while mothers often sought expert advice in order to bolster their self-confidence, the advice rarely had the desired effect. The reason may lie in the disjuncture between the experts' expressed desire to increase parents' confidence and their own need to establish themselves as experts.[130] If experts succeeded in raising parents' self-confidence to the level of self-sufficiency, they might in fact render themselves obsolete. This may account for the apparent contradiction between Spock's opening words of advice to parents to 'trust yourself. You know more than you think you do,' and the fact that the first edition of his book was 502 pages long and the second, 627 pages long!'[131]

Advice literature engendered not only confusion in its readers, but also feelings of guilt. Authors frequently castigated mothers for adhering to practices that had since fallen into disfavour. In the 1950s, for example, mothers were warned of the serious long-term psychological problems caused by early toilet training, force feeding, and rigid scheduling – all procedures advocated in the literature of the interwar years. By the late 1940s, women were accused of being inflexible, and of paying too much attention to schedules and rules and not enough to baby's needs. While an astute reader might have been able to recognize that the blame lay with the experts and not with herself, the fear of having caused their children serious, long-term problems led increasing numbers of middle-class mothers to turn to child psychologists in search of help for the children they had supposedly damaged.

Perhaps the greatest problem with the prenatal and child-rearing advice literature lies in the disjuncture between the requirements of the advice and the reality of mothers' lives, particularly during the desperate days of the Depression. Readers of advice literature were inundated with detailed descriptions of the physical requirements of infants and young children, ranging from an elaborate layette to a separate nursery and bedroom for the new arrival. While geared to a middle-class audience, Frances Lily Johnson's 1928 article 'Furnishing the Nursery' described arrangements that were clearly beyond the reach of the vast majority of Canadian families. 'If it is at all possible,' Johnson advised, 'every nursery should be provided with a wash-basin and running water.' Other essentials included a commode chair, high chair, hamper, carriage, swing, and a range of child-size furniture, including a table and chair. 'Nursery music is a most important factor in the amusement as well as the education of children.' Johnson instructed mothers, suggesting that they purchase small records and a portable phonograph for the nursery. Brightly coloured 'special nursery china' was said to act as a 'stimulant to the young appetite,' while plants taught the child a sense of responsibility. Lest the reader conclude that she might skimp on some of the nursery items, Johnson warned: 'The well-appointed and thoughtfully-planned nursery is not a luxury; it is a necessary comfort where there are children.'[132]

While the standards demanded by Helen MacMurchy's publications were less elaborate than Johnson's, they too were clearly beyond the reach of the average Canadian family during the interwar years. In one publication, for example, MacMurchy remarked, almost in an off-handed manner: 'You are not living in a flat are you? A flat is not a good place for a baby.'[133] Elsewhere she consoled: 'You haven't a bath-room? Never mind, you can do without until you can get it,' adding parenthetically, '(get it as soon as you can.)'[134] No such sympathy was offered for the mother who needed to share a bed with her new baby. MacMurchy ordered the mother, 'Never let the baby sleep with anybody!'[135] How was a mother to feel if she could not provide her baby with a room of its own, if poverty and inadequate heat led the family to share a bed with the baby in order to keep warm in winter? MacMurchy and other authors of advice literature warned that she might kill her child. But what choice did she have? Evidence from the period suggests that many families were forced to share rooms and even beds, for lack of space. A 1928 study, for example, reported that of a group of immigrant mothers in Montreal receiving mothercraft training, fully fifty per cent of the families were living in one room.[136]

The inability to meet the expectations established by advice manuals undoubtedly caused worry and anxiety for many women. Yet, ironically, one of the strongest warnings encountered in the literature concerns the dangers of worry. Time and time again, mother was exhorted to 'cheer up.'[137] In the 1923 publication *How to Take Care of the Mother*, MacMurchy warned that 'mother must not be hurried, worried, driven or oppressed. Worry is one of the greatest enemies of health and happiness.'[138] After the birth, worry was equally dangerous. MacMurchy commanded that 'passion or temper or any other bad feeling should never enter the mother's room. Great emotion spoils the nursing milk and the milk secreted under such conditions makes the child ill.'[139] Worry, then, was to be avoided at all costs, for it represented a serious danger to mother and child alike.

But how were women to avoid worrying? For many women, deprived of their husbands' incomes through death or unemployment, supplying their families with the basic necessities of life was a tremendous struggle. How was a mother-to-be to avoid worrying when she could scarcely afford to feed the children she already had? How could she help but worry about where the food would come from to feed one more mouth? As one mother noted, in a letter to Prime Minister R.B. Bennett: 'The worry of all these things is driving me mad.'[140] Another woman, a widow with four children, wrote: 'I have been fighting against worry untill I feel as I am going to break down completely.'[141]

Many of the letters to Prime Minister Bennett document the deprivation facing Canadian families. A widow in New Brunswick, struggling to provide the essentials for her five children on relief payments, told Bennett, 'In the month of January they gave me $3.00 to live.

6 persons. I don't know how I could give my children three meals a day with so Small quantity. I tell you we are suffering.'[142] Faced with drastically reduced levels of income, many women chose to do without themselves, rather than deprive their children of what little food remained. A study conducted among low-income families in the late 1930s suggests that the practice of maternal self-deprivation may, indeed, have been widespread. In the study, researchers found that 'the fathers were the best fed, young children next, then older children, and finally the mothers were most poorly fed.'[143]

An Alberta woman described how her family managed to survive on inadequate relief payments: 'We are just one of many on relief and trying to keep our place without been starved out. Have a good ½ section not bad buildings and trying to get a start without any money and 5 children all small. Have been trying to send 3 to school and live on $10.00 a month relief for everything, medicine meat flour butter scribblers. Haven't had any milk for 3 months but will have 2 cows fresh in March some time. Am nursing a 10 months old baby and doing all the work cooking washing mending on bread and potatoes some days.'[144] While she may have been aware of the importance of prenatal nutrition, such information was of little use to a family that could afford only bread and potatoes.

Many other practices recommended in the advice literature were equally difficult for women to adopt. For example, one of the most common and oft-repeated pieces of advice was the importance of regular visits to the doctor during pregnancy. Not all women, however, could afford either prenatal check-ups or a physician-attended delivery. As one expectant mother told Bennett, 'I have a poor little girl Three Years of age with hardly no cloths fit for the cold, and myself being an expectant mother for New Years I have got lots of worry as we haven't been able yet to save enough to pay the doctor I had for the one Three Years old.'[145] That not all women could afford such care was seldom acknowledged by authors of advice literature. An important exception follows. In 1934, in response to a request for suggested revisions to the *Prenatal Letters*, Ms Dykeman, R.N., director of the Public Health Nursing Service of the New Brunswick Department of Health, wrote:

In this province many of the letters go to women who are not able to have a doctor attend them at confinement or who do not see one before confinement. There is either no doctor within easy reach of them or they have not the means to bring him to them ... While the letters hold up an ideal or really the safest way to be followed, would it not be possible to include one page in the series stating briefly what the mother should expect in the woman who attends her at delivery, especially in the matter of cleanliness, the drops in the baby's eyes and the immediate care of the baby. I do not think this would be encouraging mid-wives but on the other hand would suggest to the mothers that these women were not to be taken entirely without knowing something about their methods.[146]

Despite the request, the recommendations on prenatal visits in the *Prenatal Letters* remained unchanged.

Throughout her tenure as chief of the Division of Child Welfare, Helen MacMurchy recognized that many women, particularly in outlying areas, were unable to obtain the services of a physician to supervise labour and delivery. It was for these women that the supplement to *The Canadian Mother's Book* was produced in 1923. While the supplement provided detailed information about childbirth for the 'neighbour women' who would attend to the needs of labouring women in the outpost areas, the federal government remained reluctant to distribute the supplement widely, lest it be seen as an endorsement of midwifery.[147]

Documentary evidence from the period confirms that the cost of doctors' visits would have been prohibitive for many women. A sample play, used to instruct public health nurses in prenatal visiting, included the estimated cost of a physician-attended home birth and additional nursing supervision in the 1930s. According to the script, a private-duty registered nurse would have charged five or six dollars a day. Nurses from the Victorian Order of Nurses and the St Elizabeth Visiting Nurses' Association charged five dollars for a home confinement and one dollar per visit after delivery. The expectant mother stated that her last doctor had charged $25 for delivery. Coupled with the cost of the nurse for ten days following birth, a service deemed essential by the visiting nurse, the mother's costs for a home confinement would have been $40, an amount clearly beyond the reach of many Canadian families during the Depression.[148] The cost of a hospital delivery, increasingly recommended by the 1930s, would have ranged between $50 and $70. In a 1932 article entitled 'Economy Baby,' a mother stated that her family spent $70 for a private hospital room, $50 for the doctor's services at the birth, and $20 per month for a maid. While the author described her arrangements as 'humble,' the costs amounted to more than many families received in relief payments in an entire year![149] Although Helen MacMurchy confidently reassured mothers that 'even if you have little or no money you can always have the best of care,' she did not suggest how mothers might receive such attention.[150] Letters written to the federal Department of Health during the Depression suggest that many doctors refused to attend childbirth unless they were assured that they could receive their fee in advance.[151]

One of the most eloquent descriptions of the contradiction between expert advice and the reality of women's lives appeared in an anonymous article entitled 'I Am a Canadian Mother,' published in *Chatelaine* in 1933. 'The most noble calling in the world is mine,' she wrote: 'My country realizes that my children are its greatest asset. My country knows that the wisdom and intelligence I exercise now in teaching and training my children contribute much to their usefulness but a few years hence, and that the foods used in body-building now decide whether they shall become a burden or an asset. My country knows this and spends time and money to send out useful information to mothers within its borders. *I am a Canadian mother and the recipient of more free advice than any other mortal on earth.*' Despite the 'free advice,' however, her children were 'starving and cold.' While they had bread, the family was unable to afford meat, milk, vegetables, or fruit on the meagre relief payments they received. 'The honour and glory we read about are all a myth,' she concluded. 'Who wants to starve and freeze for honour and glory?'[152]

It was not only during the Depression that advice literature set standards which many mothers were unable to meet. Throughout the middle decades of this century, authors assumed that women embraced motherhood as a full-time occupation. By the post-war era, this assumption, fuelled by the findings of Bowlby's research on maternal deprivation, had taken on the force of a dictum. Mothers were warned against working in the paid labour force and, indeed, Spock urged women to postpone taking a vacation or a new job until after the child had passed what he described as the fearful two-year-old stage. Coupled with the requirements of demand feeding, these post-war theories made the mother a virtual prisoner in her own home, unable to go out even to shop, lest the baby need to nurse or the two-year old suffer 'separation anxiety.'

Writing in *Child Development* in 1949, just three years after the appearance of Spock's famous child-rearing manual, Sibylle Escalona noted that the permissive philosophy of child rearing made it appear 'as though contentment and even normal development for the child can only be attained at the cost of great self-denial on the part of the parents.' The mother, in particular, was expected to 'subordinate her need for sleep, for recreation, for getting the housework done or for pursuing non-domestic interests at all times. Moreover, she is expected to do so with a sense of deep satisfaction and happiness.' Demand feeding, Escalona noted, 'means that all other activities must be adapted to the child's rhythm and makes it impossible to get away from home.' The philosophy of letting the child 'explore the world means endless patience and labor in cleaning up messes and in countless other ways.'[153] Escalona's analysis stands in marked contrast to that of most observers, who have described the shift to permissive child rearing as largely salutary for mother and child alike.[154]

In contrast to the assumptions of the literature, the interviews which I conducted indicate that many mothers bore considerable responsibilities in addition to demands of baby and child care. One mother, living far from friends and family, cared for her dying mother in her home, in addition to shouldering the responsibilities of raising her two children, aged eight and two and a half, while her husband travelled away from home for one to two weeks at a time. Other women also described caring for sick and elderly parents, a responsibility that would have made the demands of around-the-clock motherhood virtually impossible to meet. Furthermore, while none of the mothers I interviewed worked full time before their children reached school age, the increase in the labour force participation rates of women with young children, particularly during the 1950s, suggests that many women disregarded the prohibitions against full-time employment in order to provide for their families.[155]

How were mothers to feel if they were unable to meet the standards of middle-class motherhood established by the literature? Or if, worse still, despite all their best efforts, their children failed to turn out 'properly?' The literature reminded women time and time again that errors in child rearing were their sole responsibility. Adrienne Rich describes the experience of maternal guilt in the following excerpt from *Of Woman Born*, which documents her feelings after the birth of her first son: 'Soon I would begin to understand the full weight and burden of maternal guilt, that daily, nightly, hourly, *Am I doing what is right? Am I doing enough? Am I doing too much?* The institution of motherhood finds all mothers more or less guilty of having failed their children.'[156]

Throughout the advice literature, children's behaviour problems, ranging from feeding and sleeping difficulties to juvenile delinquency, were attributed to errors on the mother's part. While the specific nature of her failings changed over the course of these decades, her responsibility remained constant. For example, a 1928 article in the *Canadian Medical Association Journal* on eating problems of the 'nervous child,' pointed out that 'as a rule it is a nervous unstable mother who expects the doctor to prescribe a tonic ... little realizing that it is her own fretful solicitude that constitutes nine-tenths of the trouble.'[157] A 1941 article on the 'overweight child' once again blamed mothers for the problem, noting that 'the indulgent mother may develop in her child the habit of stuffing himself with ice cream and cake at all times of the day.'[158] A study of nutrition conducted on children in the Wartime Day Nurseries in Ontario during the Second World War revealed that the day nursery children exhibited far fewer feeding problems than children fed in their own homes. The author concluded that the 'lack of emotional approach to meals' at the day nursery was the prime reason for the day nurseries' success at mealtime.[159] A 1950 article in the *Canadian Nurse* attributed 'almost every feeding problem' to mothers. The authors were particularly concerned about the mother's failure to establish the proper 'emotional rapport' with her child at feeding time. 'The emotional tie between mother and infant is so close,' the authors explained, 'that an overly anxious mother makes a fretful baby and later a maladjusted child.'[160]

Mothers were held accountable for their children's psychological problems as well. In the 1932 edition of *The Normal Child*, Alan Brown reminded readers that 'the mental environment of the child is created by the mother. This is her responsibility and her opportunity.'[161] These words were echoed in countless publications throughout the period. A 1936 article in *Chatelaine* warned mothers that 'your child mirrors you and your home: if your child is a problem child, probably you are a problem mother.'[162] Indeed, by the 1950s, psychological problems, rooted in faulty maternal behaviour, had emerged as the cause of many physical childhood disorders. The following excerpt from a 1958 article on the psychological roots of atopic dermatitis demonstrates the manner in which mothers were blamed for their children's diseases: 'Mothers of children with atopic dermatitis have been described as domineering and overprotective. Even if, to all appearances, they are deeply devoted to the child, feelings of rejection for it are frequently expressed in the form of irritability. Feelings of guilt over rejecting the child are intensified by the skin disorder for which, consciously or unconsciously, they feel responsible.'[163] Mothers were cautioned to avoid the extremes of maternal deprivation/rejection and maternal overprotection, either of which could result in serious, long-term psychological damage to their offspring.[164]

The focus on maternal responsibility had significant implications for maternal and child-welfare policies of the day. Supported by medical and psychological evidence of the importance of the maternal-child connection, policy makers could reject measures of state intervention that might have helped mothers better to care for their children. State support for child-care centres, for example, was virtually non-existent throughout this period, with the exception of the limited provision of Wartime Day Nurseries in Ontario and Quebec during the Second World War. No significant efforts were made to socialize the tasks of child rearing, either through day-care centres, babysitting cooperatives, or play schools. Infants and preschool children remained the sole responsibility of their mothers; those women who failed – poor women, single parents, working mothers – had only themselves to blame.

Faced with a virtual flood of advice literature advocating a middle-class model of family life, mothers did their best to measure up to the new standards of modern motherhood. While the evidence I have presented in this chapter suggests that a few women rebelled, rejecting the advice as wrong-headed, impractical, or merely irrelevant, countless other women struggled to make sense of the dictates, to do their best for their children, in a society that, despite the lip-service paid to the citizens of the future, provided very little concrete help for its mothers and children.

For some women, the books and pamphlets represented a friendly, welcome voice in an otherwise lonely world. The advice literature provided information about the tasks of child rearing that had become, for many women, frightening, alien chores. Such information and help was purchased at a significant cost, however, for, as Veronica Strong-Boag has noted, 'in exchange ... women had to surrender power over themselves and their offspring. It was an authority they would not easily recover, however much their faith in experts proved misplaced.'[165]

Conclusion

As we approach the twenty-first century, motherhood remains a central experience in the lives of most women in Canada. Following a steady decline in the wake of the post-war 'baby boom,' fertility rates have once again begun to rise slightly.[1] Regardless of their status in the paid labour force, both married women and increasing numbers of single women are choosing to have at least one child.[2] The huge volume of child-care literature currently available attests to the fact that these women, like their counterparts in the past, are seeking information about and help with the difficult tasks they face.[3] For their part, experts have continued to offer information and advice on the many questions facing parents. Mass circulation magazines throughout Canada and the United States have featured cover stories on child rearing with titles like 'The Yuppie Generation Takes on Parenthood,' 'Are You Boring Baby?' and 'The New Baby Boom.'[4] Daily papers features regular columns on issues related to child care and parenting. In addition, specialized magazines like *Today's Parent*, *Mothering*, and the *Compleat Mother* have assumed a prominent place on the news-stands. Finally, a steady stream of experts appear on daytime television talk shows, reaching an audience the size of which was unimaginable to Helen MacMurchy and her colleagues of the interwar years.

Breast or bottle? Cloth or disposable diapers? Home-made baby food or Gerber's? Flash cards or computers? Changes in the technology of baby and child care have altered the specific questions facing new mothers, but they do not diminish the intensity of the search for the 'right way' to bring up baby. As I have argued throughout this book, new mothers in the twentieth century have confronted these issues virtually alone. Separated from their mothers by geography and generation, lacking any formal training in child care or direct experience with children, new mothers have looked to experts for information and advice.

Recent authors have argued that contradictions in child-care advice such as those documented in this book have led many parents to question the validity of expert advice, thereby removing experts from the pedestal they occupied in the early and middle decades of this century. In their book *For Her Own Good*, Barbara Ehrenreich and Deirdre English maintained that, by the early 1960s, 'the experts had lost status.' Frequent quarrels and changing views meant that '"science," applied to child raising, [had begun] to look like a chameleon which could match any national mood or corporate need.'[5] A recent article in the *Toronto Star* claimed that 'parent power' had transformed the realm of expert advice. The author quoted Nancy Hay, the mother of one child: 'We question authority. It's a generational thing. Would my mother have ever gone to the doctor and questioned anything? I don't think so.'[6]

Despite these claims, the volume of sales of child-rearing manuals and parenting magazines suggests that maternal advice literature is still a popular genre in the 1990s.[7] While much of the advice has changed over the years, the ferocity of the debates remains. One of the most contentious issues concerns the centrality of the mother-child relationship and the alleged dangers posed by alternative care during the first few years of life. Leading child-care authorities, including Burton White, T. Berry Brazelton, Penelope Leach, and Dr Benjamin Spock, continue to recommend full-time motherhood for at least the first three years of a child's life.[8] Coupled with the ever-increasing participation of women in the paid labour force, such advice has posed a considerable dilemma for working mothers seeking the best solution to their child-care needs.

One solution to the child-care crisis emerged in an unlikely place – the *Harvard Business Review*. A recent article advocated what many theorists and business leaders had been quietly discussing for years: the creation of a 'mommy track.' Written by Felice Schwartz, a self-proclaimed feminist and president of a company that advises businesses on incorporating women into executive positions, the article suggested the creation of two different career paths for women: a 'fast track' on which both men and women could compete in the race towards the top rung of the corporate ladder; and a 'mommy track,' a special, less pressured route for women who chose to combine a career and family, one that would allow for part-time employment, longer maternity leaves, and time off to care for ill children.[9] While the concept has been roundly criticized by many feminists as little more than a means to justify continued gender discrimination in hiring and promotion, articles exploring the merits of the 'mommy track' have appeared in many publications in the United States and Canada.[10]

Although the policy will probably never *officially* be put into practice, the debate reveals just how enduring the notion of maternal responsibility remains. During the early decades of this century, when faced with what they perceived to be a massive crisis in infant and child health, experts and government officials turned to mothers. A tremendous outpouring of information and advice designed to educate women in the tasks of infant and child rearing provided the ready solution to the problems of infant and child health. Since that time, conditions of child rearing have changed dramatically. Today, in all countries in the Western world, maternal, infant, and child mortality rates have reached record lows. Mothers and their children, for the most part, enjoy longer, healthier lives, relieved of the fears of epidemics and many life-threatening diseases. And yet, many problems remain. The mother of a severely disabled child still bears the overwhelming burden of her child's care virtually alone. The ever-growing number of single mothers face lives of poverty for themselves and their children with little hope of escape from the cycle.[11] Native women and women of colour continue to face historical and systemic discrimination. These are problems rooted in the very fabric of our society, problems that no amount of expert advice, however salutary, can eradicate. Yet they are ones that all of us must seek to solve in order to create better lives for society's mothers and children.

Today motherhood remains contested terrain. Lawmakers continue to debate a woman's right to choose when or indeed if she may have an abortion. Members of the anti-abortion movement appeal to a sentimentalized version of motherhood, while pro-choice activists argue that abortion should be treated as a medically insured, surgical procedure. The Royal Commission on New Reproductive Technologies has just issued its final report, concluding a lengthy process of public consultation in an effort to determine who should have access to, and, more important, who should control technologies that promise to transform the face of motherhood. Activists in the midwifery and home birth movements lobby for women's right to exert greater control over the conditions of childbirth, as they seek to reverse the medicalization of motherhood which has taken place during the course of this century.[12] At the same time, experts in neonatal medicine explore the limits of developments in medical technology that have made it possible to save the life of a baby born as early as twenty-four weeks following conception. To enable us to steer a path through these complex issues, an understanding of the changing ideas about motherhood and of the changing contexts of its practice over time is essential.

In this study, I have documented the views of experts in the fields of medicine, child psychology, nursing, and social work concerning the best ways to rear infants and young children. I have demonstrated the tremendous shifts in child-rearing advice that occurred during the first six decades of this century. I have also attempted to assess the impact that child-rearing advice had on the day-to-day lives of mothers, as they tried to balance the demands of home and family, work and recreation, with the heightened expectations of motherhood in the twentieth century. Regardless of the advice offered by child-care experts, however, mothers have often been forced to make do with what they had. As Veronica Strong-Boag has noted in her study of the interwar years, poverty rendered many families incapable of following expert advice. Instead, 'they continued to hope for the best and cope with the worst.'[13] That observation is still relevant today, as increasing numbers of mothers make decisions about what to feed their children on the basis of what is available at the local food bank rather than on the advice of some distant expert.

Interview Questions

1 BACKGROUND
- parents' occupations? number of children? ages?
- did you help take care of younger siblings, cousins, or other family members? what sorts of tasks did you do?
- did you have close ties with your family when your children were growing up?
- married? date of marriage? number of years married?
- number of children? birth dates?
- spouse's occupation? your occupation?
- decision to have children: planned? a 'matter of course'?

2 DETAILS OF PREGNANCY AND PRENATAL CARE
- did you attend a prenatal clinic?
- how often did you see a doctor and/or nurse during your pregnancy/pregnancies?
- did you receive any free books on pregnancy or prenatal care from government health services or from your doctor?
- how was your health during your pregnancy? did you change your eating habits? how did you feel?

3 BIRTH EXPERIENCES
- were your children born at home, in the hospital, maternity home?
- how did you decide where to have your baby? (e.g., followed doctor's advice, because of financial considerations, lack of access to hospital, etc.)

- if your child was born in hospital, how long did you remain there after the birth? when were you allowed to get out of bed?
- what was the father's role in the birth?
- were there any marked differences between the births of your children?

4 EARLY YEARS
- did you breast-feed your baby? if so, for how long? did you give bottles? (as a supplement, as the entire source of food, etc.)
- if you breast-fed, did anyone help you to establish this?
- if you used a formula, who helped you choose the correct formula?
- when did you first take the baby to the doctor for a check-up?
- what advice did he give at that time?
- what was the father's role in the early years of child rearing?
- what assistance (if any) did you have in your home in the early days of child rearing? (e.g., your mother, mother-in-law, nurse, friends, other relatives, visiting nurse, etc.)
- what sources of information did you use to help you with any problems that arose? (friends, your mother, books)
- did friends or family offer you much advice on taking care of your baby? do you remember any disagreements concerning what to do for the baby?
- as far as you can recall, what was the biggest influence on your first years of child rearing?
- whose advice did you follow? was it helpful?
- did you rely less on advice with your second child?
- did you feel more confident? why? (or why not?)

5 ADVICE BOOKS
- did you purchase any child-care manuals? did you consult them?
- if so, for what sort of problems? did you find them helpful?
- did you read any child-rearing manuals? advice columns in magazines (e.g., *Chatelaine*) or newspapers?
- did you receive any free books or pamphlets from the hospital, visiting nurse, government health service? if so, did you read them? did you follow any of the advice in these pamphlets, booklets?
- did this pattern change in your later years of child rearing?

6 SUPPORT NETWORK
- did you visit a well-baby clinic? if so, how often? what happened there? did a visiting nurse come to your house after the birth? what advice did she give? how did you feel about her visit(s)?
- did you have a network of friends who were raising their children at the same time as you were? did you share stories, advice, problems, etc.?
- did your child attend nursery school? day care? if yes, what sort of child-rearing advice did you receive there?

7 RECALL
- how well do you remember details of your child-rearing years?
- did you save any letters, diaries, photos, from those years?
- do other members of your family have letters, diaries, or other materials which they might be willing to share with me?

Abbreviations

AO	Archives of Ontario
CCCFW	Canadian Council on Child and Family Welfare
CHC	Canada, House of Commons
CJPH	*Canadian Journal of Public Health*
CMA	Canadian Medical Association
CMAJ	*Canadian Medical Association Journal*
CN	*Canadian Nurse*
CPHJ	*Canadian Public Health Journal*
CTA	City of Toronto Archives
DCMH	Division of Child and Maternal Hygiene
DCW	Division of Child Welfare
DMCH	Division on Maternal and Child Hygiene
DNHW	Department of National Health and Welfare
DOH	Department of Health
DOHA	Department of Health Act
NAC	National Archives of Canada
OBH	Ontario Board of Health
ODH	Ontario Department of Health
OMA	Ontario Medical Association
PHJ	*Public Health Journal*
TDPH	Toronto Department of Public Health

Notes

INTRODUCTION

1 Subsection 179c of the 1892 Criminal Code made it an indictable offence to 'offer to sell, advertise, publish an advertisement of or have for sale or disposal any medicine, drug or article intended or represented as a means of preventing conception or causing abortion (55 and 56 Victoria 1892). This law, which criminalized both abortion and birth control, was amended in 1969 (Section 251, Criminal Code, Canadian Revised Statutes, C.C-34, 1970).

2 *Morgentaler, Smoling et al v. The Queen* (1988), 82 N.R. 1, ruled that Canada's abortion law was unconstitutional. Bill C-43, passed by the House of Commons on 29 May 1990, would have placed abortion under the Criminal Code once again. Bill C-43 was defeated by the Senate on 31 Jan. 1991.

3 In *More Work for Mother: The Ironies of Household Technology from the Open Hearth to the Microwave* (New York: Basic Books 1983), Ruth Schwartz Cowan argues that the amount of time women spent in all household and domestic tasks remained constant, and, in some cases, increased over the course of this century, despite, or, perhaps, as a result of changes in household technology, in standards of cleanliness, and in ideas about child rearing. See also Joann Vanek, 'Time Spent in Housework,' *Scientific American* 231 (Nov. 1974), 116–25. Basing her article on surveys conducted during the 1920s and 1930s, and comparing those results with a time-use survey done in 1964 and 1965, Vanek found that nonemployed women in the 1960s spent slightly *more* time in housework than their counterparts in the 1920s and 1930s.

4 Adrienne Rich, *Of Woman Born: Motherhood as Experience and Institution* (New York: W.W. Norton 1976; Bantam Books 1977), 36.

5 Shulamith Firestone, *The Dialectic of Sex: The Case for Feminist Revolution* (New York: William Morrow 1970; Bantam Books 1971), 72. For a more recent statement of this position, see Jeffner Allen, 'Motherhood: The Annihilation of Women,' in Joyce Trebilcot, ed., *Mothering: Essays in Feminist Theory* (Totowa, NJ: Rowman and Allanheld 1983), 315–30.

6 See also Germaine Greer, *The Female Eunuch* (London: MacGibbon and Kee 1970; Paladin 1971).

7 Tremendous changes currently taking place in reproductive technology may, in fact, dramatically alter or even sever this connection between women and reproduction. See, e.g., Rita Arditti, Renate Duelli Klein, and Shelley Minden, eds., *Test-Tube Women: What Future for Motherhood?* (London: Pandora Press 1984).

8 For provocative discussions of cultural and historical variations in the social organization of motherhood, see, among others, Margaret Mead and Martha Wolfenstein, eds., *Childhood in Contemporary Cultures* (Chicago: University of Chicago Press, 1963) and Sheila Kitzinger, *Women as Mothers* (New York: Vintage Books 1980).

9 Rich, *Of Woman Born*, xv. For a detailed discussion of Rich's work, see Katherine Arnup, 'Adrienne Rich: Poet, Mother, Lesbian Feminist, Visionary,' *Atlantis* 8 (Fall 1982), 97–110.

10 For a fascinating discussion of the role of female support networks, see Carroll Smith-Rosenberg, 'The Female World of Love and Ritual,' *Signs: A Journal of Women in Society and Culture* 1 (Autumn 1975), 1–29.

11 For a discussion of this literature, see Christina Hardyment, *Dream Babies: Child Care from Locke to Spock* (London: Oxford University Press 1984).

12 A number of key figures during the interwar years were unmarried and childless; e.g., Helen MacMurchy and Charlotte Whitton. While this does not invalidate their ideas about child rearing, it places them in a different relationship to children than the advice-givers of the 19th century, many of whom were mothers.

13 For a discussion of working-class girls' experiences with babies, see Veronica Strong-Boag, *The New Day Recalled: Lives of Girls and Women in English Canada, 1919–1939* (Toronto: Copp Clark Pitman 1988), chap. 5.

14 For a searing critique of the use of advice literature by historians, see Jay E. Mechling, 'Advice to Historians on Advice to Mothers,' *Journal of Social History* 9 (Fall 1973), 44–63. The article was based on Mechling's doctoral dissertation, 'A Role-Learning Model for the Study of Historical Change in Parent Behavior; With a Test of the Model on the Behavior of Parents in the Great Depression' (PhD dissertation, University of Pennsylvania 1971).

15 See, *inter alia*, Celia B. Stendler, 'Sixty Years of Child Training Practices: Revolution in the Nursery,' *Journal of Pediatrics* 36 (Jan. 1950), 122–34; Clarke E. Vincent, 'Trends in Infant Care Ideas,' *Child Development* 22 (Sept. 1951), 199–209; Martha Wolfenstein, 'Fun Morality: An Analysis of Recent American Child-training Literature,' *Journal of Social Issues* 7 (1951), 15–25, reprinted in Mead and Wolfenstein, *Childhood in Contemporary Cultures*; Martha Wolfenstein, 'Trends in Infant Care,' *American Journal of Orthopsychiatry* 23 (1953), 120–30; Robert Sunley, 'Early Nineteenth-Century American Literature on Child Rearing,' in Mead and Wolfenstein, *Childhood in Contemporary Cultures*, 150–67; Michael Gordon, 'Infant Care Revisited,' *Journal of Marriage and the Family* 30 (Nov. 1968), 578–83; Abigail J. Stewart, David G. Winter, and David R. Jones, 'Coding Categories for the Study of Child-Rearing from Historical Sources,' *Journal of Interdisciplinary History* 5 (Spring 1975), 687–701; Nancy Pottishman Weiss, 'Mother, the Invention of Necessity; Dr Benjamin Spock's *Baby and Child Care*,' *American Quarterly* 24 (Winter 1977), 519–46; and Nancy Pottishman Weiss, 'The Mother-Child Dyad Revisited: Perceptions of Mothers and Children in Twentieth Century Child-Rearing Manuals,' *Journal of Social Issues* 34 (1978), 29–45.
16 For a detailed discussion of the methodological issues involved in the use of prescriptive literature, see 'The Perils of Prescriptive Literature,' in Katherine Arnup, 'Education for Motherhood: Women and the Family in 20th Century English Canada' (PhD dissertation, University of Toronto 1991).
17 Neil Sutherland, *Children in English-Canadian Society: Framing the Twentieth-Century Consensus* (Toronto: University of Toronto Press 1976), 26.
18 See Robert Craig Brown and Ramsay Cook, *Canada 1896–1921: A Nation Transformed* (Toronto: McClelland and Stewart 1974) for a discussion of the impact of the First World War on Canadian society.
19 See, e.g., Ruth Roach Pierson, *'They're Still Women After All': The Second World War and Canadian Womanhood* (Toronto: McClelland and Stewart 1986). Pierson concludes: 'The War's slight yet disquieting reconstruction of womanhood in the direction of equality with men was scrapped for a full-skirted and redomesticated post-war model, and for more than a decade feminism was once again sacrificed to femininity,' 220.
20 James Roberts, 'Insanitary Areas,' *PHJ* 3 (Apr. 1912), 182
21 Angus McLaren and Arlene Tigar McLaren, *The Bedroom and the State* (Toronto: McClelland and Stewart 1986). See also Dianne Dodd, 'The Birth Control Movement on Trial, 1936–1937,' *Histoire sociale / Social History* 16 (1983) 411–28; Gerald J. Storz with Murray A. Eaton, ' 'Pro Bono Publico':

The Eastview Birth Control Trial,' *Atlantis* 8 (1983), 51–60; and Dianne Dodd, 'Women's Involvement in the Canadian Birth Control Movement of the 1930s: The Hamilton Birth Control Clinic,' in Katherine Arnup, Andrée Lévesque, and Ruth Roach Pierson, eds., *Delivering Motherhood: Maternal Ideologies and Practices in the 19th and 20th Centuries* (London: Routledge 1990), 150–72.

22 See C. Lesley Biggs, 'The Case of the Missing Midwives: A History of Midwifery in Ontario from 1795–1900'; Jo Oppenheimer, 'Childbirth in Ontario: The Transition from Home to Hospital in the Early Twentieth Century'; and Veronica Strong-Boag and Kathryn McPherson, 'The Confinement of Women: Childbirth and Hospitalization in Vancouver, 1919–1939, in Arnup et al., *Delivering Motherhood*. See also Suzann Buckley, 'Ladies or Midwives? Efforts to Reduce Infant and Maternal Mortality,' in Linda Kealey, ed., *A Not Unreasonable Claim: Women and Reform in Canada, 1880s – 1920s* (Toronto: Women's Press 1979) 131–49.

23 Sutherland, *Children in English-Canadian Society.* Sutherland and his colleagues at the University of British Columbia are currently involved in a major work of oral history entitled the Canadian Childhood History Project. Preliminary papers based on that research were presented at the 1985 annual meeting of the Canadian Historical Association, including Neil Sutherland, 'The Role of Memory in the History of Childhood'; Jean Barman, 'Accounting for Gender and Class in Retrieving the History of Canadian Childhood.' Participants in the project conducted a round-table discussion of their work at the Biennial Conference of the Canadian History of Education Association, Oct., 1990.

24 The same limitation applies to P.T. Rooke and R.L. Schnell, eds., *Studies in Childhood History: A Canadian Perspective* (Calgary: Detselig Enterprises 1982), the focus of which is primarily on children. In a thesis on the Home and School Movement in Toronto, Kari Dehli demonstrates the active role that a group of prominent Toronto women played in establishing links between the school system and the home ('Women and Class: The Social Organization of Mothers' Relations to Schools in Toronto, 1915 to 1940,' PhD dissertation, University of Toronto 1988). This thesis forms a useful companion to my work on the mothering of young children.

25 'Intruders in the Nursery: Childcare Professionals Reshape the Years One to Five, 1920–1940,' in Joy Parr, ed., *Childhood and Family in Canadian History,* (Toronto: McClelland and Stewart 1982), 160–78. Strong-Boag develops this argument further in her chapter on motherhood in *The New Day Recalled.*

26 Norah L. Lewis, 'Advising the Parents: Child Rearing in British Columbia during the Inter-War Years' (EdD dissertation, University of British Columbia 1980); 'Creating the Little Machine: Child Rearing in British Columbia, 1919–1939,' *BC Studies* 56 (Winter 1982–3), 44–60; '"No Baby – No Nation": Mother Education, A Federal Concern 1921 to 1979,' paper presented at the Canadian History of Education Association, Vancouver, Oct. 1983

27 Katherine Arnup, 'Educating Mothers: Government Advice for Women in the Inter-War Years,' in Arnup et al., *Delivering Motherhood*, 190–210

28 Lewis, 'Creating the Little Machine,' 44

CHAPTER 1 Waging War on Infant Mortality

1 Helen MacMurchy, *Infant Mortality: Special Report* (Toronto: King's Printer 1910), 4

2 Alan Brown, 'Infant and Child Welfare Work,' *PHJ* 9, (Apr. 1918), 145

3 For detailed discussions on health and housing conditions in turn-of-the-century Canada, see Paul A. Bator, '"Saving Lives on [the] Wholesale Plan": Public Health Reform in the City of Toronto, 1900–1930' (PhD dissertation, University of Toronto 1979); Terry Copp, *The Anatomy of Poverty* (Toronto: McClelland and Stewart 1973); and Michael Piva, *The Condition of the Working Class in Toronto – 1900–1921* (Ottawa: University of Ottawa Press 1979). While there was evidence of such problems in Toronto and Montreal as early as the 1830s, the situation deteriorated considerably as the pace of urbanization increased dramatically in the latter part of the nineteenth century.

4 For a discussion of the problem of contaminated milk supplies, see Deborah Dwork, *War Is Good For Babies and Other Young Children: A History of the Infant and Child Welfare Movement in England, 1898–1918* (London: Tavistock 1987), esp. chap. 4.

5 'Although infant death rates appear to have been lower at first in most seventeenth- and eighteenth-century North American communities than they were in the less healthy cities and towns of western Europe, they began to rise in the eighteenth and nineteenth centuries as cities grew in the new world' (Beth Light and Alison Prentice, Introduction to chap. 5, 'The Work of Wives,' in Beth Light and Alison Prentice, eds., *Pioneer and Gentlewomen of British North America , 1713–1867* (Toronto: New Hogtown Press 1980, 133).

6 Piva, *Working Class in Toronto*, 114

7 MacMurchy, *Infant Mortality* (1910), 3

8 In his study of Montreal, Terry Copp states that, 'between 1897 and 1911, approximately one out of three babies died before reaching the age of twelve months. As late as 1926, the rate was still 14 per cent, a figure almost double the average for New York or Toronto' (*Anatomy of Poverty*, 93). The authors of the exhibit 'Mother and Child,' (Ontario Science Centre, 11 Dec. 1986 to 30 Apr. 1987) claimed that Montreal's infant mortality rate was the highest in the Western world.

9 It should be noted that prior to 1920, statistics on infant mortality rates cannot be considered to be accurate. Toronto's official statistician, Robert E. Mills, estimated that 28 percent of Toronto's live births were not registered in 1908. While various departments of health began collecting birth and death statistics in the first two decades of this century, as late as 1915 the TDPH would not publish its birth rate and infant mortality rate statistics because they were not dependable. In 1918 the Dominion Bureau of Statistics was established, and it, in turn, ensured that each province began to establish mechanisms for collecting and reporting birth and death statistics. In 1921 the first national figures were published (except for Quebec, which was not included until 1926). The under-reporting of births probably resulted in an overestimation of the infant death rate. For a complete discussion of this problem of estimation, see Neil Sutherland, *Children in English-Canadian Society: Framing the Twentieth-Century Consensus* (Toronto: University of Toronto Press 1976), 64.

10 Viviana A. Zelizer, *Pricing the Priceless Child: The Changing Social Value of Children* (New York: Basic Books 1985), 25

11 Lawrence Stone refers to both practices of naming in *The Family, Sex and Marriage in England, 1500–1800*, abridged and rev. ed. (Harmondsworth: Penguin 1979), 57. Ann Crawley's record of her children's births and deaths in eighteenth-century Nova Scotia indicates that she gave two of her sons the same names as siblings who had previously died ('Ann Crawley's Children,' Crawley Family Documents, MG IV.239, Public Archives of Nova Scotia, in Light and Prentice, *Pioneer and Gentlewomen*, 136).

12 Among those who argue that parents in former times did not care, see Philippe Aries, *Centuries of Childhood: A Social History of Family Life* (New York: Random House 1962); Elizabeth Badinter, *Mother Love: Myth and Reality* (New York: MacMillan 1981); and Edward Shorter, *The Making of the Modern Family* (New York: Basic Books 1975).

13 Stone, *Family, Sex, and Marriage*, 57

14 Shorter, *Making the Modern Family*, 203–4

15 Lloyd deMause, 'The Evolution of Childhood,' in Lloyd deMause, ed., *The History of Childhood* (New York: Harper and Row 1975), 1. While offering a

view generally more sympathetic to the parents' plight, Stone also refers to the 'the indifference and neglect of many parents' as one of the causes of infant and child death. 'Part of the very high mortality rate must have been due to this neglect, itself the product of poverty and ignorance,' Stone claims, adding that, 'at the same time the neglect was caused in part by the high mortality rate, since there was small reward from lavishing time and care on such ephemeral objects as small babies. It was a vicious circle' (*Family, Sex and Marriage*, 65).

16 Stephen Wilson, 'The Myth of Motherhood a Myth: The Historical View of European Child-rearing,' *Social History* 9 (May 1984), 186, 188

17 Letter from Letitia Hargrave to Mrs Dugald Mactavish (her mother), Apr. 1843, in Light and Prentice, *Pioneer and Gentlewomen*, 144

18 Linda S. Siegel, 'Child Health and Development in English Canada, 1790–1850,' in Charles Roland, ed., *Health, Disease, and Medicine: Essays in Canadian History* (Agincourt: Clarke Irwin 1983), 373

19 'Diary: 1886–1896,' Merkeley Family Papers, in Alison Prentice and Susan E. Houston, eds., *Family, School, and Society* (Toronto: Oxford University Press 1975), 267–8. The second entry was dated 1 Mar. 1891.

20 In a later entry, Mrs Merkeley recorded that her daughter had died (Merkeley Family Papers, NAC, MG29, E29). I am grateful to Alison Prentice for this reference.

21 A series of articles by Dr R. Hall Bakewell entitled 'Infant Mortality and Its Causes,' appeared in *The British Mothers' Journal* (June 1857), 141. The articles are cited in Patricia Branca, *Silent Sisterhood: Middle-Class Women in the Victorian Home* (London: Croom Helm 1975), 95.

22 Stanley Jevons, cited in Carol Dyhouse, 'Working-Class Mothers and Infant Mortality in England, 1895–1914,' *Journal of Social History* 12 (Winter 1978), 248

23 For an important discussion of these views, see Anna Davin's groundbreaking article 'Imperialism and Motherhood,' *History Workshop Journal* 5 (Spring 1978).

24 Alan Brown, 'Infant and Child Welfare Work,' *PHJ* 9 (Apr. 1918), 145–6

25 Ibid., 146, 149

26 Alan Brown, 'The Relation of the Pediatrician to the Community,' *PHJ* 10 (1919), 50

27 On the women's reform movement, see articles in Linda Kealey, ed., *A Not Unreasonable Claim: Women and Reform in Canada, 1880s–1920s* (Toronto: Women's Press 1979). On the broader social reform movement, see Richard Allen, *The Social Passion: Religion and Social Reform in Canada* (Toronto:

University of Toronto Press, 1973); Richard Allen, ed., *The Social Gospel in Canada*, (Ottawa: National Museum of Man 1975); Paul Rutherford, *Saving the Canadian City* (Toronto: University of Toronto Press 1974); and Sutherland, *Children in English-Canadian Society*. Alison Prentice documents the emergence of the social reform movement in the mid-nineteenth century in *The School Promoters: Education and Social Class in Mid-Nineteenth Century Upper Canada* (Toronto: McClelland and Stewart 1977), chap. 1.

28 MacMurchy, *Infant Mortality* (1910), 32

29 See T.R. Morrison, '"Their Proper Sphere": Feminism, the Family, and Child Centred Reform in Ontario, 1875–1900,' *Ontario History* 68 (1976), 45–64, and 68 (1976), 65–74; Linda Kealey, 'Introduction,' in Kealey, *A Not Unreasonable Claim*. For a highly critical assessment of the motives of the Canadian women's reform movement, see Carol Lee Bacchi, *Liberation Deferred? The Ideas of the English-Canadian Suffragists, 1877–1918* (Toronto: University of Toronto Press 1983). See also Mariana Valverde, *The Age of Light, Soap, and Water: Moral Reform in English Canada, 1885–1925* (Toronto: McClelland and Stewart 1991).

30 For a discussion of Hoodless's efforts, see Terry Crowley, 'Madonnas before Magdalenes: Adelaide Hoodless and the Making of the Canadian Gibson Girl,' *Canadian Historical Review* 67 (1986), 520–47; Ruth Howes, 'Adelaide Hunter Hoodless,' in Mary Quayle Innis, ed., *The Clear Spirit: Twenty Canadian Women and Their Times* (Toronto: University of Toronto Press, 1966), 103–19; Diana Pedersen, '"The Scientific Training of Mothers": The Campaign for Domestic Science in Ontario Schools, 1890–1913,' in Richard A. Jarrell and Arnold E. Roos, eds., *Critical Issues in the History of Canadian Science, Technology and Medicine* (Thornhill, Ont.: HSTC Publications 1983), 179–94.

31 Davin, 'Imperialism and Motherhood,' 12

32 The Second World War stirred up similar fears in some quarters. In several articles that appeared in the *CJPH* during the war, Ernest Couture, chief of the DCMH of the federal Department of Pensions and National Health, exhorted readers not to forget the health of the nation's children during the wartime emergency. In the same vein, in the 1943 annual report of the Canadian Welfare Council's DMCH, the author noted that 'in this, the fourth year of war, Canada is coming to realize the importance of the health of her citizens. She is beginning to realize that parents and children who are under par can never produce the virile people she needs, capable of enduring the strains of war- and post-war times' ('Annual Report of the Division on Maternal and Child Hygiene,' Canadian Welfare Council, 1 Apr. 1942 to 31 Mar. 1943, NAC, MG28, I10, vol. 66, file 010, 'CWC – Maternal and Child Hygiene Division, 1940–43, Canadian Life Insurance Officers,' 1).

33 Desmond Morton, *A Short History of Canada* (Edmonton: Hurtig 1983), 157

34 Canada's pupulation at war's end. F.H. Leacy, ed., *Historical Statistics of Canada*, 2nd ed. (Ottawa: Statistics Canada 1983), Series A1

35 One-sixth of the entire Canadian population contracted influenza during the years 1918–19. See Janis P. Dickin McGinnis, 'The Impact of Epidemic Influenza: Canada 1918–19,' in S.E.D. Shortt, ed., *Medicine in Canadian Society: Historical Perspectives* (Montreal: McGill-Queen's University Press 1981), 447–78.

36 R.E. Wodehouse, 'On the Necessity for the Careful Medical Oversight of Children of the School and Pre-School Age,' *CMAJ* 12 (1922), 428–9

37 The first Congrès des Gouttes de Lait was held in Paris in 1905. In 1906 and 1907, the first and second National Conferences on Infantile Mortality were held in London. In 1907, the second Congrès des Gouttes de Lait was held in Brussels and in 1911 the third Congress on Infantile Mortality, an international event, was held in Berlin.

38 For a full discussion of international initiatives, see G.F. McCleary, *The Early History of the Infant Welfare Movement* (London: H.K. Lewis 1933). See also Sutherland, *Children in English-Canadian Society*, 59.

39 The official history of the U.S. Children's Bureau was written by Dorothy E. Bradbury, *Five Decades of Action for Children* (Washington, DC: United States Department of Health, Education, and Welfare, 1962). See also Jacqueline K. Parker and Edward M. Carpenter, 'Julia Lathrop and the Children's Bureau: The Emergence of an Institution,' *Social Service Review* 55 (Mar. 1981), 60–77.

40 Several recent works have dealt with British efforts to combat infant mortality. See, *inter alia*, Davin, 'Imperialism and Motherhood'; Dyhouse, 'Working-Class Mothers'; Jane Lewis, *The Politics of Motherhood: Child and Maternal Welfare in England, 1900–1939* (London: Croom Helm 1980); and Dwork, *War is Good for Babies*. Dwork is highly critical of what she terms the 'social control' model used by Davin, Dyhouse, and Lewis, and is much more sympathetic towards medical officials of the day.

41 For a discussion of these and other initiatives, see Dyhouse, 'Working-Class Mothers,' 249

42 Davin, 'Imperialism and Motherhood,' 39

43 For a discussion of the relationship between the European, American, and Canadian infant welfare movements, see Sutherland, *Children in English-Canadian Society.*

44 In his recent study of eugenics in Canada, Angus McLaren noted that 'Helen MacMurchy probably did more than any other individual in Canada in the first third of the twentieth century to alert the public to the dangers posed to public health' (*Our Own Master Race: Eugenics in Canada,*

1885–1945 [Toronto: McClelland and Stewart 1990], 30).

45 For a full discussion of MacMurchy's life and career, see Kathleen McConnachie, 'Methodology in the Study of Women in History: A Case History of Helen MacMurchy, MD,' *Ontario History* 75 (Mar. 1983), and her thesis, 'Science and Ideology: The Mental Hygiene and Eugenics Movements in the Inter-War Years, 1919–1939' (PhD dissertation, University of Toronto 1987).

46 Ellen Chapman, 'New Move for Child Welfare: Dr Helen MacMurchy – Chief of a National Department,' *MacLean's Magazine* (1 May 1920), 74

47 Helen MacMurchy, *Infant Mortality: Second Special Report* (Toronto: King's Printer 1911), 3. Chapman confirms this in 'New Move for Child Welfare,' 74.

48 The 1910 report was 36 pages in length; 1911, 54 pages; and 1912, 75 pages.

49 Helen MacMurchy, *Infant Mortality: Third Report* (Toronto: King's Printer 1912), 3–4

50 Chapman, 'New Move for Child Welfare,' 74

51 MacMurchy, *Infant Mortality* (1910), 3

52 Beth Light and Joy Parr, 'Introduction,' in Beth Light and Joy Parr, eds., *Canadian Women on the Move, 1867–1920* (Toronto: New Hogtown Press and the Ontario Institute for Studies in Education, 1983), 5

53 MacMurchy, *Infant Mortality* (1910), 3

54 Ibid., 36

55 Ibid., 18, 3. Examples of military imagery abounded in the literature produced during and immediately following the First World War. Babies were frequently referred to as 'infant soldiers,' as in the posters produced for the Canadian National Exhibition by the OBH (AO, RG10, series 30-1-2, box 2, photo 2.2.10, 1918, CNE). For a recent discussion of military imagery, see Cynthia R. Abeele, '"The Infant Soldier": The Great War and the Medical Campaign for Child Welfare,' *Canadian Bulletin of the History of Medicine* 5 (1988), 99–119.

56 MacMurchy, *Infant Mortality* (1910), 30, 34–5

57 Ibid., 15. In her 1911 report she noted: 'The destruction of the poor is their poverty. The rich baby lives – the poor baby dies,' (5). In this assessment, MacMurchy met with agreement from an unlikely source – the *Western Clarion*. In an article evaluating MacMurchy's report, Moses Baritz concluded, 'Poverty means starvation. Starvation means death. And it is starvation itself, clothed many times in medical terms, that causes infantile mortality.' Baritz's solution, however, was the provision of a family wage sufficient to enable mothers to remain at home with their babies. See 'Infantile Mortality: Attracts Attention of the Capitalists When It

Threatens to Deplete the Supply of Wage Slaves,' *Western Clarion* (30 July 1910), 1.

58 MacMurchy, *Infant Mortality* (1910), 35

59 MacMurchy, *Infant Mortality* (1911), 7

60 MacMurchy, *Infant Mortality* (1910), 5

61 See, e.g., Dr A. Grant Fleming, 'Study of Infant Deaths in Toronto during the Summer of 1921,' *PHJ* 13 (1922), 199–203, in which he claimed that four times as many artificially fed babies died as breast-fed babies, 200. He concluded that the solution to the problem of infant mortality lay largely in 'securing the breast feeding of all infants,' 202. Dr George Smith argued that '10 bottle-fed babies succumb to disease to one breast-fed infant' ('The Importance of Teaching Mothers the Proper Breast-Feeding Technique,' *PHJ* 12 [1921], 522).

62 For a discussion of the dramatic increase in the use of infant formula, see Rima D. Apple, '"To Be Used Only under the Direction of a Physician": Commercial Infant Feeding and Medical Practice, 1870–1940,' *Bulletin of the History of Medicine* 54 (1980), 402–17.

63 MacMurchy, *Infant Mortality* (1910), 17, 30

64 Ibid., 17

65 Ibid., 5. To support this claim, MacMurchy offered the examples of the Siege of Paris (1870–1) when the infant mortality rate was said to have dropped 40 per cent, the cotton famine, and unspecified major strikes 'affecting women's work.'

66 Dyhouse, 'Working-Class Mothers,' 257

67 MacMurchy, *Infant Mortality* (1910), 15–16

68 See, e.g., Patricia Tomic-Trumper, 'The Care of Unwed Mothers and Illegitimate Children in Toronto, 1867–1920: A Study in Social Administration' (PhD dissertation, University of Toronto 1986). In her study of the Hôpital de la Miséricorde in Montreal, Andrée Lévesque found that of the infants born in the residence between 1929 and 1939, fully 37.7 per cent died in their first year, 'mostly from preventable diseases such as gastroenteritis or pulmonary infections' ('Deviants Anonymous: Single Mothers at the Hôpital de la Miséricorde in Montreal, 1929–1939,' *Historical Papers* [1984], 178).

69 Saleeby, cited in Davin, 'Imperialism and Motherhood,' 29

70 Helen MacMurchy, 'The Duty of a Physician to the Mother and Her Child,' *Canadian Practitioner and Review* 46 (Oct. 1921), 304

71 See NAC, RG29, vol. 1318, file 495-1-2, typescript, 'Canada, Historical Development of Services on Behalf of Mothers and Children,' Sept. 1952, 1.

72 Sutherland, *Children in English-Canadian Society*, 57

73 Fir a discussion of these and other initiatives, see Suzann Buckley, 'Ladies or Midwives? Efforts to Reduce Infant and Maternal Mortality,' in Kealey, *A Not Unreasonable Claim* 131–150.

74 CHC, *Annual Reports* (1930–1), Department of Pensions and National Health, Report of the Child Welfare Division, 134–5. The Women's Institutes were established in Canada in 1897. The Ontario Women's Institutes functioned under the wing of the provincial Department of Agriculture.

75 See NAC, RG29, vol. 1318, file 495-1-2, typescript, 'Canada, Historical Development of Services on Behalf of Mothers and Children,' Sept. 1952, 2–3

76 Sutherland, *Children in English-Canadian Society*, 85

77 This service continued until 1 Jan. 1953. (*Quarterly Bulletin for Metropolitan Nurses* 15 [Nov. 1951], 5, AO, RG10, series 30-A-1, box 3, file 3-2).

78 Bator, 'Saving Lives,' 12. For a recent discussion of the TDPH, see Heather MacDougall, *Activists and Advocates: Toronto's Health Department, 1883–1983* (Toronto: Dundurn Press 1990).

79 Bator, 'Saving Lives,' 19

80 Piva, *Working Class in Toronto*, 116

81 The Bureau was initially under the jurisdiction of OBH (Ontario, *Sessional Papers* (1917), Report of OBH, 11).

82 AO, RG62, series 1-B-1-b, box 439, file 439.1, memorandum, chief medical officer of health to the provincial secretary, 11 Mar. 1919, 4–5

83 *Statutes of Canada*, 1919, 9-10 Geo. 5, c. 24, 'An Act Respecting the Department of Health,' (DOHA)

84 NAC, DOH Records, RG29, vol. 992, file 499-3-7, part 5, 1, DCW, 'Plan of Work and General Policy.' The document is filed as if it were issued in 1930, but the pencilled date appears to read 19 and Oct. 1920, the dates of the founding conference of the Canadian Council on Child Welfare. MacMurchy also quotes the plan verbatim in a 1928 article, a further indication that the document could not have been issued in 1930.

85 Provinces, e.g., had jurisdiction over child hygiene, public health nursing, and maternal welfare, and the DOHA explicitly provided that 'nothing in this Act ... shall authorize the minister or any other officer of the department to exercise any jurisdiction or control over any provincial or municipal Board of Health or other health authority operating under the laws of any province' (Section 7).

86 Section 6 of the DOHA established the Dominion Council of Health, whose records are held in NAC, MG28, I63.

87 Helen MacMurchy, 'Handbook of Child Welfare Work in Canada,' DOH, DCW, for the year ended 31 Mar. 1922), 8

88 For information on the establishment of the Canadian Conference on Child Welfare, see CHC, *Sessional Papers* (1922), Report of the DCW (1921–2), 36.

89 From 1920 to 1929 the organization was called the Canadian Council on Child Welfare; from 1929 to 1935, the Canadian Council on Child and Family Welfare; from 1935 to 1971, the Canadian Welfare Council. The organization is now called the Canadian Council on Social Development.

90 For a discussion of the CCCFW, see Patricia Rooke and R.L. Schnell, '"Making the Way More Comfortable": Charlotte Whitton's Child Welfare Career, 1920–48,' *Journal of Canadian Studies* 17 (Winter 1982–3), 34.

91 Extensive records of the activities of the CCCFW are held at NAC. The papers of the Canadian Council on Social Development are held in MG28, I10. Charlotte Whitton's papers (MG30, E256) also include a wealth of information on the activities of the council.

92 See Sutherland, *Children in English-Canadian Society*, 85.

93 Janet Neilson, 'The History of Public Health Nursing in Toronto,' 8 Jan. 1948, typescript in 'Health Department History,' CTA, RG11, F1, box 4

94 CTA, RG11, F1, box 4, Nursing Division History file, 'The History of Public Health Nursing in Toronto, 1905–1945,' typescript, dated Dec. 1950, written by Janet Neilson and edited by Zada Keefer. For additional work on the history of public health nursing in Toronto, see Marion Royce, *Eunice Dyke: Health Care Pioneer* (Toronto: Dundurn Press 1983) and Kari Dehli, '"Health Scouts" for the State? School and Public Health Nurses in Early Twentieth Century Toronto,' *Historical Studies in Education / Revue d'Histoire de l'Education* 2 (Fall 1990), 247–64.

95 Cynthia Comacchio Abeele, '"The Mothers of the Land Must Suffer": Child and Maternal Welfare in Rural and Outpost Ontario, 1918–1940,' *Ontario History* 80 (Sept. 1988), 183

96 Arthur Newsholme, cited in Davin, 'Imperialism and Motherhood,' 14

CHAPTER 2 Creating 'An Educational Campaign'

1 Helen MacMurchy, *Infant Mortality: Special Report* (Toronto: King's Printer 1910), 31

2 'Maternal Affection,' Bridgetown, Nova Scotia, 21 Nov. 1833, 'School Exercises,' Examination Piece, Coward Collection, Public Archives of Nova

Scotia, MG IV.238, in Beth Light and Alison Prentice, eds., *Pioneer and Gentlewomen of British North America, 1713–1867* (Toronto: New Hogtown Press 1980), 140

3 B. Atlee (pseudonym), 'The Menace of Maternity,' *Canadian Home Journal* (May 1932), 9

4 Adrienne Rich, *Of Woman Born: Motherhood as Experience and Institution* (New York: W.W. Norton 1976; Bantam Books 1977), 29

5 Ruth Bloch, 'American Feminine Ideals in Transition: The Rise of the Moral Mother, 1785–1815,' *Feminist Studies* 4 (June 1978), 107

6 Ibid., 109, 113

7 Ibid., 115

8 Even today, many women, such as farm women and women who work in family businesses like corner stores, actively participate in the family economy, much as did their eighteenth- and nineteenth-century foremothers.

9 Nancy Mandell notes: 'In 1871, Darwin advanced the "maternal instinct theory" of behaviour as an explanation for women's limited intellect, emotionality, childlike behaviour and physical resemblance to children. This instinct was seen as accounting for women's piety, purity, submissiveness, intuition and sensitivity, characteristics which made her perfectly suited to child-rearing and ill-suited to wage labour' ('The Child Question: Links between Women and Children in the Family,' in Nancy Mandell and Ann Duffy, eds., *Reconstructing the Canadian Family: Feminist Perspectives* [Toronto: Butterworths 1988], 70.

10 For discussion of the changing view of childhood, see, *inter alia*, Christina Hardyment, *Dream Babies: Child Care from Locke to Spock* (London: Oxford University Press 1984); Sheila Rothman, *Woman's Proper Place: A History of Changing Ideals and Practices, 1870 to the Present* (New York: Basic Books 1978); and Neil Sutherland, *Children in English-Canadian Society: Framing the Twentieth-Century Consensus* (Toronto: University of Toronto Press 1976).

11 Celia B. Stendler, 'Sixty Years of Child Training Practices: Revolution in the Nursery,' *Journal of Pediatrics* 36 (1950), 127. A similar assessment is offered by Marilyn Helterline, 'The Emergence of Modern Motherhood: Motherhood in England 1899 to 1959,' *International Journal of Women's Studies* 3 (Nov./Dec. 1980), 590–614.

12 Lady Aberdeen's Presidential Address, 1894, cited in T.R. Morrison, '"Their Proper Sphere": Feminism, The Family, and Child-Centred Social Reform in Ontario, 1875–1900,' *Ontario History* 68 (June 1976), 65

13 See, e.g., Barbara Welter, *Dimity Convictions: The American Woman in the Nineteenth Century* (Athens: Ohio University Press 1976); Martha Vicinus, ed.,

Suffer and Be Still: Women in the Victorian Age (Bloomington: Indiana University Press 1972), and *A Widening Sphere: Changing Roles of Victorian Women* (Bloomington: Indiana University Press 1977); Patricia Branca, *Silent Sisterhood: Middle-Class Women in the Victorian Home* (London: Croom Helm 1977); Rothman, *Woman's Proper Place*; and Glenna Matthews, *'Just a Housewife:' The Rise and Fall of Domesticity in America* (New York: Oxford University Press 1987). For a thought-provoking challenge to the concept of separate spheres, see Linda K. Kerber, 'Separate Spheres, Female Worlds, Woman's Place: The Rhetoric of Women's History,' *Journal of American History* 75 (June 1988), 9–39.

14 See Marjorie Griffin Cohen, 'The Razor's Edge Invisible: Women, Markets, and Economic Development in Ontario, 1800–1911,' (PhD dissertation, York University 1985) and *Women's Work, Markets, and Economic Development in Nineteenth-Century Ontario* (Toronto: University of Toronto Press 1988).

15 Beth Light and Alison Prentice, Introduction to chap. 5, 'The Work of Wives,' in Light and Prentice, *Pioneer and Gentlewomen*, 134. Recent work suggests that women in urban Canada may have been affected by the new ideologies by the early 1800s. For a discussion of the women in one such family, see Katherine McKenna, 'Options for Elite Women in Early Upper Canadian Society: The Case of the Powell Family,' in J.K. Johnson and Bruce G. Wilson, eds., *Historical Essays on Upper Canada: New Perspectives* (Ottawa: Carleton University Press 1989), 401–23.

16 Alison Prentice, Paula Bourne, Gail Cuthbert Brandt, Beth Light, Wendy Mitchinson, and Naomi Black, *Canadian Women: A History* (Toronto: Harcourt Brace Jovanovich 1988), 83–4

17 Ibid., 83

18 *Motherhood* (1900), Toronto, published by the British Chemists Company as an advertising pamphlet, 11–12, in Beth Light and Joy Parr, eds., *Canadian Women on the Move, 1867–1920* (Toronto: New Hogtown Press and the Ontario Institute for Studies in Education 1983), chap. 3, 'Founding a Family,' 146–7

19 OBH, *The Baby* (1920), 3

20 Responding defensively to the suggestion that medical incompetence was to blame for high rates of maternal mortality, Dr Ross Mitchell countered, 'If malpractice has slain its thousands, [maternal] ignorance has slain its ten thousands' ('The Prevention of Maternal Mortality in Manitoba,' *CMAJ* 19 [1928], 296).

21 S.M. Carr Harris, 'Reasons for Parental Education,' *CN* 22 (1926), 313

22 Olive Matthews, 'Child Welfare,' *CN* 16 (1920), 15

23 Angus McLaren, *Our Own Master Race: Eugenics in Canada, 1885–1945* (Toronto: McClelland and Stewart 1990), 23. See also Kathleen Janet Anne McConnachie, 'Science and Ideology: The Mental Hygiene and Eugenics Movements in the Inter-War Years, 1919–1939' (PhD dissertation, University of Toronto 1987).

24 C.W. Saleeby, *Woman and Womanhood: A Search for Principles* (New York: Mitchell Kennerley 1911), 171–2

25 Ibid., 172–3

26 Saleeby, *Woman and Womanhood*, 177, cited in MacMurchy, *Infant Mortality* (1910), 31. Saleeby cited his own paper, 'The Human Mother,' which appeared in the *Report of the Proceedings of the National Conference on Infantile Mortality, 1908.*

27 MacMurchy, *Infant Mortality* (1912), 30

28 MacMurchy, *Infant Mortality* (1910), 31

29 E.M. Knox, *Girl of the New Day* (Toronto: McClelland and Stewart 1919), 218

30 Frances Lily Johnson, 'What of Your Child?' *Chatelaine* (Apr. 1928), 32

31 Stella Pines, 'The Baby's Routine and Management,' *Chatelaine* (Jan. 1929), 53

32 Frances Lily Johnson, 'Where a Child Can Be a Child,' *Chatelaine* (Mar. 1928), 28

33 Rothman, *Woman's Proper Place*, 97

34 Harris, 'Reasons for Parental Education,' 313

35 CCCFW, *Post-Natal Letters* 1, 1

36 K. McAllister, 'The New Mother,' *Chatelaine* (July 1932), 40

37 Lina Rogers Struthers, *The School Nurse: A Survey of the Duties and Responsibilities of the Nurse in the Maintenance of Health and Physical Perfection and the Prevention of Disease among School Children* (New York: G.P. Putnam's Sons 1917), 74

38 Harris, 'Reasons for Parental Education,' 312

39 R.P. Kinsman, 'Mental Hygiene and Its Relation to Infants and Children,' *CMAJ* 35 (1936), 541

40 R.R. Struthers, 'Recent Advances in Child Hygiene,' *CJPH* 35 (1944), 115

41 Eileen H. Troop, Department of Public Health Nursing, City of Toronto, 'Introductory Class I: Importance of Homemaking,' typescript dated 10 Mar. 1949, CTA, RG11, F1, box 1, file 'Historical Material – Maternal and Child Health.'

42 Dr Edna Guest, 'Problems of Girlhood and Motherhood,' *PHJ* 12 (1922), 198

43 Hattie B. Innis, 'Division of Child Hygiene, Vancouver Department of Health,' *CN* 19 (1923), 403

44 Knox, *The Girl in the New Day*, chap. 19, 'The Queen of Them All.' The author noted: The Professions have been so eagerly discussing the question as to which was the most honorable of them all that they are wholly taken aback at the cry: "A Mother, a Mother",' a cry that supposedly went up from 'every mother's son,' 216.

45 For a provocative discussion of the changing role of mothers within the American mothers' movement, see Barbara Ehrenreich and Deirdre English, *For Her Own Good: 150 Years of the Experts' Advice to Women* (New York: Anchor Books 1979). The authors argue that 'with the separation of home and work, private and public realms, the standards for "success" in child raising came to be set outside the home, beyond the mother's control,' 192. Domestic science was another of the women's professions that found itself increasingly subject to external regulation. See Diana Pedersen, '"Scientific Training of Mothers": The Campaign for Domestic Science in Ontario Schools, 1890–1913,' in Richard E. Jarrell and Arnold E. Roos, eds., *Critical Issues in the History of Canadian Science, Technology, and Medicine* (Ottawa: HSTC Publications 1983), 178–94.

46 For a development of this argument in the British context, see, *inter alia*, Jane Lewis, *The Politics of Motherhood*, 65, and Anna Davin, 'Imperialism and Motherhood,' *History Workshop Journal* 5 (Spring 1978), 26. It should be noted that not all historians agree with this analysis of the maternal education campaign. In her recent book, Deborah Dwork argues: 'Education was time consuming and laborious. The aids provided (milk, meals, and medical inspection as well as classes, courses, and lectures) were increasingly comprehensive and expensive. It was not a quick and easy solution. It was not a radical solution. But it was successful' (*War is Good for Babies and Other Young Children*, 220).

47 Similar services were provided for Catholic mothers by the St Elizabeth Visiting Nurses Associations. In Toronto the association was begun in 1909, 'to give nursing care to the Catholic poor, to such others as seek our care, and to promote the welfare of the sick and infirm.' The service was paid for by membership fees, donations, and patient fees. These services continued throughout this period; in 1954, e.g., St Elizabeth nurses paid 2,113 visits to new mothers (CTA, RG11, F1, box 2, file 'St. Elizabeth Visiting Nurses Associations, 1954–65,' undated pamphlet entitled 'A Short History of Visiting Nursing with special mention of St. Elizabeth Visiting Nurses Association,' 3–5).

48 K.M. Yorke, 'Saving Lives on Wholesale Plan: How Toronto Has Been Made the Healthiest of Large Cities,' citing Charles Hastings, *MacLean's* 28, 12 (July 1915), 21

49 Information on the well-baby clinics is found in A. Grant Fleming, 'Child Hygiene,' *PHJ* 14 (1923), 293, 296.

50 Yorke made reference to weekly weigh-ins. K.M. Yorke, 'Saving Lives on Wholesale Plan.' An unsigned typescript in the CTA referred to monthly visits; CTA, RG11, F1, box 5, 'Nursing Division' file, 'An Outline of the Work of the Division of Public Health Nursing, Department of Public Health, Toronto,' 1934.

51 Sutherland, *Children in English-Canadian Society*, 61

52 For a discussion of the Hamilton Babies' Dispensary, see Cynthia R. Abeele, '"The Infant Soldier": The Great War and the Medical Campaign for Child Welfare,' *Canadian Bulletin of the History of Medicine* 5 (1988), 111–12.

53 For a discussion of home visits in Toronto, see Kari Dehli, '"Health Scouts" for the State? School and Public Health Nurses in Early Twentieth-Century Toronto,' *Historical Studies in Education* 2 (1990), 247–64.

54 Fleming, 'Child Hygiene,' 295

55 Janet Neilson, 'The History of Public Health Nursing in Toronto,' typescript dated 8 Jan. 1945, CTA, RG11, F1, box 4, file 'Health Department History 1923–45'

56 Yorke, 'Saving Lives on Wholesale Plan,' 94

57 Fleming, 'Child Hygiene,' 295

58 Ibid., 294

59 Ontario, *Sessional Papers* (1918), OBH, Report of the Bureau of Child Welfare, 29

60 Ontario, *Sessional Papers* (1919), OBH, Report of the Bureau of Child Welfare, 40

61 Ontario, *Sessional Papers* (1921), OBH, Report of DMCH and Public Health Nursing, 38. For a recent discussion of the work of public health nurses in rural areas of Ontario, see Meryn Stuart, 'Ideology and Experience: Public Health Nursing and the Ontario Rural Child Welfare Project, 1920–25,' *Canadian Bulletin of Medical History* 6 (1989), 111–31. A less critical evaluation of their work is provided in Cynthia Comacchio Abeele, '"The Mothers of the Land Must Suffer": Child and Maternal Welfare in Rural and Outpost Ontario, 1918–1940,' *Ontario History* 80 (Sept. 1988), 183–205.

62 For a discussion of these initiatives, see Heather MacDougall, *Activists and Advocates: Toronto's Health Department, 1883–1983* (Toronto: Dundurn Press 1990), chap. 8.

63 CTA, RG11, F1, box 1, 'Historical Material – Maternal and Child Health,' typescript dated 5 May 1939, 'The Demonstration of a Baby's Bath at Eaton's Infants' Wear Department.' Attendance ranged from 20 to 39.

64 NAC, RG29, vol. 1318, file 495-1-2, memorandum dated 24 Nov. 1939, Dr Ernest Couture to Dr J.J. Heagerty, Director, Public Health Services, Attn. R.E. Wodehouse, 2

65 CTA, RG11, F1, box 1, typescript dated 3 Oct. 1951, 'Toronto Welfare Council - Report on Prenatal Classes from September 1950 to June 1951,' 1

66 For a discussion of these initiatives in Britain, see Lewis, *The Politics of Motherhood*, 90-5.

67 Suzann Buckley, 'Ladies or Midwives? Efforts to Reduce Infant and Maternal Mortality,' in Linda Kealey, ed., *A Not Unreasonable Claim: Women and Reform in Canada, 1880s-1920s* (Toronto: Women's Press 1979), 141

68 John Gibbon and Mary Mathewson, *Three Centuries of Canadian Nursing* (Toronto: Macmillan 1947), 317

69 E. Scholey, 'Junior Health League Classes in Toronto Schools,' *CN* (1926), 89, 91

70 Fleming, 'Child Hygiene,' 293

71 Scholey, 'Junior Health League Classes,' 89

72 Marion E. Nash, 'Little Mothers' League Classes in Mothercraft,' *CN* 22 (1926), 91

73 Montreal's school opened in 1925. Toronto's school opened its doors on 28 Jan. 1926 (Mary L. Northway, 'Child Study in Canada: A Casual History,' in Lois M. Brockman, John H. Whiteley, and John P. Zubek, eds., *Child Development: Selected Readings* [Toronto: McClelland and Stewart 1973], 11). The nursery schools are also discussed in Frances Lily Johnson, 'Where a Child Can Be a Child,' *Chatelaine* (Mar. 1928), 28, 44, 47; and in Veronica Strong-Boag, 'Intruders in the Nursery: Childcare Professionals Reshape the Years One to Five, 1920-1940,' in Joy Parr, ed., *Childhood and Family in Canadian History* (Toronto: McClelland and Stewart 1982), 167-73

74 Johnson noted that 'with the creation of the nursery school comes the Parent Education Group, at which mothers receive instruction in child guidance, and co-operate with the experts in the scientific study of human development' ('Where a Child Can Be a Child, 28). Johnson apparently saw no contradiction between the gender-neutral term 'parent education' and the fact that the participants were almost exclusively women. Records of the Parent Education Division of the St George's School are deposited at the University of Toronto, Thomas Fisher Rare Books Library, William Blatz Papers, St George's School, Parent Education Division. For a thorough discussion of the Parent Education Division, see Jocelyn Motyer Raymond, *The Nursery World of Dr Blatz* (Toronto: University of Toronto Press 1991), chap. 4.

75 Johnson, 'Where a Child Can Be a Child,' 47. It should be noted that not all parents completed the course. One of my interviewees, the mother of two children enrolled at the Institute for Child Study during the 1930s, did not attend classes, although she recalled going to one or two lectures a year given by Dr Blatz.

76 Northway, 'Child Study in Canada,' 18. For a discussion of the role of parent education groups, see Kari Dehli, 'Women and Class: The Social Organization of Mothers' Relations to Schools in Toronto, 1915 to 1940' (PhD dissertation, University of Toronto, 1988).

77 Northway, 'Child Study in Canada,' 18

78 Ibid., 27

79 Dr Sarah McVean, 'The Pageant of Motherhood,' *CPHJ* 21 (1930), 578–9

80 Sample scripts are deposited at the AO, RG10, series 30-A-1, box 7, file 7-5. One of these, entitled 'Prenatal Visit by Visiting Nurse,' bears the heading, 'Mothers' Day Festival, Royal York Hotel, Friday Evening, May 12, 1933.' The others are undated.

81 Ted Allen, 'Problem Play for Parents,' *Chatelaine* (May 1951), 95, 102. It is interesting to note that the confused mother was portrayed as someone who was always trying to remember what the advice books told her to do.

82 For example, Professor Peter Sandiford, 'Parental Responsibility,' *PHJ* 16 (Aug. 1925), 386–90; Dr J.T. Phair, 'Child Hygiene,' *PHJ* 18 (1927), 132–4; and Adelaide Plumptre, 'A Mother's Duty to the State,' *PHJ* 18 (1927), 178–81

83 CHC, *Annual Reports* (1938–9), Department of Pensions and National Health, Publicity and Health Education Division, 1939–9, 156

84 By 1944–5, 75 out of a total of 87 radio stations in Canada were providing the service free of charge to their listeners; 62 stations were broadcasting in English, andd 13 in French (CHC, *Annual Reports*, 1944–5, DNHW, Division of Information Services, 72). The number of participating stations continued to grow in the post-war period: e.g., in 1947–8, over 90 English-language and 26 French-language stations carried the broadcasts (CHC, *Annual Reports*, 1947–8, DNHW, Information Services Division, 121).

85 Scripts from radio broadcasts used during the Second World War to publicize local public health services are deposited in the CTA, Records of the Social Planning Council, SC40, box 31, file 9.

86 CHC, *Sessional Papers* (1923), DOH, Report of DCW (Mar. 1921 – Mar. 1922), 37

87 CHC, *Sessional Papers* (1943), Report of DMCH (1942–3), 43

88 Ernest Couture, 'Review of "The Birth of a Baby",' *CPHJ* 33 (1942), 513

89 CHC, *Sessional Papers* (1948), Report of DCMH (1947–8), 18

90 NAC, RG29, vol. 1318, file 495-1-2, typescript 'The Child and Maternal Health Division,' dated Apr. 1952, 3

91 The pamphlet was entitled 'Points to Remember.' CHC, *Sessional Papers* (1948), Report of DCMH (1947–8), 18

92 D.A.R. Moffatt, 'A National Health Film Service,' *CJPH* 37 (1946), 470–2

93 The Ages and Stages Series, commissioned to Crawley Films Limited by the National Film Board for DNHW. Titles included the following: 'He Acts His Age,' 'The Terrible Twos and Trusting Threes,' 'Frustrating Fours and Fascinating Fives,' and 'From Sociable Six to Noisy Nine.'

94 *The Baby* was described this way in *Chatelaine* (Apr. 1936), 28. Reference to *Information for Expectant Mothers* appeared in *Chatelaine* (Dec. 1943), 45.

95 'Her Baby Wakes up Laughing and Cooing,' *Chatelaine* (June 1928), 68

96 New editions of the *The Canadian Mother and Child* appeared in 1940, 1953, 1967, 1979, and 1991. The new edition is entitled *You & Your Baby* (Toronto: Douglas and McIntyre 1991).

97 *CMAJ* 17 (1927), 1410, 1412

98 Helen MacMurchy, 'The Division of Child Welfare,' *PHJ* 17 (1928), 517

99 CHC, *Sessional Papers* (1923), 37. Similar figures are available for succeeding years: e.g., 338,467 for 1924–5; 313,717 for 1925–6.

100 NAC, RG29, vol. 1318, file 495-1-2, typescript, 'Division of Child and Maternal Hygiene,' Spring 1943

101 CHC, *Sessional Papers* (1944), Report of DCMH, (1943–4), 56

102 NAC, RG29, vol. 1318, file 495-1-2, typescript, 'The Child and Maternal Health Division, dated Apr. 1952, 3

103 Ibid.

104 The report of DCMH for the year 1955–6 stated that 'a new policy has been established whereby the free distribution of the "Canadian Mother and Child" has been reduced by 25 percent' (CHC, *Sessional Papers*, 1956, Report of DCMH, 40). The fifth edition, *You & Your Baby*, costs $7.95.

105 *A Little Talk about the Baby*, by Helen MacMurchy. I was unable to locate a copy of this publication, but it is referred to in Helen MacMurchy, *Handbook of Child Welfare in Canada* (Ottawa: King's Printer 1923), 125.

106 Ontario, *Sessional Papers* (1920), OBH, Report of the Bureau of Child Welfare (1919), 33

107 *CPHJ* 34 (1933), 303

108 Samples of these pamphlets are held at the CTA, RG11, F1, box 7, file 'Advice for the Expectant Mother 1922–48.'

109 When my first child was born in 1982, the public health nurse responsible for my area insisted on making a home visit. She brought me a

copy of 'Infant Care,' a 16–page brochure produced by Toronto's department of public health. TDPH still provides such literature for new mothers.

110 I shall also refer to the Canadian Council on Child and Family Welfare as the CCCFW and the council.

111 For a discussion of Whitton's career, see Patricia T. Rooke and R.L. Schnell, '"An Idiot's Flowerbed" – A Study of Charlotte Whitton's Feminist Thought, 1941–50,' in Veronica Strong-Boag and Anita Clair Fellman, eds., *Rethinking Canada: The Promise of Women's History* (Toronto: Copp Clark Pitman 1986), 208–25.

112 The 1946–7 report of DMCH details this history. Transfer was completed on 1 Apr. 1947. NAC, MG28, I10, vol. 66, file 010, CWC vol. 8, Maternal and Child Hygiene, 1946–50.

113 As of Aug. 1930, the topics in the series were 1) problems in enuresis; 2) problems re: food habits; 3) problems re: temper tantrums; 4) problems re: fear and nervousness; 5) problems re: disobedience; 6) problems re: dishonesty and untruthfulness (NAC, RG29, vol. 992, file 499-3-7, part 5, Report of the Child Welfare Section of CCCFW, Nov. 1929 to 31 Mar. 1931, 6).

114 NAC, Records of the Canadian Council on Social Development, MG28, I10, vol. 5, file 19, 'Health Stories 1928'

115 Alan Brown, *The Normal Child: Its Care and Feeding* (Toronto: McClelland and Stewart 1924); Alan Brown and Frederick Tisdall, *Common Procedures in the Practice of Paediatrics* (Toronto: McClelland and Stewart 1926); and Alton Goldbloom, *The Care of the Child* (Toronto: Longmans, Green 1928)

116 'Review of *The Normal Child*,' *CMAJ* 14 (1924), 183

117 'Review of Alton Goldbloom, *The Care of the Child*,' *CMAJ* 19 (1928), 754. A reviewer in the *CN* noted that 'although designed to guide parents, [Goldbloom's book] should prove helpful to the public health nurse in providing her with those talking points so essential in home, school, and community' (44 [1948], 67).

118 Norah Lewis, 'Advising the Parents: Child Rearing in British Columbia during the Inter-War Years' (EdD dissertation, University of British Columbia 1980), 24

119 Alton Goldbloom, *Small Patients: The Autobiography of a Children's Doctor* (Toronto: Longmans, Green 1959), 216

120 In 1929, Alan Brown's *The Normal Child* cost $1.25; Goldbloom's book cost $1.50. Alice MacKay, 'Canadian Handbooks on Child Care,' *Canadian Home Journal* (May 1929), 93.

121 Robert F. de Graff to Dr Benjamin Spock, 3 Sept. 1947, 1 (courtesy, Spock Archives, George Argents Research Library, Syracuse University)
122 Goldbloom, *Small Patients*, 216
123 NAC, RG29, vol. 992, file 499-3-7, part 2, letter from Helen MacMurchy to 'Mr. Editor,' dated 4 Mar. 1921
124 CHC, *Annual Reports* (1931–2), Report of the Department of Pensions and National Health, Child Welfare Division, 130 re: The Distribution of *Maternal Care* through Women's Organizations. The author of the report noted that 456 letters had been received regarding *Maternal Care* and that 276 'of these letters stated that a meeting had been held or would soon be held to discuss the subject of maternal care and to read the publication.'
125 Strong-Boag, 'Intruders in the Nursery,' 162

CHAPTER 3 Medicalizing Motherhood

1 Helen MacMurchy, *The Canadian Mother's Book* (Toronto: King's Printer 1923), 8
2 Adrienne Rich, *Of Woman Born* (New York: W.W. Norton 1976; Bantam Books 1977), 6
3 In the city of Toronto, e.g., the average rate of infant mortality (per 1,000 live births) was as follows: 1910–14, 137.0; 1915–20, 103.2; 1921–5, 75.6; 1926–30, 73.9; 1931–5, 62.0 (typescript, 'Infant Mortality – Toronto – 1910–1935,' AO, RG10, series 30-A-1, box 10, file 10-4).
4 The actual extent of the decline is difficult to determine, because accurate national statistics were not available prior to 1921. See Neil Sutherland, *Children in English-Canadian Society: Framing the Twentieth-Century Consensus*, (Toronto: University of Toronto Press 1976), 69, for a discussion of the problem of vital statistics.
5 Prior to 1921 maternal mortality did not appear as a separate item in the records of the Dominion Bureau of Statistics (Helen MacMurchy, *Maternal Mortality in Canada*, Report of the Enquiry made by the DOH, Division of Child Welfare, Little Blue Books, National Series, no. 1 [1928], 6). It is therefore impossible to determine, with any accuracy, whether the maternal mortality rate in the 1920s was higher than in preceding decades. It does appear that the rate was rising during the 1920s. MacMurchy cited the national rate (including Quebec) as 33.85 in 1921, 4.9 in 1922 (p. 57), 5.2 in 1924 (p. 44), and 6.5 for the period from July 1, 1925 to July 1, 1926 (p. 3). In Britain, the maternal mortality rate

was also rising during the 1920s. Nonetheless, MacMurchy claimed that 'maternal mortality in Canada in 1922 was 45 per cent higher than in England.' (p. 60). For a discussion of this issue in Britain, see Ann Oakley, *The Captured Womb: A History of the Medical Care of Pregnant Women* (London: Basil Blackwell 1984), chap. 3, and Jane Lewis, *The Politics of Motherhood: Child and Maternal Welfare in England, 1900-1939* (London: Croom Helm 1980).

6 See Suzann Buckley, 'Ladies or Midwives?: Efforts to Reduce Infant and Maternal Mortality,' in Linda Kealey, ed., *A Not Unreasonable Claim: Women and Reform in Canada, 1880s-1920s* (Toronto: Women's Press 1979), 131-50. For a discussion of efforts to reduce maternal mortality in British Columbia, see Norah Lewis, 'Reducing Maternal Mortality in British Columbia: An Educational Process,' in, Barbara K. Latham and Roberta J. Pazdro, eds., *Not Just Pin Money* (Victoria: Camosun College 1984), 337-55.

7 Suzann Buckley, 'Efforts to Reduce Infant Maternity Mortality in Canada between the Two World Wars,' *Atlantis* 2 (Spring 1977), part 2, 77

8 A summary of the report was published in *Social Welfare*. Helen MacMurchy, 'Maternal Mortality,' *Social Welfare* 6 (1923), 28-30. This was the first report on the subject in Canada.

9 MacMurchy, *Maternal Mortality*, 7

10 The report covered the year between 1 July 1925 and 1 July 1926, and was released as publication no. 37 of the famous Little Blue Books Series.

11 Helen MacMurchy, *Mother: A Little Book for Women* and *Mother: A Little Book for Men*, publications no. 38 and 39 of the Little Blue Book Series (Dominion of Canada: DOH 1928)

12 Articles discussing MacMurchy's report appeared in many popular magazines of the day. See, e.g., Stella Pines, 'We Want Perfect Parents!' *Chatelaine* (Sept. 1928), 12-13; Bertha Hall, 'Must 1,532 Mothers Die?' *Chatelaine* (July 1928), 6, 61. Subsequent to the MacMurchy study, public health officials in Ontario and Manitoba also conducted exhaustive studies of the problem of maternal mortality. Their results were reported in the following articles: F.W. Jackson, R.D. Defries, and A.H. Sellers, 'A Five-Year Survey of Maternal Mortality in Manitoba, 1928-1932,' *CPHJ* 25 (1934), 103-19; and J.T. Phair and A.H. Sellers, 'A Study of Maternal Deaths in the Province of Ontario,' *CPHJ* 23 (1934), 563-79.

13 The previous rates were as follows: 1923: 4.9; 1924: 5.2; 1925: 4.9. MacMurchy, *Maternal Mortality*, 44. These rates were derived from data provided by the Dominion Bureau of Statistics.

14 Ibid., 10, 60

15 Statistics given in publication no. 143, United States Children's Bureau, Robert Morse Woodbury, PhD, cited in MacMurchy, *Maternal Mortality*, 13.

16 MacMurchy, *Maternal Mortality*, 12–13

17 Bertha E. Hall, 'Must 1,532 Mothers Die? We Lost Four Mothers Every Day in the Year,' 6. The quotation is from MacMurchy's report, 5–6.

18 Puerperal septicaemia is a 'widespread infection caused by the presence of microorganisms and their associated toxins in the blood ... Microorganisms gain access to the blood during childbirth via the cervix and the vaginal mucous membranes' (Judith Walzer Leavitt, *Brought to Bed: Childbearing in America, 1750–1950* [New York: Oxford University Press 1986], 275). Haemorrhage refers to bleeding, in this case uncontrolled bleeding following delivery. Toxaemia is a disease of pregnancy associated with high blood pressure. It can result in eclampsia – 'convulsions sometimes followed by coma and death' (Leavitt, 272).

19 MacMurchy, *Maternal Mortality*, 16. In addition, MacMurchy noted that work outside the home was cited as a factor in three deaths, and 'in 67 cases it was mentioned that the patient was overworked with the care of her children and the labours of the house and home.'

20 Ibid., 19

21 Lesley Biggs, 'The Response to Maternal Mortality in Ontario, 1920–1940' (MSc thesis, University of Toronto 1983), 47

22 MacMurchy, *Maternal Mortality*, 14. In an article in 1934, R.E. Wodehouse, deputy minister of pensions and national health, also argued that overuse of forceps was a factor in the high rate of maternal mortality. Referring to this article, Suzann Buckley observes that Wodehouse 'wanted the public to be made aware of the need for deliveries without forceps and for the profession to take action against "a few practicing brothers" whose intervention at labour or before the fetus was viable was responsible for more than one-third of maternal deaths' ('Ladies or Midwives?' note 24, 196, citing Wodehouse, 'Maternal Deaths,' *CMAJ* 34 [1934], 526).

23 Dr W.G. Cosbie, The Academy of Medicine, Toronto, in MacMurchy, *Maternal Mortality*, 45–6

24 Biggs, 'Response to Maternal Mortality,' 100–1

25 MacMurchy, *Maternal Mortality*, 10, 27, 11

26 Ibid., 12, 26

27 Joseph Nathanson, 'Prophylaxis in Obstetrics, with Special Reference to the Value and Importance of Pre-Natal Care,' *CMAJ* 14 (1924), 495

28 As Suzann Buckley observes, MacMurchy 'envisioned a simple world wherein doctors fulfilled their responsibilities by taking charge and pregnant women fulfilled their responsibilities by taking orders' ('The Search for the Decline of Maternal Mortality: The Place of Hospital Records,' in Wendy Mitchinson and Janice Dickin McGinnis, eds., *Essays in the History of Medicine* [Toronto: McClelland and Stewart 1988], 154).

29 Mrs A.M. Plumptre, 'Maternal Mortality Report,' *Canadian Child Welfare News* 4 (1928), 44

30 Blanch Emerson, 'Child Welfare,' *CN* 26 (1930), 199

31 Oakley, *Captured Womb*, 17

32 *The Baby* (1924), 3

33 Helen MacMurchy, 'The Duty of a Physician to the Mother and Her Child,' *Canadian Practitioner and Review* 46 (Oct. 1921), 303–4

34 Ernest Couture, *The Canadian Mother and Child* (Ottawa: King's Printer 1940; 1949 ed.), 3. The first edition appeared in 1940. It remained essentially unchanged until the first major revision in 1953. Since I have relied primarily on the 1949 edition of that volume, I will cite all references accordingly. Couture did not directly succeed MacMurchy, since the division was disbanded on her enforced retirement in 1933. Couture was appointed when the division was resurrected in 1937.

35 TDPH, *The Expectant Mother* (1927), 8

36 Ibid., 3–4. The same explanation appeared in *Expectant Mother* (1948), 3.

37 Helen MacMurchy, *The Canadian Mother's Book* (1931), 28. The CCCFW's *Prenatal Letters* (4, 1) told women to 'lie down for an hour or more after the noon meal.'

38 MacMurchy, *Canadian Mother's Book* (1923), 20

39 Ibid. (1932; 1935 ed.), 25. Note: *The Canadian Mother's Book* was revised in 1932; it was released, with very minor revisions, in 1934. The edition that I used bore the date 1935 and I will cite it as such.

40 Ibid., 33

41 DNHW *Canadian Mother and Child* (Ottawa: Queen's Printer 1953), 24

42 MacMurchy, *Canadian Mother's Book* (1923), 29

43 Couture, *Canadian Mother and Child* (1940; 1949 ed.), 20–1

44 DNHW, *Canadian Mother and Child* (1953), 21

45 MacMurchy, *Canadian Mother's Book* (1923), 27

46 Couture, *Canadian Mother and Child* (1940; 1949 ed.), 24

47 'It is better to discontinue sexual relations ... during the last six weeks before the baby is born, and the first six weeks afterwards. This is to avoid the possibility of infection or childbed fever' (DNHW, *Canadian Mother and Child* [1953], 26).

48 Couture, *Canadian Mother and Child* (1940; 1949 ed.), 21–2

49 Ibid., 22

50 This apparent liberalization may not always have benefited the fetus, however. While the 1940 edition recommended that pregnant women avoid smoking and drinking, the 1953 edition told women 'if you are used to a certain amount every day, it will probably do you no harm to continue' (DNHW, *Canadian Mother and Child* [1953], 25).

51 TDPH, *Pre-Natal Care: Advice for the Expectant Mother* (1922), 3

52 MacMurchy, *Mother: A Little Book for Men*, 16. She continued: 'This is partly a matter of business. You cannot pay in money for the work of a Doctor. But you, Father, are the one who pays the account. Get the right kind of Doctor.'

53 Couture, *Canadian Mother and Child* (1940; 1949 ed.), 36

54 MacMurchy, *Canadian Mother's Book* (1932; 1935 ed.), 42

55 Couture, *Canadian Mother and Child* (1940; 1949 ed.), 36

56 In a fascinating article on antenatal literature in Britain, Hilary Graham argues that the image of pregnancy as natural was 'ambiguous in several respects. There is ambiguity apparent in the depiction of pregnancy as firstly both healthy *and* a time of sickness; secondly as physiologically normal *and* emotionally stressful; and thirdly as both natural *and* medically problematic' ('Images of Pregnancy in Antenatal Literature,' in Robert Dingwall, Christian Heath, Margaret Reid, and Margaret Stacey, eds., *Health Care and Health Knowledge* [London: Croom Helm 1977], 16).

57 OBH, *Baby* (1924), 4. Helen MacMurchy placed the responsibility for securing medical attention on the father's shoulders, advising him that, 'when she tells you the Great Secret – take her to the doctor right away to make sure that all is well with her' (*How to Take Care of the Baby* [Ottawa: King's Printer 1922], 3).

58 MacMurchy, *Canadian Mother's Book* (1923), 11–12

59 Stella Pines, 'We Want Perfect Parents!' *Chatelaine* (Sept. 1928), 13

60 MacMurchy, *Canadian Mother's Book* (1923), 10–11

61 Helen MacMurchy, 'Well-Baby Centre: For Mothers and Mother-To-Be,' *Canadian Home Journal* (Oct. 1934), 54

62 MacMurchy, *Care of Baby*, 4, emphasis in the original

63 Nathanson, 'Prophylaxis in Obstetrics,' 495–6

64 MacMurchy, *Canadian Mother's Book* (1923), 13–14

65 OBH, *Baby* (1924), 9

66 TDPH, *Expectant Mother*, 3

67 Stella Pines, 'Making Ready for the Great Adventure,' *Chatelaine* (Nov. 1928), 19

68 Mary C. Ferguson, 'Mental Hygiene and Prenatal Care,' *CPHJ* 25 (1934), 350

69 Couture, *Canadian Mother and Child* (1940; 1949 ed.), 14; also, DNHW, *Canadian Mother and Child* (1953), 20

70 Kate Aitken, 'It's Fun Raising a Baby!' *Chatelaine* (Jan. 1955), 51. Similar advice appeared in Elizabeth Chant Robertson's column, 'Can a Scare Deform Your Baby?' *Chatelaine* (Jan. 1957), 54–5.

71 Oakley, *Captured Womb*, 24

72 Couture, *Canadian Mother and Child* (1940; 1949 ed.), 21–2

73 Ethel Cryderman, 'Pre-Natal Work,' quoting Carolyn Van Barclom, no original source given, *CN* 23 (1927), 536

74 Gordon P. Jackson, 'City Health Services,' article reprinted from the *Bulletin of the Academy of Medicine*, a speech given on 27 Mar. 1930, as part of a symposium on state medicine. Deposited in CTA, Records of TDPH, RG11, F1, box 4, file 'Nursing Division History 1930 to 1969,' 8, emphasis added

75 Cryderman, 'Pre-Natal Work,' 537

76 CTA, RG11, F1, box 1, 'Historical Material – Maternal and Child Health,' typescript entitled 'Suggested Content for Introductory Class I: The Importance of Homemaking,' Mar. 10, 1949, 2

77 Buckley, 'Ladies or Midwives?', 134

78 CCCFW, *Prenatal Letters*, 1, 1

79 Charlotte Whitton to Dr G.A. McIntosh, Provincial Health Officer, Nova Scotia, dated 2 Apr. 1929. NAC, MG28, I10, vol. 391, file 178, 'Post Natal Letters 1929.' Whitton was responding to a concern expressed in a letter that McIntosh had forwarded to her.

80 John Puddicombe, MD. 'The Importance of Prenatal Care,' paper presented at Hamilton on 28 May 1934 at the annual meeting of the Canadian Council on Child and Family Welfare (NAC, RG29, vol. 993, file 499-3-7, part 9, 3

81 MacMurchy, *Canadian Mother's Book* (1923), 11

82 Couture, *Canadian Mother and Child* (1940; 1949 ed.), 3, 8

83 Policy holders with Metropolitan Life Insurance were provided with prenatal visits from the company's nursing service, beginning in 1911. The service had begun in the United States in 1909 (*Quarterly Bulletin for Metropolitan Nurses* 15, 4 [Nov. 1951], 5). A limited number of other companies paid a small portion of their employees' wives' costs of maternity care. For a discussion of these services, see Norah Lewis, 'Reducing Maternal Mortality,' 343.

84 OBH, *Baby* (1920), 4

85 TDPH, *Expectant Mother,* 5

86 MacMurchy, *Mother: A Little Book for Men,* 7

87 MacMurchy, 'Well-Baby Centre,' 54

88 Elizabeth Chant Robertson, 'They Shall Inherit the Earth – We Owe Them a Good Beginning,' *Chatelaine* (Mar. 1943), 13

89 Ontario Revised Statutes, *An Act to Amend the Public Health Act* (1948), s. 74a (1): 'Every expectant mother may obtain a free medical examination upon making application on the prescribed form to a duly qualified medical practitioner.'

90 Couture, *Canadian Mother and Child* (1940; 1949 ed.), 3

91 Toronto's first prenatal clinic was established at Toronto General Hospital in 1915. The first prenatal home visit took place in 1913. By 1927, Toronto boasted 19 clinics in 6 hospitals and 5 neighbourhood clinics per week (Cryderman, 'Pre-Natal Work,' 536).

92 Ibid., 537. Cryderman also noted that while 11.3 per cent of all pregnant women were attending a clinic, only 2 per cent of the total client population had personally requested a class or home visit.

93 Constance Gray, 'Prenatal Classes in Greater Toronto,' *CN* 46 (1950), 962

94 CTA, RG11, F1, box 4, file – Nursing Division History, 1930–1969, typescript entitled 'The History of Public Health Nursing in Toronto, 1905–1945,' dated Dec., 1950, 13

95 Jean Webb, 'Observations on Maternal and Infant Health in Canada,' *CJPH* 45 (Jan. 1954), 3. Webb was appointed acting chief in 1953. In 1954, she was named chief, a position she held until 1967.

96 Norah Lewis suggests this as one possible reason for the lack of success of clinics during the interwar years. 'Although public health workers, the VON, and Red Cross nurses urged mothers to seek prenatal care for themselves and their unborn child, less progress was made in this area than in any other stage of child development. Whether from embarassment or from financial constraints, many women were reluctant to attend prenatal clinics or seek prenatal care' ('Advising the Parents: Child Rearing in British Columbia During the Inter-War Years,' (EdD dissertation, University of British Columbia 1980), 52).

97 Webb, 'Observations,' 3

98 As Veronica Strong-Boag has observed, 'childbirth was often the occasion which initiated a doctor's association with a family and its illnesses.' 'Canada's Women Doctors: Feminism Constrained,' in Linda Kealey, *A Not Unreasonable Claim,* 111–12.

99 *Historical Statistics of Canada,* 2nd ed., ed. F.H. Leacy (Ottawa: Statistics Canada, 1983), B1–14

100 Forceps: 'an instrument with two blades and handles for pulling; utilized to extract the fetus by the head from the maternal passages during delivery.' An anaesthetic is 'a substance which when ingested by inhalation or injection produces a loss of sense of touch or pain.' An episiotomy is a 'surgical incision in the perineal tissues [the tissues in the region of the body between the anus and the vulva] to facilitate delivery' (Leavitt, *Brought to Bed*, 271–4).

101 Wendy Mitchinson, 'The Medical Treatment of Women,' in Sandra Burt, Lorraine Code, and Lindsay Dorney, eds., *Changing Patterns: Women in Canada* (Toronto: McClelland and Stewart 1988), 254. Mitchinson notes that the perceived need for routine prenatal care and for hospitalization at childbirth was part of a general trend of medicalization in society.

102 For an excellent review of the American and British literature, see Deborah Gorham, 'Birth and History,' *Histoire sociale / Social History* 17, 34 (Nov. 1984), 383–94. For Britain, see, among others, Jean Donnison, *Midwives and Medical Men: A History of Inter-Professional Rivalries and Women's Rights* (London: Hinemann 1977); Lewis, *The Politics of Motherhood*, which deals with both changes in birthing practices and women's attitudes towards and demands for those changes; Oakley, *The Captured Womb*. For the United States, see Leavitt, *Brought to Bed*; Richard W. and Dorothy C. Wertz, *Lying In: A History of Childbirth in America* (New York: Free Press 1977); Jane B. Donegan, *Women and Men Midwives: Medicine, Morality, and Misogyny in Early America* (Westport, Conn.: Greenwood Press 1978); Judy Barett Litoff, *American Midwives: 1869 to the Present* (Westport, Conn.: Greenwood Press 1978); Nancy Schrom Dye, 'History of Childbirth in America,' *Signs* 6 (Autumn 1980), 97–108; and articles by Catherine Scholten, Judith Walzer Leavitt and Whitney Walton, Virginia G. Drachman, and Judith Walzer Leavitt in Judith Walzer Leavitt, ed., *Women and Health in America*, (Madison: University of Wisconsin Press 1984).

103 See, among others, C. Lesley Biggs, '"The Case of the Missing Midwives": A History of Midwifery in Ontario from 1795–1900.' Helene Laforce, 'The Different Stages in the Elimination of Midwives in Quebec,' Jo Oppenheimer, 'Childbirth in Ontario: The Transition from Home to Hospital in the Early Twentieth Century,' and Veronica Strong-Boag and Kathryn McPherson, 'The Confinement of Women: Childbirth and Hospitalization in Vancouver, 1919–1939,' in Katherine Arnup, Andrée Lévesque, and Ruth Roach Pierson, eds., *Delivering Motherhood: Maternal Ideologies and Practices in the 19th and 20th Centuries* (London: Routledge 1990); Wendy Mitchinson, 'Historical Attitudes Toward Women and Childbirth,'

Atlantis 4 (1979), 13–35; Buckley, 'Ladies or Midwives'; Veronica Strong-Boag, *New Day Recalled: Lives of Girls and Women in English Canada, 1919–1939* (Toronto: Copp Clark Pitman 1988), chap. 5; and Wendy Mitchinson, *The Nature of Their Bodies: Women and Their Doctors in Victorian Canada* (Toronto: University of Toronto Press 1991), chap. 6–7

104 MacMurchy, *Mother – A Little Book for Women*, 11

105 B.E. Harris, 'Pre-Natal Education in the Home,' *CN* 20 (1924), 341

106 TDPH, *Pre-Natal Care* (1922), 5. The reference to midwives was omitted in subsequent editions.

107 Lewis, 'Reducing Maternal Mortality,' 342–3. Similar provisions held force across Canada.

108 For a discussion of doctors' lobbying efforts during the nineteenth century, see Biggs, 'Case of the Missing Midwives.' For a fascinating history of midwifery in Canada, see Appendix A to the *Report of the Task Force on the Implementation of Midwifery in Ontario* (Ontario, Government Publications, 1987).

109 For a discussion of these efforts, see Buckley, 'Ladies or Midwives?'

110 Dr John W.S. McCullough, 'Should Canada Have Midwives?' *Chatelaine* (Oct., 1931), 53. The medical profession has continued its opposition to midwifery right up to the present day, and its powerful lobby has been a key factor in preventing the legalization of midwifery in Canada.

111 For a discussion of the 1923 supplement to *The Canadian Mother's Book*, see Dianne Dodd, paper presented at the Annual Meeting of the CHA, Queen's University, June 1991, and 'Advice to Parents: The Blue Books, Helen MacMurchy, MD, and the Federal Department of Health, 1920–34,' *Canadian Bulletin of Medical History* 8 (1991), 203–30. An important variation in the practice of midwifery can be seen in Newfoundland, where 'granny midwives' have provided services to labouring women throughout this century, and continue to provide such services in outlying areas of the island (Cecilia Benoit, *Midwives in Passage*, [St John's, Newfoundland: Institute of Social and Economic Research 1991]).

112 Dominion Council of Health, Minutes of the 9th Meeting, 11–13 Dec. 1923, NAC, Microfilm Reel C-9814, cited in Dodd, 'Advice to Parents,' 219

113 Dodd, 'Advice to Parents,' 219

114 Couture, *Canadian Mother and Child* (1940; 1949 ed.), 68, emphasis in original

115 Ibid., 50

116 DNHW, *Canadian Mother and Child* (1953), 54

117 The 1943–44, report of DCMH provided national figures on physician-attended births. The percentage of births that took place without a medical attendant had declined from 10.1 per cent in 1935 to 6.1 per cent in 1942. At the same time the percentage of births which took place in hospital steadily increased, from 32 per cent of total confinements in 1935 to 53 per cent in 1942 (CHC, *Annual Reports*, 1943–4, Department of Pensions and National Health, DCMH, 53–4). The first record of the percentage of physician-attended births in British Columbia appeared in 1952. At that time, 98 per cent of births were attended by doctors. That number had risen to 99 per cent by 1960 (Lewis, 'Reducing Maternal Mortality,' 343).

118 TDPH, *Pre-Natal Care* (1922), 8

119 The 1922 edition of *Pre-Natal Care* included a section on home confinement. That section did not appear in the 1927 edition, but was included in the expanded 1931 edition. The 1920 edition of Ontario's *The Baby* contained no information on preparations for a home confinement. The 1924 edition did include a section on 'things you need' 'if the mother is not going to the hospital,' 10. Later editions also included instructions on home confinement.

120 OBH, *Baby* (1920), 7. Toronto's pamphlet *Pre-Natal Care* (1922) used almost identical words: 'There should be a soft, warm blanket to receive the baby,' 8.

121 Kate McIlraith, 'Nurses' Part in a Prenatal Program,' *CN* 46 (1950), 959, emphasis in original

122 CCCFW, *Prenatal Letters* 6, 1

123 Couture, *Canadian Mother and Child* (1940; 1949 ed.), 64

124 Mrs A.M. Plumptre, 'Maternal Mortality Report,' *Canadian Child Welfare News* 4, 2 (1928), 44–5. The Canadian Council on Child Welfare concurred: 'Do not listen to the stories of difficult labour that some gossip will want to tell you' (*Prenatal Letters* 6, 1).

125 Couture, *Canadian Mother and Child* (1940; 1949 ed.), 66

126 Alison Prentice, et al., *Canadian Women: A History* (Toronto: Harcourt Brace Jovanovich 1988), 167

127 TDPH, *Pre-Natal Care* (1922), 8. This phrase was repeated in the 1927 and 1931 editions on pages 16 and 68 respectively.

128 OBH, *Baby* (1924), 10

129 TDPH, *Expectant Mother* (1931), 67

130 Ibid., (1948), 18

131 DBH, *Baby* (1933), 11

132 MacMurchy, *Canadian Mother's Book* (1923), 14. This advice was repeated in the 1931 edition on page 15.

133 Ibid., 14

134 Lewis states that in 1921, Vancouver doctors usually charged $35 for a normal delivery, $50 if the woman haemorrhaged, $45 for an instrument delivery, and $35 for a miscarriage. She notes that, in contrast, an office visit usually cost $2.50. In addition, the woman would be required to pay the costs of the hospital bed. In Vancouver General Hospital in 1906, the weekly rate was $10 ('Reducing Maternal Mortality,' 342). In an article in *Chatelaine*, an anonymous author noted that her combined hospital and surgical costs for a caesarean delivery totalled $345 in 1927 ('Just One Baby?' *Chatelaine* [Mar. 1931], 15).

135 In British Columbia, half of all births took place in hospital by 1928–9. Ontario reached that mark in 1938, and Quebec, in 1945 (Prentice, et al. *Canadian Women*, 248). By 1942 more than half of all births in Canada took place in hospital (F.H. Leacy, ed., *Historical Statistics of Canada*, 2nd Ed., [Ottawa, Statistics Canada 1983], B1–14).

136 Couture, *Canadian Mother and Child* (1940; 1949 ed.), 60

137 Ibid., 61–2

138 DNHW, *Canadian Mother and Child* (1953), 45

139 Benjamin Spock, *Baby and Child Care* (New York: Pocket Books 1946), 12–13

140 Ibid., 13. The same advantages were cited in the 1957 edition, with the omission of the final sentence, 'All of these are real compensations.' As with *The Canadian Mother and Child*, the section on home birth followed the section on hospital births, a subtle but important shift in emphasis.

141 Spock, *Baby and Child Care* (1946), 13

142 Ibid. (1957), 40–1

143 TDPH, *Expectant Mother* (1927), 17

144 MacMurchy, *Canadian Mother's Book* (1932; 1935 ed.), 102

145 Couture, *Canadian Mother and Child* (1940; 1949 ed.), 87. Toronto's *The Expectant Mother* (1948) recommended that 'if there are no complications, her physician may allow her to sit up in a chair about the fifth day and to walk about at the end of the first week,' 13.

146 The 1974 maternal mortality rate for Canada was 0.1 per 1,000 live births. (F.H. Leacy, ed., *Historical Statistics of Canada*, 2nd Ed., B58).

147 A 1987 article reported that 'in 1983 the mortality rate among native infants was 2 times higher for Indians and 4 times higher for Inuit than the national rate; the postneonatal rate was 3.5 to 4 times higher respectively' (Chandrakant P. Shah, Meldon Kahan, and John Krauser, 'The Health of Children of Low-Income Families,' *CMAJ* 137 [Sept. 1987],

487). At the 1990 conference of the Canadian Public Health Association in Toronto, Ellen Bobet, a researcher with Health and Welfare Canada, reported that the infant mortality rate among status Indians remains 'almost twice the rate of the national average' (Kelly Toughhill, 'Natives' Health Still Worse Than Average,' *Toronto Star* 27 June 1990, A25).

148 For an example of an article which blames women's 'casual' attitude towards pregnancy for high rates of infant mortality, see Frank Croft, 'Why Do So Many Canadian Babies Die?' *Chatelaine* (Feb. 1957), 62. Commenting on Canada's high rate of infant mortality, Croft stated that 'one person who came in for scolding from all quarters was you – the Canadian woman. Far too many of you are charged with failing in your obligations as mothers or mothers-to-be. Your attitude toward pregnancy is casual compared with women in other countries.'

149 See Peter Carlyle-Gordge, 'Inuit Fight Loneliness for Safe Births,' *Toronto Star* 23 Mar. 1987, C1, C4.

CHAPTER 4 'Bringing Up Baby'

1 William E. Blatz and Helen McM. Bott, *Parents and the Pre-School Child* (Toronto and London: J.M. Dent 1928), 83

2 Benjamin Spock, MD, *The Pocket Book of Baby and Child Care* (Montreal: Pocket Books 1946), 3. This edition is referred to hereafter unless otherwise specified.

3 Jane Brickman, 'Mother Love – Mother Death: Maternal and Infant Care: Social Class and the Role of the Government' (PhD dissertation, City University of New York 1978), 188

4 For a discussion of Holt's relationship with the Rockefeller family, see Barbara Ehrenreich and Deirdre English, *For Her Own Good: 150 Years of the Experts' Advice to Women* (New York: Anchor Books 1979), 85

5 Alan Brown was resident physician under Dr Holt at New York Babies' Hospital. Goldbloom was a junior intern under Holt. Regarding the influence of Holt's book, Blatz and Bott noted: 'It conveyed to the mothers of the generation to which it was addressed the idea of a positive regime of right physical habits as essential to the child's health and well-being. Previous to this mothers had brought their children up by rule of thumb, the child's demands being the gauge of the mother's behaviour' (*Parents and the Pre-School Child*, 54).

6 John B. Watson, *Psychological Care of the Infant and Child* (London: George Allen and Unwin 1928). For a discussion of Watson's views on child rear-

ing, see Ben Harris, '"Give Me a Dozen Healthy Infants ... ": John B. Watson's Popular Advice on Childrearing, Women, and the Family,' in Miriam Lewis, ed., *In the Shadow of the Past: Psychology Portrays the Sexes – A Social and Intellectual History* (New York: Columbia University Press 1984), 126–54.

7 Frances Lily Johnson, 'The Making and Breaking of Habits,' *Chatelaine* (June 1928), 37

8 In 1899 Frederick Taylor demonstrated that a worker at Bethlehem Steel could increase his productivity nearly four-fold when the principles of scientific management were applied. Taylor's ideas were quickly translated into the private sphere by Christine Frederick, whose series of articles, entitled 'The New Housekeeping,' was serialized in the *Ladies' Home Journal* between September and December 1912. Frederick began each article with a reference to Taylor's accomplishments at Bethlehem Steel, suggesting, by implication, that housewives could improve their productivity in a similar manner. For a discussion of scientific management in the United States, see Ehrenreich and English, *For Her Own Good*, 162.

9 Johnson, 'Making and Breaking Habits,' 38

10 The advocation of rigid scheduling could already be found in literature of the late nineteenth century. L. Emmett Holt, e.g., told parents that the baby could be taught proper habits of eating and sleeping 'by always feeding at regular intervals and putting to sleep at exactly the same time every day and evening' (L.E. Holt, *The Care and Feeding of Children* [1894], cited in Elizabeth Lomax, *Science and Patterns of Child Care* [San Francisco: W.H. Freeman 1978], 18 n11).

11 CCCFW, *Post-Natal Letters* 1,a, 1–2

12 OBH, *The Baby* (1920), 10

13 CCCFW, *Post-Natal Letters* 1,a, 1. The suggestion was accompanied by a drawing of two rabbits gazing earnestly at a clock.

14 For a discussion of the key role of science in Victorian Canada, see Suzanne Zeller, *Inventing Canada: Early Victorian Science and the Idea of a Transcontinental Nation* (Toronto: University of Toronto Press 1987). Zeller notes, 'science became the gauge by which Canadians assessed what their country and, through it, they themselves could one day become.' Zeller refers to the frequent use of 'scientific metaphors applied to the issues of the day' (*Inventing Canada*, 6).

15 The *Manual for Foster Parents* urged readers to establish 'routine health habits' for baby so that he might come to 'expect his feeding, bathing, sleep and all other attentions with clock-like regularity' (J. Vera Moberly, *Manual for Foster Parents*, undated pamphlet, AO, Records of the Ministry of

Health, RG10, series 30-A-1, box 5, file 5-3, 'Historical – Pamphlets and Literature. Manual for Foster Parents c. 1930.' Moberly was the executive secretary of the Toronto Infants' Home at the time of writing.

16 Alan Brown, *The Normal Child: Its Care and Feeding* (Toronto: McClelland and Stewart 1932), 223. These same words appeared in the 1920 edition of the OBH publication, *The Baby*, 36. In virtually the same words, Frederick Tisdall noted that 'it is remarkable how these infants learn to wake up at or shortly before the appointed time. After a few days' training they behave like little machines' (*The Home Care of the Infant and Child* [New York: William Morrow 1942], 72). Such terminology reflected the fascination with machines and technology that characterized the early decades of this century. An article by Stella Pines was the sole exception I found to this approach. While including the standard advice that 'sleeping times, bathing, outings all need regulating,' Pines reassured women that 'you need not be afraid he will become a machine. Nature guards against that in his development.' Lest readers take such reassurance too far, she admonished, 'Do not leave too much to nature' ('The Baby's Routine and Management,' *Chatelaine* [Jan. 1929], 53).

17 Brown, *Normal Child*, 223

18 TDPH, *Expectant Mother* (1931), 11

19 Adelaide A. Plumptre, 'A Mother's Duty to the State,' Radio Talk, Canadian Social Hygiene Council, delivered on CKCL, 5 Apr. 1927, published in *PHJ* 18 (1927), 179

20 Frances Lily Johnson, 'Learning to Eat,' *Chatelaine* (Sept. 1928), 36

21 CCCFW, *Post-Natal Letters* 1, 2

22 Pines, 'Baby's Routine and Management,' 53

23 For a discussion of developmental theory, see Elizabeth Lomax, *Science and Patterns of Child Care*, chap. 5 (San Francisco: W.H. Freeman 1978). Benjamin Spock was also influenced by the views of Sigmund Freud, and studied for a number of years at the New York Psychoanalytic Institute. On the influences on Spock's work, see Benjamin Spock and Mary Morgan, *Spock on Spock: A Memoir of Growing Up with the Century* (New York: Pantheon Books 1989) and Lynn Z. Bloom, *Dr Spock: Biography of a Conservative Radical* (Indianapolis: Bobbs-Merrill 1972). For a general discussion of Freud's influence on child-rearing advice, see Geoffrey H. Steere, 'Freudianism and Child-Rearing in the Twenties,' *American Quarterly* 20 (1968), 759–67. A similar time-lag took place between the development of child-centred education, promoted as early as 1905 by Thomas Dewey, and its application within the public school system. The ideas of progressive education did not gain wide-scale prominence in Canada until after the Second World War.

24 Canada, DNHW, *Up the Years from One to Six* (Ottawa: King's Printer, 1950), 38

25 Margaret Laine, 'When Baby Cries,' *Chatelaine* (Feb. 1932), 40

26 Spock, *Baby and Child Care*, 18–19

27 Elizabeth Chant Robertson, 'They *Want* to Be Good,' *Chatelaine* (May 1954), 110. The article was subtitled 'Training a Child for Living Is More Important Than Just Proving You're Boss.'

28 Spock, *Baby and Child Care*, 19

29 OBH, *Early Years* (1954; 1957 ed.), 91

30 Spock, *Baby and Child Care*, 194

31 Robertson, 'They *Want* to Be Good,' 112

32 Spock, *Baby and Child Care*, 20

33 DNHW, *Canadian Mother and Child* (1953), 106

34 Elizabeth Chant Robertson, 'Enjoy Your Baby,' *Chatelaine* (Apr. 1951), 90

35 Couture, *Canadian Mother and Child* (1940), 166

36 OBH, *Expectant Mother* (1931), 11. Those remarks did not appear in the 1927 edition of that publication.

37 Tisdall, *Home Care*, 41

38 Ibid., 41–3

39 CCCFW, *Post-Natal Letters* 6, 2

40 Frances Lily Johnson, 'What of Your Child? Learning to Sleep.' *Chatelaine* (Oct. 1928), 42

41 OBH, *Baby* (1933), 28

42 Tisdall, *Home Care*, 57–8

43 Blatz and Bott, *Parents and the Pre-School Child*, 117

44 Tisdall, *Home Care*, 58

45 OBH, *Baby* (1933), 46

46 Couture, *Canadian Mother and Child* (1940; 1949 ed.), 152

47 DNHW, *Canadian Mother and Child* (1953), 95–6

48 Spock, *Baby and Child Care*, 95

49 DNHW, *Canadian Mother and Child* (1953), 95–6

50 Canada, DNHW, *Up the Years from One to Six* (1950), 9. *Up the Years from One to Six* was a joint project of the Division of Child and Maternal Health, the Mental Health Division, Nutrition Division, Dental Health Division, and the Physical Fitness Division. Ernest Couture, director of the Child and Maternal Health Division, was the chairman of the editorial board for the publication.

51 Ibid., 56

52 Spock, *Baby and Child Care*, 246

53 DNHW, *One to Six*, 56

54 Ibid., 55–6

55 Early toilet training became popular in the late eighteenth and early nineteenth centuries once the fashion of swaddling clothes for infants was abandoned. For a discussion of toilet training in the nineteenth century, see Christina Hardyment, *Dream Babies: Child Care from Locke to Spock* (London: Oxford University Press 1984), 59–60.

56 OBH, *Baby* (1920), 45–6. Mothers in the interwar years, caring for infants in an age before disposable or ready-made diapers, washing machines, or, in many cases, hot and cold running water, might well have appreciated the advantages of early toilet training!

57 OBH, *Baby* (1933), 30

58 TDPH, *The Care of the Infant and Young Child* (1931), 44

59 Ibid., 45. OBH, *Baby* (1943) stressed that *'unchanging regularity of time, place and conditions are essential in forming good toilet habits,'* 46, emphasis in original

60 CCCFW, *Post-Natal Letters* 6, 3

61 Ibid., 5, 1

62 Ibid., 12, 2

63 OBH, *Baby* (1943), 46

64 Couture, *Canadian Mother and Child* (1940), 168

65 TDPH, *Infant and Young Child* (1944), 56

66 Blatz and Bott, *Parents and the Pre-School Child*, 138. Nowhere in any of the publications is reference made to the father's role in toilet training.

67 OBH, *Baby* (1943), 46

68 DNHW, *Canadian Mother and Child* (1953), 97

69 Spock, *Baby and Child Care*, 185. Differing from the writers of almost all manuals produced during the interwar years, Blatz and Bott made a similar observation regarding early toilet training in 1928. Noting 'how absurd it is for mothers to boast of having trained in bladder control at two or three months,' the authors pointed out that 'the mother may have good luck in anticipating accidents, but the control is hers, not the child's, and this may actually militate against real control on the child's part' (*Parents and the Pre-School Child*, 133).

70 ODH, *Early Years* (1954; 1957 ed.), 93

71 DNHW, *One to Six*, 58. Thus, mothers who had followed expert advice from the interwar years and trained their babies early were now held responsible for psychological problems which allegedly resulted from such early training.

72 Ibid., 60

73 Spock, *Baby and Child Care*, 187

74 ODH, *Early Years* (1954; 1957 ed.), 93–4, emphasis in original

75 Spock, *Baby and Child Care*, 187

76 ODH, *Early Years* (1954; 1957 ed.), 93

77 Spock, *Baby and Child Care*, 189

78 DNHW, *Canadian Mother and Child* (1953), 98

79 Spock, *Baby and Child Care*, 184; 189-90, emphasis in original

80 ODH, *Early Years* (1954; 1957 ed.), 93

81 DNHW, *One to Six* (1950), 60

82 ODH, *Early Years* (1954; 1957 ed.), 94

83 Spock, *Baby and Child Care*, 190

84 Elizabeth Chant Robertson, 'Training Your Baby (Part Two),' *Chatelaine* (Feb. 1949), 65. This stands in marked contrast to an earlier article by Robertson in which she recommended beginning bowel training at one to three months of age ('Training Our Infants,' *Chatelaine* [Dec. 1941], 70-1).

85 Helen MacMurchy, *Infant Mortality: Special Report* (1910), 5

86 TDPH, *Infant and Young Child* (1931), 6

87 Stella Pines, 'Making Ready for the Great Arrival,' *Chatelaine* (Nov. 1928), 19

88 Couture, *Canadian Mother and Child* (1940), 108

89 Urban J. Gareau, 'Nutrition in Childhood,' *CN* 23 (1927), 294

90 The Hospital for Sick Children, *Dr Alan Brown* (Toronto: Hospital for Sick Children Alumni Association 1984), 35-6. A similar statement was attributed to Brown in an article about his work by Dorothy Sangster ('Alan Brown of Sick Kids,' *Maclean's* [1 Aug. 1952], 34).

91 'Dr Alan Brown, Child Specialist,' *Toronto Star*, 8 Sept. 1960. Toronto Public Library Scrapbooks, vol. 17, 121

92 John W.S. McCullough, 'The Baby Clinic, no. 3: Feeding,' *Chatelaine* (Apr. 1933), 68

93 John W.S. McCullough, 'Chatelaine's Baby Clinic, no. 8: The Nursing Mother,' *Chatelaine* (Sept. 1933), 64-5

94 Dr John W.S. McCullough, 'The Importance of Breast Feeding' *Chatelaine* (Aug. 1940), 48

95 For a discussion of these factors, see chap. 5 of this book.

96 Dr John W.S. McCullough, 'Artificial Feeding,' *Chatelaine* (Mar. 1941), 66

97 Among the advantages of breast-feeding are the following: breast milk contains antibodies which render the baby less likely to develop allergies; breast milk is easier to digest than formula; breast-fed babies have fewer problems with rapid weight gain; breast-feeding is less expensive and more convenient than bottle feeding.

98 Elizabeth Chant Robertson, 'Is Breast Feeding Worth the Effort?' *Chatelaine* (May 1942), 75, 78. In a 1960 article, Robertson claimed that about 85 per cent of 'healthy mothers' were able to breast-feed their ba-

bies if they wanted to. 'Just a few seem physically unable to do it and there are a few who find the whole idea upsetting, but that is quite unusual' ('The Care and Feeding of Baby ... *and* Yourself,' *Chatelaine* [Oct. 1960], 166).

99 Elizabeth Chant Robertson, 'Now We *Know* Breast Feeding Is Best,' *Chatelaine* (Sept. 1955), 79

100 Spock, *Baby and Child Care* (1946), 30–2

101 For a discussion of the increasing use of commercial infant formula in the United States over the course of this century, see Rima D. Apple, '"To be Used Only under the Direction of a Physician": Commercial Infant Feeding and Medical Practice, 1870–1940,' *Bulletin of the History of Medicine* 54 (1980), 402–17. Apple attributes the steady decline in breast–feeding rates between the 1870s and the 1930s to several factors, including 'the rise of pediatrics, the growing availability of pure milk and infant-food products, the increase in hospital births, the changing role and image of women, and, most importantly, the development of a new relationship between commercial infant-food manufacturers and the medical profession,' 402. See also Rima D. Apple, *Mothers and Medicine: A Social History of Infant Feeding, 1890–1950* (Madison: University of Wisconsin Press 1987).

102 MacMurchy, *How to Take Care of the Baby* (1923), 11

103 MacMurchy, *The Canadian Mother's Book* (1923), 30–1

104 Ibid., (1933; 1935 ed.), 117

105 See, e.g. CCCFW, *Post-Natal Letters* 2, 2. 'Your doctor will give you directions for preparing the milk, and you must follow these directions exactly. Never experiment with the preparation or formula of modified food for your baby, and do not feed him the various patent foods that your neighbours may suggest.'

106 OBH, *Baby* (1920), 15 emphasis in original

107 Ibid., 17

108 TDPH, *Infant and Young Child* (1931), 16

109 ODH, *Early Years* (1954; 1957 ed.), 23

110 Couture, *Canadian Mother and Child* (1940; 1949 ed.), 136

111 DNHW, *Canadian Mother and Child* (1953), 81

112 For a discussion of these practices in American hospitals, see Apple, *Mothers and Medicine*, 128

113 DNHW, *Canadian Mother and Child* (1953), 80

114 Tisdall, *Home Care*, 72. Tisdall ended this section of his book with a phrase that echoed the words of his colleague, Alan Brown. 'After a few days' training they [the infants] behave like little machines.'

115 Blatz and Bott, *Parents and the Pre-School Child*, 78
116 Tisdall, *Home Care*, 71
117 See, e.g., ibid., 28.
118 For a discussion of this problem, see 'Doctoring the Family, part three,' radio program, 'Ideas,' CBC Radio, Apr. 1985, 25.
119 Tisdall, *Home Care*, 76–7
120 Brown, *Normal Child*, 86
121 Ibid., 79
122 Tisdall, *Home Care*, 76
123 Brown, *Normal Child*, 88
124 MacMurchy, *Canadian Mother's Book* (1923), 32
125 R.R. MacGregor, 'Supplemental Feeding in Gastro-Intestinal Disturbances of the Breast Fed Infant,' *CMAJ* 13 (1923), 180
126 Arthur B. Chandler, 'Recent Studies in Problems connected with Lactation and Infant Feeding,' *CMAJ* 11 (1921), 62
127 CCCFW *Post-Natal Letters* 1a, 2
128 ODH, *Early Years* (1954; 1957 ed.), 26
129 Couture, *Canadian Mother and Child* (1940; 1949 ed.), 109
130 TDPH, *Infant and Young Child* (1948), 9. Lest the reader interpret this as a completely unstructured program, the author added the following: 'Regularity of feeding makes the baby feel comfortable and secure and keeps the milk secretion uniform.'
131 Couture, *Canadian Mother and Child* (1940; 1949 ed.), 110
132 DNHW, *Canadian Mother and Child* (1953), 75
133 C.K. Rowan-Legg, 'Self-Demand Feeding of Infants,' *CMAJ* 60 (Apr. 1949), 390
134 Ethel B. Cooke, 'Nutrition of Infants,' *CN* 51 (1955), 382
135 Spock, *Baby and Child Care*, 24
136 Ibid., 25
137 Ibid.
138 In a letter, Spock noted that 'the accusation that I was permissive never came in the first 22 years after $B + CC$ was published; it came out of a sermon by Rev Norman Vincent Peal, a supporter of the Vietnam War, two weeks after I was indicted for my opposition to the war, in 1968' (to the author, 28 Mar. 1988). That comment notwithstanding, it would seem that Spock did find it necessary to account for the shift in emphasis between the first and second editions of his book. In 'A Letter to the Reader of This New Edition,' Spock explained that 'When I was writing the first edition, between 1943 and 1946, the attitude of a majority of people toward infant feeding, toilet training, and general child manage-

ment was still fairly strict and inflexible ... Since then a great change in attitude has occurred, and nowadays there seems to be more chance of a conscientious parent's getting into trouble with permissiveness than with strictness. So I have tried to give a more balanced view' (*Baby and Child Care* [1957], 1–2).

139 Ibid., 53
140 Ibid., 54
141 Ibid., 53
142 OBH, *Baby* (1920) recommended that the mother feed by the breast 'without other food' until the baby was 9 or 10 months old. MacMurchy advised that the mother begin to switch from nursing to feeding at nine months, but that she make this switch 'slowly and gradually' (*How to Take Care of the Baby* [1923], 20).
143 Brown, *Normal Child*, 106
144 Tisdall, *Home Care*, 97
145 TDPH, *Infant and Young Child* (1931), 12
146 Tisdall, *Home Care*, 93
147 'During recent years tremendous strides have been made in our knowledge of the parts played by different foods in the production and maintenance of health. This knowledge, which is absolsutely essential in the selection of the proper diet for your infant or child, has been gained through laborious and painstaking observations made under the most carefully controlled conditions. The details of these fascinating studies ... are unfortunately beyond the scope of this book. However a few of the essential facts are listed here as they will be of interest to the modern mother who wishes to know why certain diets are recommended' (Tisdall, *Home Care*, 34).
148 TDPH, *Infant and Young Child* (1931), 34
149 Couture, *Canadian Mother and Child* (1940; 1949 ed.), 125, emphasis in original
150 ODH, *Early Years* (1953; 1957 ed.), 38
151 OBH, *Baby* (1933), 48
152 Johnson, 'What of Your Child? Learning to Eat,' 37
153 Blatz and Bott, *Parents and the Pre-School Child*, 97
154 CCCFW, *Pre-School Letters* 4, 1
155 Blatz and Bott, *Parents and the Pre-School Child*, 105
156 Brown, *Normal Child*, 151
157 Blatz and Bott, *Parents and the Pre-School Child*, 101
158 Elizabeth Chant Robertson, 'Feeding Difficulties,' *Chatelaine* (Oct. 1943), 87

159 Elizabeth Chant Robertson, 'Don't Fight to Make Him Eat,' *Chatelaine* (May 1956), 84

160 DNHW, *One to Six* (1953), 51–2

161 DNHW, *Canadian Mother and Child* (1953), 91

162 DNHW, *One to Six* (1953), 54

163 Ibid., 52

164 Spock, *Baby and Child Care* (1946), 210. This stands in marked contrast to the battle of wills posed in the literature of the interwar years. See, e.g., Blatz and Bott, who warned that 'the loss of a meal by the child is insignificant in importance to the loss by the parent of control in a fundamental relation' (*Parents and the Pre-School Child*, 100).

165 *NAC*, National Film, Television and Sound Archives, National Film Board Collection, 'Why Won't Tommy Eat' (NFB 1948), 16-mm sd b & w, 17 min., acc. no. 7708-273

166 DNHW, *Canadian Mother and Child* (1953), 91

167 'Stork Club Conversation,' *Chatelaine* (Sept. 1957), 93

168 'Swifts' Meats for Babies,' *Chatelaine* (June 1953), 95

169 'Heinz Meats for Babies,' *Chatelaine* (May 1955), 95

170 W.A. Cochrane, 'Nutritional Excess in Infancy and Childhood,' *CMAJ* 81 (1959), 454

171 For a fascinating discussion of the relationship between mothers and paediatricians in the United States, see Kathleen Jones, 'Sentiment and Science: The Late Nineteenth Century Pediatrician as Mother's Adviser,' *Journal of Social History* 17 (Fall 1983), 79–96.

172 John and Elizabeth Newson, 'Cultural Aspects of Child-Rearing in the English-speaking World,' in Martin P.M. Richards, ed., *The Integration of a Child into a Social World*, (London: Cambridge University Press 1974), 60

173 Alan Brown, cited in 'Doctoring the Family,' part three,' radio program, 'Ideas,' CBC Radio, Apr. 1985, 26. Brown made a similar observation in 'Preventive Pediatrics and Its Relation to the General Practitioner,' *CMAJ* 24 (1931), 517.

174 Tisdall, *Home Care*, 231

175 Ibid., 233

176 Couture, *Canadian Mother and Child* (1940; 1949 ed.), for example, recommended that 'if possible' a mother should have the doctor 'regularly supervise the progress' of her child. 'Failing this,' the author continued, 'you will be well advised to visit a Well Baby Health Centre, or obtain the regular visits of a public health nurse,' 84.

177 Tisdall, *Home Care*, 33

178 TDPH, *Infant and Young Child* (1936), 37

179 CCCFW, *Post-Natal Letters*, preface

180 Ibid., 12, 5

181 Spock, *Baby and Child Care*, both the 1946 and the 1957 editions

182 Elizabeth Chant Robertson, 'The Critical First Year,' *Chatelaine* (Mar. 1943), 65. In a fascinating article which appeared just five months later, Robertson felt obliged to warn mothers not to waste their doctors' time 'with [their] theories of why the child reacted the way he did. Sometimes an intelligent child, provided he isn't too sick, can give a more helpful story of his illness than his highly excited mother.' ('You and Your Doctor,' *Chatelaine* [Aug. 1943], 61). Robertson was particularly concerned because the war had caused a shortage of doctors, and as a result the time of those doctors remaining at home was at a premium. 'The main responsibility for maintaining health in your home rests squarely on your shoulders,' Robertson told mothers.

183 DNHW, *One to Six* (1953), 161

184 Spock, *Baby and Child Care* (1957), 1. A similar warning also appeared in the first edition. However, the 1957 section was even more strongly worded and had been moved to the beginning of the book.

185 OBH, *Baby* (1920), 37

186 OBH, *Baby* (1933), 54

187 Brown, *Normal Child*, 213

188 CCCFW, *Post-Natal Letters* 9, 3

189 For example, the preceding quotation regarding the mother's responsibility for creating the mental environment of the child was followed with this statement: 'Wise management plays an important part in both the mental and physical health of children. Good temper and happiness mean a wise management while constant crying, fretfulness, broken sleep, and bad food habits, and fears, indicate bad management on the part of the parents' (ibid.).

190 MacMurchy, *Take Care of Baby*, 7

CHAPTER 5 Thoroughly Modern Mother

1 Charles A. Hodgetts, Chief of the Division of Statistics and Publicity, 'Statistics and Publicity in Child Welfare Work,' *PHJ* 12 (1921), 107

2 CTA, RG11, F1, box 1, 'Historical Material – Maternal and Child Health,' Dr G.P. Jackson, Deputy Medical Officer of Health, City of Toronto, 'The Pre-School Child,' typescript of speech given on 19 Mar. 1929, 2

3 Veronica Strong-Boag, *The New Day Recalled: Lives of Girls and Women in English Canada, 1919–1939* (Toronto: Copp Clark Pitman 1988), 171

4 Beth Light and Joy Parr, 'Managing the Family,' chap. 4 in Beth Light and Joy Parr, eds., *Canadian Women on the Move, 1967–1920* (Toronto: New Hogtown Press and the Ontario Institute for Studies in Education 1983), 154

5 CHC, *Sessional Papers* (1923), DOH, Report of DCW (Mar. 1921–Mar. 1922), 37

6 Population statistics are derived from F.H. Leacy, ed., *Historical Statistics of Canada*, 2nd ed., (Ottawa: Statistics Canada 1983), series A78–93. I have included all women between the ages of 15 and 50 for the census year 1921.

7 Norah Lewis makes this observation in her paper '"No Baby – No Nation": Mother Education, A Federal Concern – 1921 to 1979,' presented at the Canadian History of Education Conference, Vancouver, Oct. 1983, 3.

8 During the 1930s, e.g., the CCCFW reported distribution rates of hundreds of thousands of pieces of literature each year: 1933–4, 128,215 sets or partial sets of literature; 1934–5, 206,494; 1935–6, 232,343 NAC, MG28, I10, vol. 66, file 010, 'CWC Maternal and Child Hygiene 1935–39,' Report of DMCH, 2).

9 Canada, *Annual Reports*, Report of the Division of Publicity and Health Education (1940–1), 163

10 The 1941–2 report of the Publicity and Health Education Service noted that 'the most popular book in both languages was *The Canadian Mother and Child*, of which it was impossible to keep an adequate stock to meet the public demand. Several thousand names have been filed by the Division awaiting receipt of the next printing,' 151.

11 Canada, *Annual Reports*, Report of DCMH (1943–4), 56. Elsewhere, Ernest Couture noted that 'it is likely that everyone here finds mothers today keener than ever before to secure information on maternal and child care. The character of the letters we receive, and the ever-increasing demand for literature, attest to this fact. For instance, we have distributed upon request, in the course of the last three years, some 350,000 copies of our publication "The Canadian Mother and Child"' ('Maternal Hygiene in Wartime,' *CJPH* 35 [May 1944], 179).

12 Canada, *Annual Reports*, Report of the Publicity and Health Education Service (1943–4), 67

13 F--- C---, Bellingham, Washington, to Julia Lathrop, 23 Feb. 1915, file 8-6-6-2-9, CB, cited in 'Mother, The Invention of Necessity: Dr. Benjamin Spock's *Baby and Child Care*,' *American Quarterly* 24 (Winter 1977), 523

14 Kay Macpherson, e.g., referred to magazine articles which circulated among her 'lot of friends.' Interview, 24 Feb. 1986. C. Dora Arnup made a similar observation.

15 NAC, Records of DNHW, RG29, vol. 992, file 499-3-7, part 6, minutes of the 4th Annual Meeting of the Child Hygiene Section of CCCFW, 4

16 Helen MacMurchy, *Handbook of Child Welfare Work in Canada* (Ottawa: King's Printer 1923), 9. Unfortunately, most of those letters have been destroyed.

17 I have been unable to determine the proportion of copies distributed in response to individual requests. MacMurchy did note in her 1930-1 report that the demands for *The Canadian Mother's Book* were 'nearly all personal requests' (Canada, *Annual Reports*, Report of DCW, 1930-1, 144).

18 MacMurchy, *Child Welfare Work*, 9

19 'A Personal Service in Child Training,' *Chatelaine* 2 (Nov. 1929), 52

20 Norah Lewis has drawn upon women's letters to the women's pages of farm and ranch magazines in a recent article, 'Goose Grease and Turpentine: Mother Treats the Family's Illnesses,' *Prairie Forum* 15 (Spring 1990), 67–84. One writer, 'Anxious Mother,' requested feeding suggestions for a baby who was not gaining properly. A number of mothers responded to her request, offering suggestions and even volunteering to lend her their copy of E.L. Holt's *The Care and Feeding of Children*. I am grateful to Dr Lewis for bringing this article to my attention.

21 Alton Goldbloom, *Small Patients: The Autobiography of a Children's Doctor* (Toronto: Longmans, Green 1959), 217

22 See, e.g., letters from mothers held at the Spock Archives, George Argents Library, Syracuse University. Letters to Dr Allan Roy Dafoe, physician to the world-famous Dionne Quintuplets, are held in AO, Dafoe Collection, MS 598, series B-1. Dafoe began to receive a great number of personal requests when he began his radio broadcast throughout Canada and the United States. The correspondence to the U.S. Children's Bureau is discussed in Nancy Pottishman Weiss, 'Mother: The Invention of Necessity: Dr. Benjamin Spock's *Baby and Child Care*,' *American Quarterly* 29 (Winter 1977), 529–47, and 'The Mother-Child Dyad Revisited: Perceptions of Mothers and Children in Twentieth-Century Childrearing Manuals,' *Journal of Social Issues* 34 (1978), 29–45, as well as in Molly Ladd-Taylor, *Raising a Baby the Government Way: Mothers' Letters to the Children's Bureau, 1915–1932* (New Brunswick: Rutgers University Press 1986).

23 Jane France, Wiarton, Ontario, letter to author, 2 Apr. 1986. Other working-class women in my interview sample also indicated that they used baby books and child-care literature.

24 Winnie Weatherstone, interview, 23 Jan. 1986

25 Kay Herrington, interview, 12 Feb. 1986

26 Kay Macpherson, interview, 24 Feb. 1986

27 V.T., interview, 13 Feb. 1986

28 C. Dora Arnup, interview, 26 Feb. 1986. She continued: "I don't think I did have any women's magazines then ... When I was sitting in the pediatrician's office I used to read things called *Baby Talk* or something but I never came across anything too startling that was going to change my life.' My own experience with advice literature was in many respects similar to my mother's. Given a copy of Penelope Leach's *Your Baby and Child: From Birth to Age Five* during my pregnancy, I devoured the first two hundred pages before my daughter was born. After her birth, I continued to read the book, searching for reassurances during her naptimes. I found, however, that the amount of time I spent reading advice literature decreased in direct proportion to the amount of time Jesse slept. By the time my second child had arrived six years later, I still had not managed to read the last two hundred pages of the book. And today, as she nears five and a half, I notice that my bookmark remains in the section marked, 'The First Six Months.'

29 Reported in the *Labour Gazette*, cited in Marion Royce, *Eunice Dyke: Health Care Pioneer* (Toronto: Dundurn Press 1983), 52. A description of the ferry experiment can also be found in Eunice Dyke's Brown Book, deposited in the CTA, RG11, F1, box 5, 328.

30 CTA, RG11, F1, box 1, file 'Historical Material – Maternal and Child Health,' typescript dated 5 May 1939, 'The Demonstration of a Baby's Bath at Eaton's Infants' Wear Department.' The attendance figures were: Mon., 25; Tues., 35; Wed., 20; Thurs., 39; and Fri., 27.

31 For a review of the history of child development research, see, *inter alia*, Robert L. Sears, 'Your Ancients Revisited: A History of Child Development,' in E. Mavis Herrington, ed., *Review of Child Development Research*, vol. 5 (Chicago: University of Chicago Press 1975), 1–74; and Elizabeth M.R. Lomax, *Science and Patterns of Child Care* (San Francisco: W.H. Freeman 1978). A number of early studies investigated the relationship between social class and advice-seeking behaviour. See Urie Bronfenbrenner, 'Socialization and Social Class through Time and Space,' in Eleanor Maccoby, Theodore Newcomb, and Eugene L. Hartley, eds., *Readings in Social Psychology*, 3rd ed. (New York: Henry Holt, 1958), 400–25; Donald Miller and Guy Swanson, *The Changing American Parent* (1958); Robert F. Winch, 'Rearing by the Book,' chap. 14 in *The Modern Family* (New York: Holt, Rinehart and Winston 1963); and Robert Sears, Eleanor Maccoby, and Harry Levin, *Patterns of Child Rearing* (Stanford: Stanford University Press 1976).

32 Nathan Maccoby, 'The Communication of Child-Rearing Advice to Parents,' *Merrill-Palmer Quarterly* 7 (July 1961), 203

33 Melvin S. Brooks, Douglas L. Rennie, and Roger F. Sondag, 'Sociological Variables in the Reaction of Parents to Child-Rearing Information,' *Merrill-Palmer Quarterly* 8 (July 1962), 175-82

34 Alison Clarke-Stewart, 'Popular Primers for Parents,' *American Psychologist* 33 (Apr. 1978), 361, 365, 368

35 Michael J. Geboy, 'Who Is Listening to the "Experts"? The Use of Child Care Materials by Parents,' *Family Relations* 3 (Apr. 1981), 206-7

36 Jay Mechling, 'Advice to Historians on Advice to Mothers,' *Journal of Social History* 9 (Fall 1973), 45

37 Interview with Mrs Smith, reprinted in Cathy Urwin, 'Constructing Motherhood: The Persuasion of Normal Development,' in Carolyn Steedman, Cathy Urwin, and Valerie Walkerdine, eds., *Language, Gender, and Childhood* (London: Routledge and Kegan Paul 1985), 187

38 Urwin, 'Constructing Motherhood,' 171, 184

39 Sheila Kitzinger, *Women as Mothers* (New York: Vintage Books 1980), 170

40 Beatrice B. Whiting, 'Folk Wisdom and Child Rearing,' *Merrill-Palmer Quarterly* 20 (Jan. 1974), 11

41 Alison Prentice, written comment on Katherine Arnup's thesis proposal, 26 Apr. 1985

42 Kay Herrington, interview, 12 Feb. 1986

43 Kay Macpherson, interview, 24 Feb. 1986

44 Goldbloom, *Small Patients*, 307

45 Whiting, 'Folk Wisdom and Child Rearing,' 17

46 Couture, *Mother and Child* (1940), 122

47 Goldbloom, *Small Patients*, 307. He continued: 'Every article of clothing, every procedure, every choice in matters where choice is of no consequence or importance, becomes a subject of decision for the overworked pediatrician.'

48 CCCFW, *Pre-School Letters* 9, 2

49 K. McAllister, 'The New Mother,' *Chatelaine* (July 1932), 40

50 AO, RG10, series 30-A-1, box 3, file 3-3, *Bulletin of the Division of Maternal and Child Hygiene and Public Health Nursing* (Feb.–Mar. 1923), no page indicated. The 'Holt in the hand' is a reference to L. Emmett Holt's child-care manual, *The Care and Feeding of Children*.

51 June Callwood, 'What to Do after the Doctor Leaves,' *Chatelaine* (May 1953), 33

52 Stella Pines, 'Making Ready for the New Arrival,' *Chatelaine* (Nov. 1928), 19

53 Ina May Gaskin, interview for 'Doctoring the Family, part 3,' radio program, 'Ideas,' CBC Radio, Apr. 1985

54 Ibid.

55 V.M. MacDonald, 'Child Welfare Work in Montreal,' *CN* 19 (1923), 663

56 CTA, RG11, F1, box 1, file 'Historical Material – Maternal and Child Health, 1936–65,' 'Secretary's Report on prenatal education from September 1949 to July 1950,' 4

57 CTA, RG11, F1, box 1, file 1936–65, 'Historical Material – Maternal and Child Health,' 'Toronto Welfare Council – Report on Prenatal Classes from September 1950 to June 1951,' typescript dated 3 Oct. 1951, 3

58 Nursing Sister Phyllis M. Reay, 'Royal Canadian Naval Well Baby Health Service,' *CN* 40 (1944), 470

59 CTA, SC40, box 31, file 9, typescript 'Material on Public Health Services Which Might Be Adapted for Broadcasting,' dated 11 Apr. 1940

60 For information on the 'language nurses,' see Royce, *Eunice Dyke*, 63–6.

61 CTA, RG11, F1, box 4, 'Health Department History, 1923–1945,' typescript dated 8 Jan. 1945, Janet Neilson, 'The History of Public Health Nursing in Toronto,' 5

62 Writing about the efforts to 'Americanize' immigrant mothers in the United States, Jane Brickman notes that 'antithetical to social workers' desires to make motherhood scientific were the immigrant mothering customs of demand feeding, swaddling the new born, and the use of the pacifier' (Jane Brickman, 'Mother Love – Mother Death: Maternal and Infant Care – Social Class and the Role of the Government' [PhD dissertation, City University of New York 1978], 440). Brickman notes that all three are practices currently in vogue.

63 Royce, *Eunice Dyke*, 65–6. Although immigrant mothers, like their Canadian-born counterparts, may have welcomed a visit from the public health nurse, it is likely that many of them preferred to hold onto their traditional methods of infant and child care.

64 For a discussion of immigrant women's use of city services during the 1950s, see Heather MacDougall, *Activists and Advocates: Toronto's Health Department, 1883–1983* (Toronto: Dundurn Press 1990), 171–3.

65 Blanch Emerson, 'Child Welfare,' *CN* 26 (1930), 199, emphasis mine

66 B.E. Harris, 'Pre-Natal Education in the Home,' *CN* 30 (1934), 340–1

67 Jane Lewis has argued with respect to Britain that women campaigned for and welcomed the provision of direct aid. *The Politics of Motherhood: Child and Maternal Welfare in England, 1900–1939* (London: Croom Helm 1980)

68 In *The Politics of Motherhood*, Lewis indicates that 'none of the 83 working

class women interviewed had read an infant care manual,' chap. 2, n119. As I have noted above, my interviews turned up a different result. Five of the six working-class women I interviewed indicated that they had used baby books and child-care literature.

69 Winnie Weatherstone, interview, 23 Jan. 1986
70 Eleanor Enkin, interview, 20 Mar. 1986
71 NAC, MG28, I19, vol. 66, file 010 'CWC – Maternal and Child Hygiene Division 1940–43, Canadian Life Insurance Officers,' Report of DMCH, Canadian Welfare Council, 1 Apr. 1942 to 31 Mar. 1943, 5–6
72 Mrs Fernando Plourde, Rimouski, Quebec, 31 Aug. 1931, NAC, MG28, I10, vol. 39, file 168, 'Insurance Companies 1931'
73 Mrs Romeo Payne, Hull, Quebec, 21 Aug. 1931, to Canadian Council on Child and Family Welfare, fowarded to Helen MacMurchy by the secretary of the French Section of CCCFW, NAC, RG29, vol. 992, file 499-3-7, part 5
74 Mrs Helen Watling, Kapuskasing, Ontario, to CCCFW, 16 Dec. 1935, NAC, RG29, vol. 991, file 499-3-2, part 2
75 Mrs F.D., Quebec. Letter to the U.S. Children's Bureau, 18 Dec. 1921. Mrs F.D. was originally from Minneapolis, but had moved to Quebec with her husband. The letter was the only one from a Canadian included in Ladd-Taylor, *Raising a Baby the Government Way*, 110–11.
76 Mrs W.E. Corbett, Maloy, Alberta, to CCCFW, 28 Aug. 1935, NAC, RG29, vol. 991, file 499-3-2, part 2
77 Weiss, 'Mother, The Invention of Necessity,' 522
78 Mrs A.H. Etekella (spelling difficult to determine), to Dr Allan Roy Dafoe, 29 Jan. 1937, AO, Dafoe Collection, MS598, series B-1, vol. 1
79 Mrs Robt. Averbeck to Dr Allan Roy Dafoe, 19 Jan. 1937, AO, Dafoe Collection, MS598, series B-1, vol. 1
80 Phyllis Knight and Rolf Knight, *A Very Ordinary Life* (Vancouver: New Star Books 1974), 164–5
81 Mona Gould, 'Modern Mother,' *Chatelaine* (Nov. 1932), 26
82 I have been unable to determine what became of these letters. I do not wish to imply that a conspiracy of silence took place. Their disappearance is more likely the result of office house-keeping than of a deliberate attempt to alter the historical record.
83 Charlotte Whitton to Mr E.E. Reid, managing director, London Life Insurance Company, 18 Sept. 1933, NAC, MG28, I10, vol. 39, file 168, 'CWC Division – Maternal and Child Hygiene – Canadian Life Insurance 1933.' The letter was accompanied by ten appreciative letters from mothers.

84 See, e.g., the following letter from Charlotte Whitton to Dr R.E. Wode-house, 26 Dec. 1935. 'I thought that you and possibly the Minister would be interested in the copy of a letter which I enclose, and the snapshot which accompanies it. You will notice that this is one of our mothers in Northern Ontario and I think that this is a very real tribute to the value of our letter service' (NAC, RG29, vol. 991, file 499-3-2, part 2).

85 Mrs Leonard Renaud, Wawbewawa, to DOH, 10 July 1935, NAC, RG29, vol. 993, file 499-3-7, part 10

86 Doris Denman, Sudbury, to minister of DOH, 7 Jan. 1937, NAC, RG29, vol. 991, file 499-3-2, part 3, pp. 7, 10.

87 Emile Dupuis, Noelville, Ontario, to Helen MacMurchy, 7 Sept. 1931, NAC, RG29, vol. 992, file 499-3-7, part 5. Dupuis reminded MacMurchy that 'I was in correspondence few months ago with you relating that many of our mother were dieing [sic] because they have not had medical care.'

88 No name indicated, letter reprinted in CHC, *Annual Reports* (1929–30), Report of DCW, 124

89 'Dr. Helen MacMurchy to Be Honoured Again,' *Toronto Star* 6 Jan. 1940, n.p. Toronto Public Library Scrapbooks, Helen MacMurchy

90 Adrienne Rich, *Of Woman Born: Motherhood as Experience and Institution* (New York: W.W. Norton 1976; Bantam Books 1977), 282

91 CHC, *Sessional Papers* (1947–8), Report of the Child and Maternal Health Division, 20

92 Esther J. Robertson, 'Nurses and New Parents,' *CN* 54 (1958), 950

93 Norah L. Lewis, 'Reducing Maternal Mortality in British Columbia: An Educational Process,' in Barbara K. Latham and Roberta J. Pazdro, eds., *Not Just Pin Money,* (Victoria: Camosun College 1984), 339–40

94 Ibid., 346

95 Ibid., 349

96 Catherine Lesley Biggs, 'The Response to Maternal Mortality in Ontario, 1920–1940' (MSc thesis, University of Toronto 1983), 49

97 Ibid., 47

98 Ibid., 106

99 Jo Oppenheimer, 'Childbirth in Ontario: The Transition from Home to Hospital in the Early Twentieth Century,' in Katherine Arnup, Andrée Lévesque, and Ruth Roach Pierson, eds., *Delivering Motherhood: Maternal Ideologies and Practices in the 19th and 20th Centuries,* (London: Routledge 1990), 67

100 Suzann Buckley, 'The Search for the Decline of Maternal Mortality: The Place of Hospital Records,' in Wendy Mitchinson and Janice Dickin

McGinnis, eds., *Essays in the History of Canadian Medicine*, (Toronto: McClelland and Stewart 1988), 161

101 Harry Ebbs, Alan Brown, F.F. Tisdall, Winifred Hoyle, and Marjorie Bell, 'The Influence of Improved Prenatal Nutrition upon the Infant,' *CMAJ* 46 (1942), 8

102 For an examination of the impact of prenatal nutrition on infant birth weight in the nineteenth century, see W. Peter Ward and Patricia C. Ward, 'Infant Birth Weight and Nutrition in Industrializing Montreal,' *American Historical Review* (Feb. 1984), 324-45. For a review of the literature on the effect of maternal nutrition on fetal growth, see Jack Metcoff, 'Association of Fetal Growth with Maternal Nutrition,' in Frank Falkner and J.M. Tanner, eds., *Human Growth*, vol. 1, *Principles and Prenatal Growth*, (New York: Plenum 1978), 415-60.

103 Ernest Couture, 'Maternal Hygiene in Wartime,' *CJPH* 35 (May 1944), 177

104 Norah L. Lewis, 'Creating the Little Machine: Child Rearing in British Columbia, 1919-1939,' *BC Studies* 56 (Winter 1982-3), 44

105 Neil Sutherland, *Children in English-Canadian Society: Framing the Twentieth-Century Consensus* (Toronto: University of Toronto Press 1976), 68

106 Cecilia Benoit notes that women enjoyed their stay at the Burgeo cottage hospital because it enabled them to get away from their household responsibilities for a few days. As one midwife reported, during their confinement in the hospital, the new mothers 'were able to get away from a lot. Someone went in and took over their household while they were away. I guess it was a kind of holiday, or at least a rest' (Lou-Anne, cited in *Midwives in Passage*, St John's: Institute of Social and Economic Research [1991], 3). Meg Luxton made a similar observation in her 1980 study of Flin Flon, Manitoba: 'Whatever their opinions, women unanimously noted one major advantage that hospital births have over home births. It is socially acceptable for a women giving birth to spend four or five days in hospital where she is not responsible for anything. Women considered their hospital stays as vacations or holidays' (*More Than a Labour of Love*, [Toronto: Women's Press 1980], 100).

107 C. Dora Arnup, interview, 26 Feb. 1986

108 Mrs E.H. Ross, interview, 24 Jan. 1986

109 For a discussion of the campaign for twilight sleep in the United States, see Judith Walzer Leavitt, 'Birthing and Anesthesia: The Debate over Twilight Sleep,' in Judith Walzer Leavitt, ed., *Women and Health in America* (Madison: University of Wisconsin Press 1984), 175-85. The drug was known under the name scopolamine in the United States.

110 'Doctoring the Family, part two,' radio program, 'Ideas,' CBC Radio, Apr. 1985

111 Leavitt, 'Birthing and Anesthesia,' 177

112 Bertha Van Hoosen, 'Scopolamine-Morphine Anaesthesia,' (1915), 101, cited in Leavitt, 'Birthing and Anesthesia,' 176

113 Mrs Eleanor Enkin, interviewed for 'Doctoring the Family, part two.'

114 Mrs E.H. Ross, interview, 24 Jan. 1986

115 Winnie Weatherstone, interviewed for 'Doctoring the Family, part three,' radio program, 'Ideas,' CBC Radio, Apr. 1985

116 For a discussion of the impact of hospital procedures on American women's breast-feeding practices, see Rima D. Apple, *Mothers and Medicine: A Social History of Infant Feeding, 1890–1950* (Madison: University of Wisconsin Press 1987), chap. 9. Debate over supplying infant formula to hospitals still rages today. Across North America, hospitals continue to receive financial inducements for using a specific brand of formula in their nurseries, despite official policies which prohibit such arrangements. See 'Drug Firms Fight to Donate Formula,' *Globe and Mail*, 27 Oct. 1991, A1, A4. Perhaps this can account for the steady decline in rates of breast-feeding during the 1980s, despite vigorous campaigns to promote maternal nursing. See, e.g., 'Breast-feeding Declining, Study Finds,' *Toronto Star* 27 Sept. 1991, B1. The survey, conducted by Ross Laboratories, reported that while 62 per cent of mothers breast-fed their babies in hospital in 1982, that percentage had dropped to 52 per cent by 1989.

117 Hilary B. Bourne, 'Breast Feeding,' *Canadian Nurse* 46 (Dec. 1950), 969. The author did not indicate the source of her 'well-known fact.' She explained the reasons for the poor showing of North American women as follows: 'The North American woman of today is not sufficiently impressed during her adolescent years of the importance and advantages offered by breast feeding.' She urged her medical colleagues to impress upon their prenatal patients the importance of attempting to breast-feed once the baby arrived.

118 CTA, RG11, F1, box 1, file 'Historical Material – Maternal and Child Health,' typescript entitled 'Data from Prenatal Questionnaires, August 1950 – July 1951 inclusive,' 4

119 CTA, RG11, F1, box 1, file 'Historical Material – Maternal and Child Health, 1936–1965,' typescript 'Secretary's Report on Prenatal Education from September 1949 – July 1950,' 2

120 ODH, *The Early Years* (1954; 1957 ed.), 94

121 Benjamin Spock, *Baby and Child Care* (1946), 185

122 John and Elizabeth Newson, 'Cultural Aspects of Child-Rearing in the

English-speaking World,' in Martin P.M. Richards, ed., *The Integration of a Child into a Social World* (London: Cambridge University Press 1974), 61–2

123 C. Dora Arnup, interview, 26 Feb. 1986

124 Win Hall, interview, 12 Mar. 1986

125 Mary Bolton, cited in Barbara Ehrenreich and Deirdre English, *For Her Own Good: 150 Years of the Experts' Advice to Women* (New York: Anchor Books 1979), 214

126 See, e.g., 'A Letter to the Reader of This New Edition,' *Baby and Child Care* (1957), 1–2.

127 Charles H. Gundry, Trenna G. Hunter, Ruby A. Kerr, and Beverley E. Hopkins, 'Anticipatory Guidance,' *CN* 50 (1954), 118

128 E. McKerlie and Laura Einarson, 'The Psychological Impact of and on the New Arrival,' *CN* 50 (1954), 263

129 Lillian E. Frank, 'Expansion to Meet Expansion,' *CN* 50 (1954), 647

130 Alison Clarke-Stewart makes a similar argument in 'Popular Primers for Parents,' *American Psychologist* 33 (Apr. 1978), 368.

131 Spock, *Baby and Child Care*, 3. The first edition (1946) was 482 pages long without the index and 502 pages long including the index. The second edition (1957) was 597 pages long without the index and 627 pages including the index.

132 Frances Lily Johnson, 'Furnishing the Nursery,' *Chatelaine* (May 1928), 6, 48

133 MacMurchy, *Canadian Mother's Book* (1933), 25

134 MacMurchy, *Care of Mother* (1922), 7

135 MacMurchy, *Care of the Baby* (1922), 10

136 Flora F. Stewart, 'Teaching Public Health to Groups of Mothers,' *CN* 24 (1928), 550

137 One example, among many, is the following advice from Helen Mac-Murchy. 'Don't be down-hearted – there is no reason you should be. Don't be frightened. Cheer up. We are all standing by you' (*Canadian Mother's Book* [1923], 29).

138 MacMurchy, *Care of Mother* (1923), 24

139 MacMurchy, *Canadian Mother's Book* (1923), 32

140 Dorothy Franklin, Kent, Ontario, letter to R.B. Bennett, 15 Dec. 1931, in L.M. Grayson and Michael Bliss, eds., *The Wretched of Canada: Letters to R.B. Bennett, 1930–1935* (Toronto: University of Toronto Press 1971), 16

141 Mrs Rose Artimus, Calgary, letter to R.B. Bennett, 13 May 1935, in Grayson and Bliss, *Wretched of Canada*, 145

142 Mrs Daria Collinet, Upsalquitch, New Brunswick, letter to R.B. Bennett, 2 Feb. 1934, in *Wretched of Canada*, 73

143 E.W. McHenry, 'Nutrition and Child Health,' *CJPH* 33 (1942), 153

144 Mrs R. Paddy, Burton, Alberta, letter to R.B. Bennett, 19 Feb. 1935, in *Wretched of Canada*, 117–8

145 Mrs Hubert Provost, McAlpine, Ontario, letter to R.B. Bennett, 3 Oct. 1935, in *Wretched of Canada*, 194

146 Ms Dykeman, to Dr Puddicombe, 22 Oct. 1934, NAC, MG28, I10, vol. 18, file 74 (1934), 'Prenatal Letters'

147 For a discussion of the Supplement, see Dianne Dodd, 'Advice to Parents: The Blue Books, Helen MacMurchy, MD, and the Federal Department of Health, 1920–34,' *Canadian Bulletin of Medical History* 8 (1991), 203–30.

148 AO, RG10, series 30-A-1, box 7, file 7–5, typescript 'Demonstration of First Visit of Public Health Nurse to Expectant Mother,' undated but filed with material dated 1933, 3

149 F. Hope, 'The Economy Baby,' *Chatelaine* (May 1932), 24

150 MacMurchy, *Canadian Mother's Book* (1931), 15. Earlier, MacMurchy told mothers, 'The right kind of Doctor will charge a reasonable fee for all the care you need. Don't have any other kind of doctor. It might be well for you to mention what you can afford when you first go to see the Doctor' (Ibid., 14–15). She did not suggest where mothers ought to turn if the doctor was not prepared to accept that amount.

151 See, e.g., the eloquent letter from Mrs Leonard Renaud, Wawbewawa, Ontario, 10 July 1935, to Dr J.J. Heagerty, chief executive assistant, Department of Pensions and National Health, NAC, RG29, vol. 993, file 499-3-7, part 10. Mrs Renaud was unable to persuade one of the nearby town's two doctors to attend her birth and was forced to give birth without medical attention. Heagerty forwarded the letter to the CCCFW, OMA, ODH, and CMA. The general secretary of the CMA noted, in reply, that 'I am in possession of personal information ... and know that the Doctors presumably to whom she refers have been very concerned as to how they were going to pay their bills. So few patients seem to be in a position to pay them' (Dr T.C. Routley, Toronto, To Dr J.J. Heagerty, 24 July 1935, NAC, RG29, vol. 993, file 499-3-7, part 10).

152 Anonymous, 'I Am a Canadian Mother,' *Chatelaine* (Apr. 1933), 18, emphasis mine

153 Sibylle Escalona, 'A Commentary upon Some Recent Changes in Child Rearing Practices,' *Child Development* 20 (Sept. 1949), 160

154 A similar assessment is offered by Nancy Pottishman Weiss, 'The Mother-Child Dyad Revisited: Perceptions of Mothers and Children in Twentieth Century Child-Rearing Manuals,' *Journal of Social Issues* 34

(1978), 29–45. Weiss writes: 'The task of the mother in permissive literature is freighted with new significance, replacing the earlier concerns
over physical survival of the child. Now a misstep could spell both psychological and cognitive harm, just as earlier mistaken care could result
in severe physical illness,' 53.

155 While only 11.2 per cent of married women participated in the paid labour force in 1951, that number had increased to 22 per cent by 1961.
Monica Boyd, 'Changing Canadian Family Forms: Issues for Women' (in
Nancy Mandell and Ann Duffy, eds., *Reconstructing the Canadian Family: Feminist Perspectives* [Toronto: Butterworths 1988], 92). By 1985, that percentage had increased to 55 per cent.

156 Rich, *Of Woman Born*, 223, emphasis in original

157 W.L. Denney, 'The Nervous Child,' *CMAJ* 18 (1928), 555

158 Lionel M. Lindsay, 'The Overweight Child,' *CMAJ* 44 (1941), 505

159 H. Jean Leeson, 'Nutrition Problems of Pre-School Children' *CJPH* 37
(1946), 282.

160 McKerlie and Einarson, 'Psychological Impact,' 264

161 Alan Brown, *The Normal Child* (Toronto: McClelland and Stewart 1932),
220

162 Evelyn Seeley, 'Debunking the Mother Myth,' *Chatelaine* (Feb. 1936), 4,
citing Dr Ellaine Elmore, a psychologist

163 E.D. Wittkower and B.R. Hunt, 'Psychological Aspects of Atopic Dermatitis in Children,' *CMAJ* 79 (1958), 813

164 The dangers posed by these conditions are discussed in Hyman Caplan
and Hedley G. Dimock, 'The Student Nurse in a Pediatric Setting,' *CN* 52
(Dec. 1956), 959–62. A recent survey suggests that mother-blaming continues today. A 1990 study which surveyed 93 articles published in four
major U.S. family therapy journals concluded that 'blaming mothers unfairly for the problems of their children and families is a serious and
widespread problem in family therapy' (Sean Fine, 'Mothers Unfairly
Blamed,' *Globe and Mail*, 23 Nov. 1990, A5).

165 Strong-Boag, *The New Day Recalled*, 150

CONCLUSION

1 In 1989 the birth rate in Canada had its biggest increase since the 1950s
baby boom, increasing 3.5 per cent over the 1988 birth rate. Despite that
increase, however, in 1989, women on average bore only 1.77 children, in
comparison with the 1959 average of 4 children per woman (Alanna Mitchell, 'Babies' Numbers Bounce,' *Globe and Mail* 2 Mar. 1991, A1).

2 The number of reported births to unmarried women rose from 27,800 in 1975 to 62,700 in 1986 (Bali Ram, *Current Demographic Analysis: New Trends in the Family*, [Ottawa: Statistics Canada 1990], 32). 'From 1981 to 1989, the birth rate for single women aged 30 to 34 shot up 142 per cent, while that for single women 35 to 39 jumped 145 per cent, according to Statistics Canada. There were 12,513 babies born to single women aged 30 to 39 in Canada in 1989' (Louise Kinross, 'Going It Alone,' *Toronto Star*, 21 Dec. 1991, E1).

3 A 1986 article reported that there were 40 titles on pregnancy in local bookstores and over 50 books on the subject at Metro Toronto Reference Library (Leslie Fruman, 'Use Common-Sense Approach to Protect Your Unborn Child' *Toronto Star*, 21 Apr. 1986, D5). The 1990–1 edition of *Books in Print* included 400 titles on child rearing and over 5 pages of listings under the heading 'parent and child.'

4 *Time* magazine's cover story on 22 Feb. 1982 was entitled 'The New Baby Boom.' Others included *Maclean's*, 20 May 1985, 'Bringing Up Babies – The Yuppie Generation Takes on Parenthood'; *Toronto Life*, Aug. 1985, 'Are You Boring Baby?'; and *Saturday Night*, Dec. 1989, 'Bringing Up Baby.' *Chatelaine* regularly features articles on motherhood; see, e.g., 'Mommy Wars: Who Mothers Best: Careerists or Stay-at-Homes?' Mar. 1990.

5 Barbara Ehrenreich and Deirdre English, *For Her Own Good: 150 Years of the Experts' Advice to Women* (New York: Anchor Books 1979), 264

6 Dana Flavelle, 'Parent Power, '50s and '60s Generation Challenges Experts, Gets Involved,' *Toronto Star*, 7 Mar. 1989, F1

7 By 1986, Spock's *Baby and Child Care* had sold 32 million copies and had been translated into 38 languages, a fact which suggests the interest in advice literature was not limited to North America (Nancy J. White, 'Don't Push Children So Hard, Spock Says,' *Toronto Star*, 22 Oct. 1986, E1, E13). Spock continues to speak before large and enthusiastic audiences across North America.

8 Burton White, *The First Years of Life* (New York: Prentice Hall 1990); T. Berry Brazelton, *Infants and Mothers: Differences in Development* (New York: Delta / Seymour Lawrence 1983); Benjamin Spock and Michael Rothenberg, *Baby and Child Care* (New York: Pocket Books 1985); Penelope Leach, *Your Baby and Child* (New York: Knopf 1981)

9 Felice Schwartz, 'Management Women and the New Facts of Life,' *Harvard Business Review* (Jan./Feb. 1989). It should be noted that Schwartz did not, in fact, use the term 'mommy track.' She referred, instead, to 'career-primary' and 'career-and-family' women.

10 For a searing criticism of the concept of the mommy-track, see Barbara

Ehrenreich and Deirdre English, 'Blowing the Whistle on the "Mommy Track",' *Ms.* (July/Aug. 1989), 56, 58. The authors note that 'the "mommy track" story rated prominent coverage in the *New York Times* and *USA Today*, a cover story in *Business Week*, and airtime on dozens of talk shows,' 56.

11 For a discussion of the attendant health problems faced by poor families, see Chandrakant P. Shah, Meldon Kahan, and John Krauser, 'The Health of Children of Low-Income Families,' *CMAJ* 137 (15 Sept. 1987), 485–90. Infant and child mortality rates were twice as high among the children of low-income families. As well, poor children suffered from 'iron deficiency anemia, dental caries, chronic ear infections, mental retardation, learning disabilities, poor school performance, and increased suicide rates,' 485.

12 Ontario's establishment of a degree program for midwives represents an important step in the integration of midwives into the health-care system. Twenty-six students will begin the four-year program in September 1993, studying at McMaster University, Laurentian University, and Ryerson Polytechnic Institute. By 1996 the number of students will rise to 122 (Kelly Toughill, 'Ontario to Pay for All Midwife Services,' *Toronto Star* 21 Dec. 1992, A1).

13 Veronica Strong-Boag, *The New Day Recalled: Lives of Girls and Women in English Canada, 1919–1939* (Toronto: Copp Clark Pitman 1988), 146

A Note on Sources

Since child-rearing advice emanates from a number of different sectors of society, including the medical profession, various levels of government, and private authors, it is important to consider the information provided by each of these sectors. In order to view changes which have taken place in maternal advice, I have drawn on publications of the medical and nursing professions, examining the complete run from 1920 to 1960 of three key medical journals: *Canadian Medical Association Journal*; the *Canadian Journal of Public Health*,[1] official organ of the Canadian Public Health Association; and *Canadian Nurse*, journal of the Canadian National Association of Trained Nurses (later, Canadian Nurses Association). Because members of the medical and nursing professions played a critical role in the preservation of child health during this period, I was particularly interested in examining their professional journals to see the ways in which they discussed issues concerning the health and welfare of mothers and children. Circulation for all three publications remained below 5,000 throughout the period under consideration, a relatively low figure in comparison with the rates of mass-circulation magazines.[2] Actual readership, however, probably far exceeded these rates, as doctors and nurses consulted their professional journals in medical libraries and reading rooms. In addition, subscribers often lent a copy of their journal to a friend or colleague, thereby increasing readership substantially.[3]

To view the advice literature produced by the various levels of government, I examined the records of the federal, provincial, and municipal departments of health, looking, in particular, at the activities of the various divisions of child welfare and their respective publications. Whenever possible, I examined every edition of each publication in order to view changes which may have taken place over time. In order to gather information on circulation and distribution of literature I also examined the annual departmental reports of the departments of health of all three levels of government for the period 1920 to 1960.

The voluntary sector also played a significant role in the production and distribution of prenatal and child-care literature during the first half of this century. In particular, the Canadian Council on Child and Family Welfare produced several sets of monthly letters to mothers. At the National Archives of Canada, I viewed the entire holdings of the council with respect to child care during the period from 1920 to 1960, in addition to the relevant materials in the Charlotte Whitton Collection.[4]

A key figure in child care during the middle decades of this century was Dr William E. Blatz, founder and director of the St George's School for Child Study at the University of Toronto (later, the Institute of Child Study) and author of a number of key works on child study. To investigate Blatz's ideas on child care, I read all his major works, in addition to examining the Blatz papers, which are deposited at the Thomas Fisher Rare Book Library at the University of Toronto. I also considered the case of the Dionne Quintuplets, perhaps the most highly documented example of the implementation of a scientific approach to child rearing. I have examined all the major books and articles written about the quintuplets, including the papers of Dr Allan Roy Dafoe, the Dionne Quintuplets' personal physician for the first years of their lives.[5]

During this period, the question of child rearing was dealt with extensively in the popular media. Virtually every mass circulation magazine and newspaper contained a regular column offering advice to mothers on the care and feeding of their children. The volume of this literature is in itself staggering. I therefore chose to focus on *Chatelaine*, examining every issue of the magazine from its inception in 1928 until 1960. I selected *Chatelaine* primarily because of its large circulation to Canadian women.[6] In many respects *Chatelaine* typified the perspective of the growing middle class, a key audience for advice literature during these decades.[7] In addition to *Chatelaine*, I looked at selected child-care articles in *Canadian Home Journal* and *Maclean's*.

The availability of relatively inexpensive paper and, after the Second World War, the advent of mass-market paperback books, meant that increasing numbers of Canadian mothers purchased books on child rearing. I considered the major mass-market books available to Canadian mothers during the period 1920 to 1960. *The Normal Child* by Dr Alan Brown[8] and the *Care of the Child* by Dr Alton Goldbloom[9] were two key child-care manuals in the interwar years. Following the war, Dr Benjamin Spock's famous *Baby and Child Care* was published. Although written by an American doctor, the book sold widely in Canada, and had a profound influence on many Canadian mothers and their child-rearing habits. Accordingly, I considered the two editions of *Baby and Child Care* which were published before 1960.[10]

By drawing upon the literature produced by several key sectors, I was able to demonstrate that a high degree of unanimity existed in the advice offered by child-rearing experts in all areas of society. This can in part be explained by the fact that considerable overlap existed between various sectors: members of the medical profession, for example, held key government posts, penned columns for newspapers and women's magazines, and spoke on the radio. Most of the authors of advice manuals in the twentieth century were located in the key institutions of Canadian society, occupying positions of responsibility in government, social welfare, and medicine. As a consequence, manual writers were responsible not only for producing pamphlets and booklets for Canadian mothers, but for establishing laws and social policies which affected women's day-to-day lives. As well, their strategic locations enabled them to meet with one another frequently, to share information, and to compare ideas about child care.

One of the major goals of this study was to assess women's response to the child-rearing advice they received. As Nancy Pottishman Weiss has argued, in the past 'scholars have assessed rules for rearing the young, but have neglected to ask questions about what these rules have meant for adults.[11] Reminding readers that child-rearing manuals are also 'mother-rearing tracts,[12] Weiss points out that 'behind every rule concerning desirable child behavior,' there was 'a message to mothers ... advising them on how to act and recommending the right, proper, and moral way to conduct their own lives.[13] To document the impact of advice literature on mothers, Weiss draws upon the enormous volume of correspondence received by the United States Children's Bureau and by Dr Benjamin Spock. In the letters, women revealed a great deal about the day-to-day conditions of their lives. Like their American counterparts, Canadian mothers wrote to the authors of child-care manuals, seeking assistance and advice. Despite a reference in one article to 'thousands of mothers' letters' on file,[14] it appears that most of this correspondence has been destroyed. A small number of letters do remain, however, and, I have used these in addition to letters to advice columnists and other authors including Dr Spock and Dr Allan Roy Dafoe.

In addition to written sources, I turned to oral history as another means to assess women's response to the child-rearing advice.[15] Since the interviews were intended primarily to supplement the literary sources, I decided to conduct a small number of interviews with women who had reared their children between 1920 and 1960. I hoped to interview six women from the period 1920–40 and six from the period 1940–60. It was also my intention to select an equal number of working-class and middle-class women.[16] With these plans in mind I set out to find my subjects. I began with my mother, a logical starting point, perhaps, when one is writting about motherhood. She agreed to be interviewed herself, and willingly offered the names of her friends as well.

As well as relying on personal contacts, I placed advertisements in a number of community papers. Each time a woman contacted me, I sent her a list of proposed questions,[17] contacting her two weeks later to see whether she was still willing to be interviewed. Several women declined to participate at this point. The remaining women were interviewed in their homes during the winter of 1986. Each woman signed a release form at the time of the interview, granting me permission to use the material and indicating whether she wished her name to be deleted from the study. I interviewed twelve women in total, six from the period 1920–40 and six from 1940–60. The women were equally divided between working class and middle class. All but one of the women had reared her children in an urban centre in southern Ontario.

There has been considerable scholarly debate in recent years over the reliability of information obtained through interviews.[18] It should be noted that, despite many of the women's fears that they would have little to say, all of the women I interviewed spoke for at least an hour, and all recalled in vivid detail specific information about birth weight, hospital procedures, breast- and bottle-feeding, and the introduction of solid foods. It is my contention that supplementing the interviews with documentary evidence in the form of letters, diaries, and other materials written at the time of child rearing has helped to overcome some of the problems of 'maternal recall.' Coupling the interviews with letters to child-care experts has enabled me to evaluate women's responses to the child-rearing advice they received.

1 This has been the title of the journal since 1943. Before that it was called the *Public Health Journal* (1913–28) and then the *Canadian Public Health Journal* (1929–42).

2 The circulation of the *Canadian Medical Association Journal* was 2,750 (1930), 3,742 (1932), 3,437 (1935), and 6,046 (1945). The circulation of the *Canadian Public Health Journal* was 1,750 (1930), 3,000 (1935), and 3,000 plus (1940). The circulation of the *Canadian Nurse* was 2,750 (1930), 3,000 (1936), 4,916 (1944), 40,000 (1958). Figures are taken from McKim's *Directory of Canadian Publications*, various years.

3 A reader survey of *Canadian Nurse* conducted in 1958 indicated that 31.1 per cent of subscribers lent their copy of the journal to a colleague, thereby increasing the circulation rate from approximately 40,000 per issue to 65,000 readers per issue (*CN* 54 [1958], 216).

4 Copies of the council's publications, *Prenatal Letters*, *Post-Natal Letters*, *Pre-School Letters*, and *School-Age Letters*, are held in the records of the Canadian Council on Social Development.

5 For a detailed discussion of the advice given by the experts in charge of the quintuplets, see Katherine Arnup, 'Raising the Dionne Quintuplets: Lessons for Modern Mothers,' forthcoming in *Rethinking the Dionne Quintuplets*.

6 In 1930, two years after its establishment, the monthly circulation had reached 74,278. By 1931, this figure had climbed to 121,760; by 1934, 198,303; and by 1935, 215,353. Circulation figures were provided in the magazine on a regular basis.

7 For a discussion of *Chatelaine*'s changing editorial policies see Inez Houlihan, 'The Image of Women in *Chatelaine* Editorials, Mar. 1928 to Sep. 1977' (MA thesis, University of Toronto 1984). See also Mary Vipond, 'The Image of Women in Mass Circulation Magazines in the 1920s,' in Susan Mann Trofimenkoff and Alison Prentice, eds., *The Neglected Majority: Essays in Canadian Women's History*, vol. 1, (Toronto: McClelland and Stewart 1977).

8 Toronto: McClelland and Stewart 1928

9 Toronto: Longmans, Green 1945

10 New York: Pocket Books 1946, and 1957

11 Nancy Pottishman Weiss, 'Mother, the Invention of Necessity: Dr. Ben-

jamin Spock's *Baby and Child Care*,' *American Quarterly* 24 (Winter 1977), 519–46. This quotation appears on 519. See, also, Nancy Pottishman Weiss, 'The Mother-Child Dyad Revisited: Perceptions of Mothers and Children in Twentieth Century Child-Rearing Manuals,' *Journal of Social Issues* 34 (1978), 29–45.

12 Weiss, 'The Mother-Child Dyad Revisited, 31

13 Weiss, 'Mother, the Invention of Necessity, 520

14 Helen MacMurchy, 'The Division of Child Welfare: Department of Pensions and National Health,' *PHJ* 19 (1928), 517

15 In recent years, increasing numbers of historians have used oral history as a means of recovering the experiences of people whose lives might otherwise remain undocumented. A pioneer in this work is Paul Thompson, whose book, *The Voice of the Past*, has influenced countless historians. (Oxford: Oxford University Press 1978). For an example of the use of oral sources in women's history, see the special issue on women's oral history of *Frontiers: A Journal of Women's History* 2 (Summer 1977).

16 For the purposes of this study, I identified the women's class in terms of their husbands' occupations, since none of the women was employed in the paid labour force during her years of early mothering. I recognize, of course, that the question of class is far more complex than this measure suggests.

17 See Appendix.

18 See, among others, M.K. Pyles, H.R. Stolz, and J.W. MacFarlane, 'The Accuracy of Mothers' Reports on Birth and Developmental Data,' *Child Development* 6 (1935), 165–76; Myrtle B. McGraw and Louise B. Molloy, 'The Pediatric Anamnesis: Inaccuracies in Eliciting Developmental Data,' *Child Development* 12 (1941), 255–65; Sarnoff A. Mednick and John B.P. Shaffer, 'Mothers' Retrospective Reports in Child-Rearing Research,' *American Journal of Orthopsychiatry* 33 (1963), 457–61; Charles Wenar, 'The Reliability of Mothers' Histories,' *Child Development* 32 (1961), 491–500; Vaughn J. Crandall and Anne Preston, 'Patterns and Levels of Maternal Behavior,' *Child Development* 16 (1955), 274–76; Marvin Zuckerman, Beatrice H. Barrett, and Raymond M. Bragiel, 'The Parental Attitudes of Parents of Child Guidance Cases,' *Child Development* 31 (1960), 401–17; Lillian Cukier Robbins, 'The Accuracy of Parental Recall of Aspects of Child Development and Child-Rearing Practices,' *Journal of Abnormal and Social Psychology* 66 (1963), 267; and Joan and William McCord, 'Cultural Stereotypes and the Validity of Interviews for Research in Child Development,' *Child Development* 32 (1961), 171–85.

Bibliography

Primary Sources

MANUSCRIPT COLLECTIONS AND GOVERNMENT RECORDS

National Archives of Canada
Canadian Council on Social Development (MG28, I10)
Department of Health, Division of Child Welfare (RG29)
Dominion Council of Health (MG28, I63)
National Council of Women (MG28, I25)
John R. Ross Papers (MG30, B107)
Charlotte Whitton Papers (MG30, E256)

Province of Ontario Archives
Allan Roy Dafoe Collection (MS598)
Provincial Board of Health (RG62)
Ministry of Health, Public Health Nursing Branch (RG10)

City of Toronto Archives
Association of Neighbourhood Services (SC14)
Paul Bator Collection (SC215)
Canadian Mothercraft (SC112)
Central Neighbourhood House (SC5)
Department of Public Health (RG11)
Neighbourhood Workers (SC136)
Social Planning Council (SC40)
University Settlement House (SC24)

Thomas Fisher Rare Books Library
William E. Blatz Papers

NEWSPAPERS AND PERIODICALS

Canadian Medical Association Journal, 1919–60
Canadian Nurse, 1919–60
Canadian Journal of Public Health, 1915–60
Chatelaine, 1928–60
Canadian Home Journal (selected articles)
Maclean's (selected articles)
Social Welfare (selected articles)

GOVERNMENT DOCUMENTS: ANNUAL AND MONTHLY REPORTS

Canada, Department of Health, 1920–7
Canada, Department of Pensions and National Health, 1928–44
Canada, Department of National Health and Welfare, 1945–60
Ontario, Department of Health
Ontario, Provincial Board of Health
Toronto, *City Council Minutes: Appendix A.* Monthly Reports of the Local Board
   of Health

INTERVIEWS

C. Dora Arnup
Mrs C. Carson
Eleanor Enkin (by telephone)
Jane France (by mail)
Win Hall
Kay Herrington
Kay Macpherson
Eila I. Hopper Ross
Dr John R. Ross
Winnie Weatherstone
Three additional mothers who chose to remain anonymous

ARTICLES AND BOOKS

Blatz, William E. *The Five Sisters: A Study of Child Psychology.* Toronto: McClelland
   and Stewart, 1938

- *Understanding the Young Child.* Toronto: Clarke Irwin, 1944
- and Helen McM. Bott. *Parents and the Pre-School Child.* Toronto: J.M..Dent, 1928
- *The Management of Young Children.* Toronto: McClelland and Stewart, 1930.
Blatz, W.E., N. Chant, M.W. Charles, M.I. Fletcher, N.H.C. Ford, A.L. Harris, J.W. MacArthur, M. Mason, and D.A. Millichamp. *Collected Studies on the Dionne Quintuplets.* St George's School for Child Study, University of Toronto: University of Toronto Press, 1937
Brittain, Horace L. 'The Administration of the Toronto Department of Public Health.' *PHJ* 6 (July 1915), 309–15 and *PHJ* 6 (Aug. 1915), 365–75
Brown, Alan. 'Infant and Child Welfare Work.' *PHJ* 9 (Apr. 1918), 145–56
- 'Problems of the Rural Mother in the Feeding of Her Children.' *PHJ* 8 (July 1918), 297–301
- 'The Relation of the Pediatrician to the Community.' *PHJ* 10 (Feb. 1919), 49–55
- 'The General Practitioner and Preventive Pediatrics.' *CPHJ* 21 (1930), 267–74.
- *The Normal Child: Its Care and Feeding: Its Care and Feeding.* Toronto: McClelland and Stewart, 1932
- and Frederick Tisdall. *Common Procedures in the Practice of Pediatrics.* Toronto: McClelland and Stewart, 1926
Canada, Department of National Health and Welfare. *Up the Years from One to Six.* Ottawa: King's Printer, 1950
- *Canadian Mother and Child.* Ottawa: Queen's Printer, 1953
Canadian Council on Child and Family Welfare. *Prenatal Letters.* Ottawa: Canadian Council on Child and Family Welfare, 1926
- *Post-Natal Letters.* Ottawa: Canadian Council on Child and Family Welfare, 1930
- *Pre-School Letters.* Ottawa: Canadian Council on Child and Family Welfare, 1934
- *School-Age Letters.* Ottawa: Canadian Council on Child and Family Welfare, 1939
Chapman, Ethel M. 'The New Move for Child Welfare: Dr. Helen MacMurchy – Chief of a National Department.' *MacLean's* 33 (1 May 1920), 74, 77
City of Toronto, Department of Public Health. *Pre-Natal Care.* Toronto: Department of Public Health, 1922.
- *The Expectant Mother.* Toronto: Department of Public Health, 1927 (1931, 1943, 1948)
- *The Care of the Infant and Young Child.* Toronto: Department of Public Health, 1931 (1933, 1936, 1944)
Couture, Ernest. *The Canadian Mother and Child.* Ottawa: King's Printer, 1940

Dafoe, Allan Roy. 'The Dionne Quintuplets.' *Journal of the American Medical Association* 103 (Sept. 1934), 673–77
– 'Further History of the Care and Feeding of the Dionne Quintuplets.' *CMAJ* 34 (Jan. 1936), 26–32
– and William A. Dafoe. 'The Physical Welfare of the Dionne Quintuplets.' *CMAJ* 37 (Nov. 1937), 415–23
de Kiriline, Louise. *The Quintuplets' First Year: The Survival of the Famous Dionne Babies and Its Significance for All Mothers.* Toronto: Macmillan, at St Martin's House, 1936.
Goldbloom, Alton. *The Care of the Child.* Toronto: Longmans, Green, 1928 (1935, 1940, 1945)
Knox, E.M. *Girl of the New Day.* Toronto: McClelland and Stewart, 1919
McCleary, G.F. *The Early History of the Infant Welfare Movement.* London: H.K. Lewis, 1933
MacMurchy, Helen. *Infant Mortality: Special Report.* Toronto: King's Printer, 1910
– 'What We Can Do for Posterity.' *Canadian Therapeutist and Sanitary Engineer* 1 (June 1910), 305–6
– *Infant Mortality: Second Special Report.* Toronto: King's Printer, 1912
– *Infant Mortality: Third Report.* Toronto: King's Printer, 1911
– 'The Baby's Father.' *PHJ* 9 (July 1918), 315–19
– *The Canadian Mother's Book.* Ottawa: King's Printer, 1921. The Little Blue Books: The Mother's Series, no. 2. (1923, 1927, 1930, 1932)
– 'The Duty of a Physician to the Mother and Her Child.' *Canadian Practitioner and Review* 46 (Oct. 1921), 302–7
– *How to Take Care of the Baby.* The Little Blue Books: Mother's Series, no. 2. Ottawa: King's Printer, 1922
– *How to Take Care of Mother.* The Little Blue Books: Home Series, no. 8. Ottawa: King's Printer, 1922
– *How to Take Care of the Family.* The Little Blue Books: Home Series. no. 9. Ottawa: King's Printer, 1922
– *How to Take Care of the Children.* The Little Blue Books: Home Series, no. 11. Ottawa: King's Printer, 1922
– *Beginning a Home in Canada.* The Little Blue Books: Home Series, no. 7. Ottawa: King's Printer, 1923
– *Handbook of Child Welfare in Canada.* Ottawa: King's Printer, 1923
– *How to Manage Housework in Canada.* The Little Blue Books: Household Series, no. 14. Ottawa: King's Printer, 1923
– *How to Take Care of the Father and the Family.* The Little Blue Books: Mother's Series, no. 5. Ottawa: King's Printer, 1923

- *How to Take Care of the Mother*. The Little Blue Books: Mother's Series, no. 3. Ottawa: King's Printer, 1923
- 'The Division of Child Welfare: Department of Pensions and National Health.' *PHJ* 19 (1928), 514–21
- *Maternity Mortality in Canada: Report of the Enquiry Made by the Department of Health, Division of Child Welfare*. The Little Blue Books: National Series, no. 1. Ottawa: King's Printer, 1928
- *Mother: A Little Book for Men*. The Little Blue Books: National Series, no. 3. Ottawa: King's Printer, 1928
- *Mother: A Little Book for Women*. The Little Blue Books: National Series, no. 2. Ottawa: King's Printer, 1928

Newman, George. *Infant Mortality*. New York: E.P. Dutton, 1907

Ontario, Department of Health. *The Baby*. Toronto: Ontario Department of Health, 1920 (1921, 1924, 1933, 1940, 1943)
- *The Early Years*. Toronto: Ontario Department of Health, 1953

The Physiology of Motherhood. Toronto: British Chemists Company, 1900

Read, Mary L. *The Mothercraft Manual*. Boston: Little, Brown, 1916

Saleeby, C.W. *Woman and Womanhood*. London: Mitchell Kennerley, 1911

Spock, Benjamin. *The Pocket Book of Baby and Child Care*. Montreal: Pocket Books, 1946 (1957)

Stopes, Marie Carmichael. *Radiant Motherhood: A Book for Those Who Are Creating the Future*. Toronto: Musson, 1920

Thornton, Willis. *The Country Doctor*. New York: Grosset and Dunlap, 1936

Tisdall, Frederick F. *The Home Care of the Infant and Child*. New York: William Morrow, 1942

Yorke, K.M. 'Saving Lives on Wholesale Plan: How Toronto Has Been Made the Healthiest of Large Cities.' *MacLean's* 28 (July 1915), 20–2, 93–5.

FILMS

National Archives of Canada: National Film, Television, and Sound Archives
National Film Board Collection:
Before They Are Six (1943)
Small Fry (1946)
Mother and Her Child (1947), acc. no. 8220-771-5
Why Won't Tommy Eat (1948), acc. no. 7708-273
He Acts His Age (1949), acc. no. 8220-978
Terrible Twos and Trusting Threes (1950), acc. no. 7906-1888
Frustrating Fours and Fascinating Fives (1952), acc. no. 7906-1861

From Sociable Six to Noisy Nine (1953), acc. no. 7906-1859

Secondary Sources

PUBLISHED MATERIALS

Abeele, Cynthia R. '"The Infant Soldier": The Great War and the Medical Campaign for Child Welfare.' *Canadian Bulletin of Medical History* 5 (1988), 99–119

Abeele, Cynthia Comacchio.'"The Mothers of the Last Must Suffer": Child and Maternal Welfare in Rural and Outpost Ontario, 1918–1940.' *Ontario History* 80 (September 1988), 183–205

Abella, Rosalie Silberman. 'The Critical Century: The Rights of Women and Children from 1882–1982.' *Law Society Gazette* 18 (1984), 40–53

Apple, Rima D. '"To Be Used Only under the Direction of a Physician": Commercial Infant Feeding and Medical Practice, 1870–1940.' *Bulletin of the History of Medicine* 54 (1980), 402–17

– *Mothers and Medicine: A Social History of Infant Feeding, 1890–1950.* Madison: University of Wisconsin Press, 1987

Aries, Philippe. *Centuries of Childhood: A Social History of Family Life.* Translated by Robert Baldick. New York: Random House, 1962

Arnup, Katherine. 'Adrienne Rich: Poet, Mother, Lesbian Feminist, Visionary.' *Atlantis* 8 (Fall 1982), 97–110

– 'Educating Mothers: Government Advice for Women in the Inter-War Years.' In Katherine Arnup, Andrée Lévesque, and Ruth Roach Pierson, eds. *Delivering Motherhood: Maternal Ideologies and Practices in the 19th and 20th Centuries,* 190–210. London: Routledge, 1990

– Andrée Lévesque, and Ruth Roach Pierson, eds. *Delivering Motherhood: Maternal Ideologies and Practices in the 19th and 20th Centuries.* London: Routledge, 1990

Bach, William G. 'The Influence of Psychoanalytic Thought in Benjamin Spock's *Baby and Child Care.' Journal of the History of the Behavioral Sciences* 10 (Jan. 1974), 91–4

Backhouse, Constance B. 'Shifting Patterns in Nineteenth-Century Canadian Custody Law.' In David H. Flaherty, ed., *Essays in the History of Canadian Law,* vol. 1, 212–48. Toronto: University of Toronto Press, 1981

– 'Desperate Women and Compassionate Courts: Infanticide in Nineteenth-Century Canada.' *University of Toronto Law Journal* 34 (Fall 1984), 447–78

– '"Pure Patriarchy": Nineteenth-Century Canadian Marriage.' *McGill Law Journal* 31 (1986), 264–312

Badinter, Elizabeth. *Mother Love: Myth and Reality.* New York: Macmillan, 1981

Barrett, Michele, and Mary McIntosh. *The Anti-social Family.* London: Verso, 1982

Beddoe, Dierdre. *Discovering Women's History: A Practical Manual.* London: Pandora Press, 1983

Beekman, Daniel. *The Mechanical Baby: A Popular History of the Theory and Practice of Child Rearing.* Westport, Conn.: Lawrence Hill, 1977

Benoit, Cecilia. 'Mothering in a Newfoundland Community: 1900-1940.' In Katherine Arnup, Andrée Lévesque, and Ruth Roach Pierson, eds. *Delivering Motherhood: Maternal Ideologies and Practices in the 19th and 20th Centuries,* 173-89. London: Routledge, 1990

- *Midwives in Passage.* St John's, Newfoundland: Institute of Social and Economic Research, 1991

Bernard, Jessie. *The Future of Motherhood.* New York: Penguin, 1975

Berton, Pierre. *The Dionne Years: A Thirties Melodrama.* Toronto: McClelland and Stewart, 1977

Biggs, C. Lesley. 'The Case of the Missing Midwives: A History of Midwifery in Ontario from 1795-1900.' *Ontario History* 75 (March 1983), 21-35. Reprinted in Katherine Arnup, Andrée Lévesque, and Ruth Roach Pierson, eds., *Delivering Motherhood: Maternal Ideologies and Practices in the 19th and 20th Centuries,* 20-35. London: Routledge, 1990

Birnbaum, Lucille C. 'Behaviorism in the 1920's.' *American Quarterly* 7 (Spring 1955), 15-30

Blau, Zena Smith. 'Exposure to Child-Rearing Experts: A Structural Interpretation of Class-Color Differences.' *American Journal of Sociology* 69 (May 1964), 596-608

Bliss, Michael. '"Pure Books on Avoided Subjects": Pre-Freudian Sexual Ideas in Canada.' *Historical Papers* (1970), 89-108

Bloch, Ruth. 'American Feminine Ideals in Transition: The Rise of the Moral Mother, 1785-1815.' *Feminist Studies* 4 (June 1978), 101-26

Bloom, Lynn Z. *Doctor Spock: Biography of a Conservative Radical.* Indianapolis: Bobbs-Merrill, 1972

- '"It's All for Your Own Good": Parent-Child Relationships in Popular American Child Rearing Literature, 1820-1970.' *Journal of Popular Culture* 10 (Summer 1976), 191-8

Boulton, Mary Georgina. *On Being a Mother: A Study of Women with Pre-School Children.* New York: Tavistock, 1983

Bradbury, Dorothy E. *Five Decades of Action for Children: A History of the Children's Bureau.* Washington, D.C.: U.S. Department of Health, Education, and Welfare, 1962

Branca, Patricia. *Silent Sisterhood: Middle-Class Women in the Victorian Home.* London: Croom Helm, 1977

Broadfoot, Barry. *Ten Lost Years, 1929–1939: Memories of Canadians Who Survived the Depression.* Don Mills, Ont.: Paper Jacks, 1975

Bronfenbrenner, Urie. 'Socialization and Social Class through Time and Space.' In Eleanor E. Maccoby, Theodore M. Newcomb, and Eugene L. Hartley, eds., *Readings in Social Psychology,* 3rd ed., New York: Henry Holt, 1958, 400–24

Brooks, Melvin S., Douglas L. Rennie, and Roger Sondag. 'Sociological Variables in the Reaction of Parents to Child-Rearing Information.' *Merrill-Palmer Quarterly* 8 (July 1962), 175–82

Buckley, Suzann. 'Efforts to Reduce Infant Maternity Mortality in Canada between the Two World Wars.' *Atlantis* 2 (Spring 1977), 76–84

– 'Ladies or Midwives? Efforts to Reduce Infant and Maternal Mortality.' In Linda Kealey, ed., *A Not Unreasonable Claim: Women and Reform in Canada, 1880s–1920s.* Toronto: Women's Press, 1979, 131–49

– 'The Search for the Decline of Maternal Mortality: The Place of Hospital Records.' In Wendy Mitchinson and Janice Dickin McGinnis, eds., *Essays in the History of Medicine.* Toronto: McClelland and Stewart, 1988, 148–63

Cable, Mary. *The Little Darlings: A History of Child Rearing in America.* New York: Charles Scribner's Sons, 1975

Caldwell, Bettye M., and Julius B. Richmond. 'The Impact of Theories of Child Development.' *Children* 9 (March–April 1962), 73–8

Charles, Enid. 'The Changing Size of the Family in Canada.' Ottawa: King's Printer, 1948

Chodorow, Nancy. *The Reproduction of Mothering: Psychoanalysis and the Sociology of Gender.* Berkeley: University of California Press, 1978

Clarke-Stewart, K. Alison. 'Popular Primers for Parents.' *American Psychologist* 33 (1978), 359–69

Cleverley, John, and D.C. Phillips. *From Locke to Spock: Influential Models of the Child in Modern Western Thought.* Carlton, Victoria: Melbourne University Press, 1976

Coburn, Judi. '"I See and Am Silent": A Short History of Nursing in Ontario.' In Janice Acton, ed., *Women at Work: Ontario, 1850–1930.* Toronto: Women's Press, 1974

Contratto, Susan. 'Mother: Social Sculptor and Trustee of the Faith.' In Miriam Lewin, ed., *In the Shadow of the Past: Psychology Portrays the Sexes: A Social and Intellectual History.* New York: Columbia University Press, 1974, 226–55

Cook, Ramsay, and Wendy Mitchinson, eds. *The Proper Sphere: Women's Place in Canadian Society.* Toronto: Oxford University Press, 1976

Copp, Terry. *The Anatomy of Poverty*. Toronto: McClelland and Stewart, 1973

Coulter, Rebecca. 'Perspectives on Motherhood: A Review Essay.' *Atlantis* 10 (Spring 1985), 127–37

Cowan, Ruth Schwartz. *More Work for Mother: The Ironies of Household Technology from the Open Hearth to the Microwave*. New York: Basic Books, 1983

Crowley, Terry. 'Madonnas before Magdalenes: Adelaide Hoodless and the Making of the Canadian Gibson Girl.' *Canadian Historical Review* 67 (1986), 520–47

Dally, Ann. *Inventing Motherhood: The Consequences of an Ideal*. New York: Schocken, 1983

Davies, Margaret Llewelyn, ed. *Maternity: Letters from Working Women*. Women's Co-operative Guild, 1915; reprint, London: Virago, 1978

– *Life as We Have Known It*. Women's Co-operative Guild, 1931; reprint, New York: Norton, 1975

Davies, Megan J. '"Services Rendered, Rearing Children for the State": Mothers' Pensions in British Columbia, 1919–1931.' In Barbara K. Latham and Roberta J. Pazdro, eds., *Not Just Pin Money*. Victoria: Camosun College, 1984, 249–63

Davin, Anna. 'Imperialism and Motherhood.' *History Workshop Journal* 5 (Spring 1978), 9–65

Degler, Carl. 'What Ought to Be and What Was: Women's Sexuality in the Nineteenth Century.' *American Historical Review* 79 (Dec. 1974), 1467–90

Dehli, Kari. '"Health Scouts" for the State? School and Public Health Nurses in Early Twentieth Century Toronto.' *Historical Studies in Education / Revue d'Histoire de l'Education* 2 (Fall 1990), 247–64

deMause, Lloyd, ed. *The History of Childhood*. New York: Harper and Row, 1975

Dodd, Dianne. 'The Birth Control Movement on Trial, 1936–37.' *Histoire sociale / Social History* 16 (1983), 411–28

– 'Advice to Parents: The Blue Books, Helen MacMurchy, MD, and the Federal Department of Health, 1920–34.' *Canadian Bulletin of Medical History* 8 (1991), 203–30

Dyhouse, Carol, 'Towards a "Feminine" Curriculum for English Schoolgirls: The Demands of Ideology, 1870–1963.' *Women's Studies International Quarterly* (1978), 297–311

– 'Working-Class Mothers and Infant Mortality in England, 1895–1914.' *Journal of Social History* 12 (Winter 1978), 248–67

– *Girls Growing Up in Late Victorian and Edwardian England*. London: Routledge and Kegan Paul, 1981

Dwork, Deborah. *War Is Good for Babies and Other Young Children: A History of the Infant and Child Welfare Movement in England, 1898–1918*. London: Tavistock, 1987

Ehrenreich, Barbara, and Deirdre English. *For Her Own Good: 150 Years of the Experts' Advice to Women*. Garden City, NY: Anchor Books, 1979

Emory, Florence. *Public Health Nursing in Canada*. Toronto: Macmillan, 1945

Escalona, Sibylle. 'A Commentary upon Some Recent Changes in Child Rearing Practices.' *Child Development* 20 (Sept. 1949), 157–62

Fellman, Anita Clair, and Michael Fellman. *Making Sense of Self: Medical Advice Literature in Late Nineteenth-Century America*. Philadelphia: University of Pennsylvania Press, 1981

Geboy, Michael J. 'Who Is Listening to the "Experts"? The Use of Child Care Materials by Parents.' *Family Relations* 30 (Apr. 1981), 205–10

Gee, Ellen. 'Female Marriage Patterns in Canada: Changes and Differentials.' *Journal of Comparative Family Studies* 11 (1980), 457–73

Gibbon, John Murray, and Mary S. Mathewson. *Three Centuries of Canadian Nursing*. Toronto: Macmillan, 1947

Gieve, Katherine, ed. *Balancing Acts: On Being a Mother*. London: Virago, 1989

Goldbloom, Alton. *Small Patients: The Autobiography of a Children's Doctor*. Toronto: Longmans, Green, 1959

Gordon, Michael. '*Infant Care* Revisited.' *Journal of Marriage and the Family* 30 (Nov. 1968), 578–83

Gorham, Deborah. 'Birth and History.' *Histoire sociale / Social History* 17, 34 (Nov. 1984), 383–94

Graham, Hilary. 'Images of Pregnancy in Antenatal Literature.' In Christian Heath, Margaret Reid, and Margaret Stacey, eds., *Health Care and Health Knowledge*. London: Croom Helm, 1977, 13–37

– '"Prevention and Health: Every Mother's Business": A Comment on Child Health Policies in the 1970s.' In Chris Harris, ed., *The Sociology of the Family: New Directions for Britain*. Keele: University of Keele, 1979, 160–85

– 'Caring: A Labour of Love.' In Janet Finch and Dulcie Groves, eds., *A Labour of Love: Women, Work, and Caring*. London: Routledge and Kegan Paul, 1983, 13–30

– *Women, Health and the Family*. Sussex: Wheatsheaf Books, 1984

– and Ann Oakley. 'Competing Ideologies of Reproduction: Medical and Maternal Perspectives on Pregnancy.' In Helen Roberts, ed., *Women, Health and Reproduction*. London: Routledge and Kegan Paul, 1981

Grayson, L.M., and Michael Bliss, eds. *The Wretched of Canada: Letters to R.B. Bennett, 1930–1935*. Toronto: University of Toronto Press, 1971

Hall, Catherine. 'The Early Formation of Victorian Domestic Ideology.' In Sandra Burman, ed., *Fit Work for Women*. London: Croom Helm, 1979, 15–32

Hardyment, Christina. *Dream Babies: Child Care from Locke to Spock*. London: Oxford University Press, 1984

Hareven, Tamara K. 'An Ambiguous Alliance: Some Aspects of American Influences on Canadian Social Welfare.' *Histoire sociale / Social History* 3 (Apr. 1969), 82–98

Harris, Ben. '"Give Me a Dozen Healthy Infants ... "': John B. Watson's Popular Advice on Childrearing, Women, and the Family.' In Miriam Lewin, ed., *In the Shadow of the Past: Psychology Portrays the Sexes – A Social and Intellectual History*. New York: Columbia University Press, 1984

Helterline, Marilyn. 'The Emergence of Modern Motherhood: Motherhood in England, 1899 to 1959.' *International Journal of Women's Studies* 3 (Nov./Dec. 1980), 590–614

Hess, Robert D. 'Experts and Amateurs: Some Unintended Consequences of Parent Education.' In Mario D. Fantini and Rene Cardenas, eds., *Parenting in a Multicultural Society*. New York: Longmans, 1980, 141–59

Jones, Kathleen W. 'Sentiment and Science: The Late Nineteenth Century Pediatrician as Mother's Advisor.' *Journal of Social History* 17 (Fall 1983), 79–96

Kaledin, Eugenia. *American Women in the 1950s: Mothers and More*. Boston: Twayne, 1984

Kealey, Linda, ed. *A Not Unreasonable Claim: Women and Reform in Canada, 1880s–1920s*. Toronto: Women's Press, 1979

Kern, Stephen. 'The History of Childhood: A Review Article.' *Journal of the History of the Behavioral Sciences* 9 (Oct. 1973), 406–11

Kessen, William. 'Research in the Psychological Development of Infants: An Overview.' *Merrill-Palmer Quarterly* 9 (1963), 83–94

Kitzinger, Sheila. *Women as Mothers*. New York: Vintage Books, 1984

Klapper, Zelda S. 'The Impact of the Women's Liberation Movement on Child Development Books.' *American Journal of Orthopsychiatry* 41 (Oct. 1971), 725–32

Klaus, Alisa. 'Women's Organizations and the Infant Health Movement in France and the United States, 1890–1920.' In Kathleen D. McCarthy, ed., *Lady Bountiful Revisited: Women, Philanthropy, and Power*. New Brunswick, NJ: Rutgers University Press, 1990, 157–73

Ladd-Taylor, Molly. *Raising a Baby the Government Way: Mothers' Letters to the Children's Bureau, 1915–1932*. New Brunswick, NJ: Rutgers University Press, 1986

Leavitt, Judith Walzer. *Brought to Bed: Childbearing in America, 1750–1950*. New York: Oxford University Press, 1986

- ed. *Women and Health in America*. Madison: University of Wisconsin Press, 1984
LeShan, Eda. 'Child Care.' *New York Times Book Review* (20 Feb. 1977), 26–7
Lévesque, Andrée. 'Deviants Anonymous: Single Mothers at the Hôpital de la Miséricorde in Montreal, 1929–1939.' *Historical Papers* (1984), 168–84. Reprinted in Katherine Arnup, Andrée Lévesque, and Ruth Roach Pierson, eds., *Delivering Motherhood: Maternal Ideologies and Practices in the 19th and 20th Centuries*. London: Routledge, 1990, 108–25
Lewin, Miriam, ed. *In the Shadow of the Past: Psychology Portrays the Sexes: A Social and Intellectual History*. New York: Columbia University Press, 1984
Lewis, Jane. *The Politics of Motherhood: Child and Maternal Welfare in England, 1900–1939*. London: Croom Helm, 1980
- '"Motherhood Issues" in the Late Nineteenth and Twentieth Centuries.' In Katherine Arnup, Andrée Lévesque, and Ruth Roach Pierson, eds., *Delivering Motherhood: Maternal Ideologies and Practices in the 19th and 20th Centuries*. London: Routledge, 1990, 1–19
- ed. *Labour and Love: Women's Experience of Home and Family, 1850–1940*. Oxford: Basil Blackwell, 1986
Lewis, Norah L. 'Creating the Little Machine: Child Rearing in British Columbia, 1919–1939.' *BC Studies* 56 (Winter 1982–3), 44–60
- 'Reducing Maternal Mortality in British Columbia: An Educational Process.' In Barbara K. Latham and Roberta J. Pazdro, eds., *Not Just Pin Money*. Victoria: Camosun College, 1984, 337–55
- 'Goose Grease and Turpentine: Mother Treats the Family's Illnesses.' *Prairie Forum* 15 (Spring 1990), 67–84
Light, Beth, and Joy Parr, eds. *Canadian Women on the Move, 1867–1920*. Toronto: New Hogtown Press and the Ontario Institute for Studies in Education, 1983
Light, Beth, and Ruth Roach Pierson, eds. *No Easy Road: Women in Canada, 1920s to 1960s*. Toronto: New Hogtown Press, 1990
Light, Beth, and Alison Prentice, eds. *Pioneer and Gentlewomen of British North America*. Toronto: New Hogtown Press, 1980
Lomax, Elizabeth M.R. *Science and Patterns of Child Care*. San Francisco: W.H. Freeman, 1978
Luxton, Meg. *More Than a Labour of Love: Three Generations of Women's Work in the Home*. Toronto: Women's Press, 1980
McCarthy, Kathleen D., ed. *Lady Bountiful Revisited: Women, Philanthropy, and Power*. New Brunswick, NJ: Rutgers University Press, 1990
McConnachie, Kathleen. 'Methodology in the Study of Women in History: A

Case Study of Helen MacMurchy, MD.' *Ontario History* 75 (Mar. 1983), 61–70

MacDougall, Heather. 'Public Health in Toronto's Municipal Politics, 1883–1890.' *Bulletin of the History of Medicine* 55 (1981), 186–202

MacIntyre, Sally. '"Who Wants Babies?" The Social Construction of "Instincts."' In Diana Baker Leonard and Sheila Allen, eds., *Social Divisions and Society: Process and Change*. London: Tavistock, 1976, 150–73

McKenna, Katherine. 'Options for Elite Women in Early Upper Canadian Society: The Case of the Powell Family.' In J.K. Johnson and Bruce G. Wilson, eds., *Historical Essays on Upper Canada: New Perspectives*. Ottawa: Carleton University Press, 1989, 401–23

McLaren, Angus. *Our Own Master Race: Eugenics in Canada, 1885–1945*. Toronto: McClelland and Stewart, 1990

– and Arlene Tigar McLaren. *The Bedroom and the State: The Changing Practices and Politics of Contraception and Abortion in Canada, 1880–1980*. Toronto: McClelland and Stewart, 1986

Maccoby, Nathan. 'The Communication of Child-Rearing Advice to Parents.' *Merrill-Palmer Quarterly* 7 (July 1961), 199–204

Margolis, Maxine L. *Mothers and Such: Views of American Women and Why They Changed*. Berkeley: University of California Press, 1985

Maroney, Heather Jon. 'Embracing Motherhood: New Feminist Theory.' In Marilouise and Arthur Kroker, Pamela McCallum, and Mair Verthuy, eds., *Feminism Now: Theory and Practice*. Montreal: New World Perspectives, 1985, 40–64

Mason, Jutta, and David Cayley. 'Doctoring the Family.' Radio Program, CBC Radio, Apr. 1985

Matthews, Glenna. *'Just a Housewife': The Rise and Fall of Domesticity in America*. New York: Oxford University Press, 1987

Maynard, Rona. 'Motherhood: New Choices and Challenges.' *Chatelaine* 58 (June 1985), 55, 138, 140–5

Mechling, Jay. 'Advice to Historians on Advice to Mothers.' *Journal of Social History* 9 (Fall 1973), 44–63

Mitchinson, Wendy. 'Historical Attitudes toward Women and Childbirth.' *Atlantis* 4 (Spring 1979), 13–34

– 'The Medical Treatment of Women.' In Sandra Burt, Lorraine Code, and Lindsay Dorney, eds., *Changing Patterns: Women in Canada*. Toronto: McClelland and Stewart, 1988, 237–63

– *The Nature of Their Bodies: Women and Their Doctors in Victorian Canada*. Toronto: University of Toronto Press, 1991

Morrison, T.R. '"Their Proper Sphere": Feminism, the Family, and Child-Centred Social Reform in Ontario, 1875–1900.' *Ontario History* 68 (Mar./June 1976), 45–64, 65–74

Newson, John and Elizabeth. 'Cultural Aspects of Child-Rearing in the English-speaking World.' In Martin P.M. Richards, ed., *The Integration of a Child into a Social World*. London: Cambridge University Press, 1974, 53–82

Newton, Niles. *Maternal Emotions*. New York: Paul B. Hoeber, 1955.

Northway, Mary L. 'Child Study in Canada: A Casual History.' In Lois M. Brockman, John H. Whitely, and John P. Zubek, eds., *Child Development: Selected Readings*. Toronto: McClelland and Stewart, 1973, 11–46

Northway, Mary L. *Laughter in the Front Hall*. Toronto: Longmans, 1966

Oakley, Ann. 'The Trap of Medicalised Motherhood.' *New Society* 34 (18 Dec. 1975), 639–41

– *Becoming a Mother*. New York: Schocken, 1980

– *Women Confined: Towards a Sociology of Childbirth*. New York: Schocken, 1980

– 'Normal Motherhood: An Exercise in Self Control?' In Bridget Hutter and Gillian Williams, eds., *Controlling Women: The Normal and the Deviant*. London: Croom Helm, 1981, 79–107

– 'Women and Health Policy.' In Jane Lewis, ed., *Women's Welfare, Women's Rights*. London: Croom Helm, 1983, 103–29

– *The Captured Womb: A History of the Medical Care of Pregnant Women*. Oxford: Oxford University Press, 1984

Oppenheimer, Jo. 'Childbirth in Ontario: The Transition from Home to Hospital in the Early Twentieth Century.' In Katherine Arnup, Andrée Lévesque, and Ruth Roach Pierson, eds., *Delivering Motherhood: Maternal Ideologies and Practices in the 19th and 20th Centuries*. London: Routledge, 1990, 51–74

Orkin, Mark M. *The Great Stork Derby*. Don Mills, Ontario: General Publishing, 1981

Palmer, Charlene D. 'Child Development Articles in Popular Periodicals.' *Merrill-Palmer Quarterly* 6 (Fall 1959), 52–7

Parker, Jacqueline K., and Edward M Carpenter. 'Julia Lathrop and the Children's Bureau: The Emergence of an Institution.' *Social Service Review* 55 (Mar. 1981), 60–77

Parr, Joy, ed. *Childhood and Family in Canadian History*. Toronto: McClelland and Stewart, 1982

Pedersen, Diana. '"The Scientific Training of Mothers": The Campaign for Domestic Science in Ontario Schools, 1890–1913.' In Richard A. Jarrell and Arnold E. Roos, eds., *Critical Issues in the History of Canadian Science, Technology, and Medicine*. Thornhill, Ontario: HSTC Publications, 1983, 179–94

Pierson, Ruth Roach. *'They're Still Women After All': The Second World War and Canadian Womanhood*. Toronto: McClelland and Stewart, 1986

Piva, Michael. *The Conditions of the Working Class in Toronto: 1900-1921.* Ottawa: University of Ottawa Press, 1979

Prentice, Alison, Paula Bourne, Gail Cuthbert Brandt, Beth Light, Wendy Mitchinson, and Naomi Black. *Canadian Women: A History.* Toronto: Harcourt Brace Jovanovich, 1988

Raymond, Jocelyn Motyer. *The Nursery World of Dr Blatz.* Toronto: University of Toronto Press, 1991

Reiger, Kerreen M. *The Disenchantment of the Home: Modernizing the Australian Family, 1880-1940.* Melbourne: Oxford University Press, 1985

Rich, Adrienne. *Of Woman Born: Motherhood as Experience and Institution.* New York: W.W. Norton, 1976; Bantam, 1977

- 'Motherhood: The Contemporary Emergency and the Quantum Leap.' In *On Lies, Secrets and Silence: Selected Prose, 1966-1978.* New York: W.W. Norton, 1979, 258-273

- 'Motherhood in Bondage.' In *On Lies, Secrets, and Silence: Selected Prose, 1966-1978.* New York: W.W. Norton, 1979, 195-7

Riley, Denise. *War in the Nursery: Theories of the Child and Mother.* London: Virago, 1983

Roberts, Wayne. 'Six New Women: A Guide to the Mental Map of Women Reformers in Toronto.' *Atlantis* 3 (Fall 1977), 145-65

- '"Rocking the Cradle for the World": The New Woman and Maternal Feminism, Toronto, 1877-1914.' In Linda Kealey, ed., *A Not Unreasonable Claim: Women and Reform, 1880s-1920s.* Toronto: Women's Press, 1979, 15-45

Rooke, Patricia. 'Public Figure, Private Woman: Same Sex Support Structures in the Life of Charlotte Whitton.' *International Journal of Women's Studies* 6 (Nov./Dec. 1983), 412-28

- and R.L. Schnell. 'Child Welfare in English Canada, 1920-1948.' *Social Service Review* 55 (Sept. 1981), 484-506

- '"Making the Way More Comfortable": Charlotte Whitton's Child Welfare Career, 1920-48.' *Journal of Canadian Studies* 17 (Winter 1982-3), 33-45

- *Discarding the Asylum: From Child Rescue to the Welfare State in English-Canada (1800-1950).* Lanham, Md.: University Press of America, 1983

- '"An Idiot's Flowerbed": A Study of Charlotte Whitton's Feminist Thought, 1941-50.' In Veronica Strong-Boag and Anita Clair Fellman, eds., *Rethinking Canada: The Promise of Women's History.* Toronto: Copp Clark Pitman, 1986, 208-25

- eds. *Studies in Childhood History: A Canadian Perspective.* Calgary: Detselig Enterprises, 1982

Rosenberg, Charles, ed. *The Family in History.* Philadelphia: University of Pennsylvania Press, 1975

Rothman, Barbara Katz. *The Tentative Pregnancy: Prenatal Diagnosis and the Future of Motherhood.* New York: Viking Penguin, 1986

– *Recreating Motherhood: Ideology and Technology in a Patriarchal Society.* New York: W.W. Norton, 1990

Rothman, Sheila M. *Woman's Proper Place: A History of Changing Ideals and Practices, 1870 to the Present.* New York: Basic Books, 1978

Royce, Marion. *Eunice Dyke: Health Care Pioneer.* Toronto: Dundurn Press, 1983

Ruddick, Sara. 'Maternal Thinking.' In Joyce Trebilcot, ed., *Mothering: Essays in Feminist Theory.* Totowa, NJ: Rowman and Allanheld, 1983, 213–230

Schulz, Patricia Vanderbelt. 'Day Care in Canada, 1850–1962.' In Kathleen Gallagher Ross, ed., *Good Day Care: Fighting for It, Getting It, Keeping It.* Toronto: Women's Press, 1978, 137–58

Sears, Robert R. 'Your Ancients Revisited: A History of Child Development.' In E. Mavis Hetherington, ed., *Review of Child Development Research,* vol. 5, Chicago: University of Chicago Press, 1975, 1–74

– *Patterns of Child Rearing.* Stanford, Calif.: Stanford University Press, 1976

Shields, Stephanie A. '"To Pet, Coddle, and Do For": Caretaking and the Concept of Maternal Instinct.' In Miriam Lewin, ed., *In the Shadow of the Past: Psychology Portrays the Sexes.* New York: Columbia University Press, 1984, 256–73

Shorter, Edward. *The Making of the Modern Family.* New York: Basic Books, 1975

Siegel, Linda S. 'Child Health and Development in English Canada, 1790–1850.' In Charles G. Roland, ed., *Health, Disease, and Medicine: Essays in Canadian History.* Agincourt: Clarke Irwin, 1983, 360–80

Smith-Rosenberg, Carroll. 'The Female World of Love and Ritual.' *Signs: A Journal of Women in Society and Culture* 1 (Autumn 1975), 1–29

Snell, James G. '"The White Life for Two": The Defence of Marriage and Sexual Morality in Canada, 1890–1914.' *Histoire sociale / Social History* 16 (May 1983), 111–28

Spock, Benjamin, and Mary Morgan. *Spock on Spock: A Memoir of Growing Up with the Century.* New York: Pantheon Books, 1989

Steere, Geoffrey H. 'Freudianism and Child-Rearing in the Twenties.' *American Quarterly* 20 (1968), 759–67

Stendler, Celia B. 'Sixty Years of Child Training Practices: Revolution in the Nursery.' *Journal of Pediatrics* 36 (1950), 122–34

Stewart, Abigail J., David G. Winter, and A. David Jones. 'Coding Categories for the Study of Child-Rearing from Historical Sources.' *Journal of Interdisciplinary History* 5 (Spring 1975), 687–701

Stone, Lawrence. 'The Massacre of the Innocents.' *New York Review of Books* 21 (14 Nov. 1974), 25–31

– *The Family, Sex, and Marriage in England, 1500–1800,* rev. ed. Harmondsworth: Penguin, 1979

Strong-Boag, Veronica. 'Canada's Women Doctors: Feminism Constrained.' In Linda Kealey, ed., *A Not Unreasonable Claim: Women and Reform in Canada, 1880s–1920s.* Toronto: Women's Press, 1979, 109–29

– '"Wages for Housework": Mothers' Allowances and the Beginnings of Social Security in Canada.' *Journal of Canadian Studies* 14 (Spring 1979), 24–34

– 'Intruders in the Nursery: Childcare Professionals Reshape the Years One to Five, 1920–1940.' In Joy Parr, ed., *Childhood and Family in Canadian History.* Toronto: McClelland and Stewart, 1982, 160–78

– *The New Day Recalled: Lives of Girls and Women in English Canada, 1919–1939.* Toronto: Copp Clark Pitman, 1988

– and Kathryn McPherson. 'The Confinement of Women: Childbirth and Hospitalization in Vancouver, 1919–1939.' In Katherine Arnup, Andrée Lévesque, and Ruth Roach Pierson, eds., *Delivering Motherhood: Maternal Ideologies and Practices in the 19th and 20th Centuries,* London: Routledge, 1990, 75–107

Stuart, Meryn. 'Ideology and Experience: Public Health Nursing and the Ontario Rural Child Welfare Project, 1920–25.' *Canadian Bulletin of Medical History* 6 (1989), 111–31

Sulman, A. Michael. 'The Humanization of the American Child: Benjamin Spock as a Popularizer of Psychoanalytic Thought.' *Journal of the History of the Behavioral Sciences* 9 (July 1973), 258–68

Sunley, Robert. 'Early Nineteenth-Century American Literature on Child Rearing.' In Margaret Mead and Martha Wolfenstein, eds., *Childhood in Contemporary Cultures.* Chicago: University of Chicago Press, 1955; Phoenix Books, 1963, 150–67

Sutherland, Neil. 'Towards a History of English-Canadian Youngsters.' In Michael B. Katz and Paul H. Mattingly, eds., *Education and Social Change.* New York: New York University Press, 1975, xi–xxxi

– *Children in English-Canadian Society: Framing the Twentieth Century Consensus.* Toronto: University of Toronto Press, 1976

Takanishi, Ruby. 'Childhood as a Social Issue: Historical Roots of Contemporary Child Advocacy Movements.' *Journal of Social Issues* 34 (1978), 8–27

Thompson, Paul. *The Voice of the Past: Oral History.* Oxford: Oxford University Press, 1978

Thorne, Barry, ed., with Marilyn Yalom. *Rethinking the Family: Some Feminist Questions.* New York: Longman, 1982

Trebilcot, Joyce, ed. *Mothering: Essays in Feminist Theory.* Totowa, NJ: Rowman and Allanheld, 1983

Urwin, Cathy. 'Constructing Motherhood: The Persuasion of Normal Development.' In Carolyn Steedman, Cathy Urwin, and Valerie Walkerdine, eds.,

Language, Gender, and Childhood. London: Routledge and Kegan Paul, 1985, 164–202

Vanek, Joann. 'Time Spent in Housework.' *Scientific American* 231 (Nov. 1974), 116–25

Vincent, Clark E. 'Trends in Infant Care Ideas.' *Child Development* 22 (Sept. 1951), 199–209

Vipond, Mary. 'The Image of Women in Mass Circulation Magazines in the 1920s.' In Susan Mann Trofimenkoff and Alison Prentice, eds., *The Neglected Majority: Essays in Canadian Women's History,* vol. 1. Toronto: McClelland and Stewart, 1977, 116–24

Ward, W. Peter and Patricia C. 'Infant Birth Weight and Nutrition in Industrializing Montreal.' *American Historical Review* 89 (1984), 324–45

Wearing, Betsy. *The Ideology of Motherhood.* Sydney: George Allen and Unwin, 1984

Weiss, Nancy Pottishman. 'Mother, the Invention of Necessity: Dr. Benjamin Spock's *Baby and Child Care.' American Quarterly* 24 (Winter 1977), 519–46

– 'The Mother-Child Dyad Revisited: Perceptions of Mothers and Children in Twentieth Century Child-Rearing Manuals.' *Journal of Social Issues* 34 (1978), 29–45

Weisskopf, Susan. 'Maternal Guilt and Mental Health Professionals: A Reconfirming Interaction.' *Michigan Occasional Papers* 5 (Fall 1978), 1–16

Wertz, Richard W. and Dorothy C. *Lying In: A History of Childbirth in America.* New York: Free Press, 1977

Whiting, Beatrice B. 'Folk Wisdom and Child Rearing.' *Merrill-Palmer Quarterly* 20 (Jan. 1974), 9–20

Wilson, Adrian. 'The Infancy of the History of Childhood: An Appraisal of Philippe Aries.' *History and Theory* 19 (1980), 132–53

Wilson, Stephen. 'The Myth of Motherhood a Myth: The Historical View of European Child-Rearing.' *Social History* 9 (May 1984), 181–98

Winch, Robert F. 'Rearing by the Book.' Chapter in *The Modern Family.* New York: Holt, Rinehart, and Winston, 1963

Wishy, Bernard. *The Child and the Republic: The Dawn of Modern American Child Nurture.* Philadelphia: University of Pennsylvania Press, 1968

Wolfenstein, Martha. 'Trends in Infant Care.' *American Journal of Orthopsychiatry* 23 (1953), 120–30

– 'Fun Morality: An Analysis of Recent American Child-Training Literature.' *Journal of Social Issues* 7 (1951), 15–25. Reprinted in Margaret Mead and Martha Wolfenstein, eds., *Childhood in Contemporary Cultures,* Chicago: University of Chicago Press, 1955; Phoenix Books, 1963, 168–77

Zelizer, Viviana A. *Pricing the Priceless Child: The Changing Social Value of Children.* New York: Basic Books, 1985

Zuckerman, Michael. 'Dr. Spock: The Confidence Man.' In Charles Rosenberg, ed., *The Family in History.* Philadelphia: University of Pennsylvania Press, 1975

UNPUBLISHED MATERIALS

Theses

Abeele, Cynthia Comacchio. '"Nations Are Built of Babies": Maternal and Child Welfare in Ontario, 1914–1940.' PhD dissertation, University of Guelph, 1987

Bator, Paul Adolphus. '"Saving Lives on [the] Wholesale Plan": Public Health Reform in the City of Toronto, 1900–1930.' PhD dissertation, University of Toronto, 1979

Biggs, Catherine Lesley. 'The Response to Maternal Mortality in Ontario, 1920–1940.' MSc thesis, University of Toronto, 1983

Brickman, Jane. 'Mother Love – Mother Death: Maternal and Infant Care: Social Class and the Role of the Government.' PhD dissertation, City University of New York, 1978

Dehli, Kari. 'Women and Class: The Social Organization of Mothers' Relations to Schools in Toronto, 1915 to 1940.' PhD dissertation, University of Toronto, 1988

Houlihan, Inez. 'The Image of Women in *Chatelaine* Editorials, March 1928 to September 1977.' MA thesis, University of Toronto, 1984

Lewis, Norah Lillian. 'Advising the Parents: Child Rearing in British Columbia During the Inter-War Years.' EdD dissertation, University of British Columbia, 1980

Lomax, Elizabeth Raine. 'Advances in Pediatrics and in Infant Care in Nineteenth Century England.' PhD dissertation, University of California, Los Angeles, 1972

McConnachie, Kathleen Janet Anne. 'Science and Ideology: The Mental Hygiene and Eugenics Movements in the Inter-War Years, 1919–1939.' PhD dissertation, University of Toronto, 1987

MacDougall, Heather. '"Health is Wealth": The Development of Public Health Activity in Toronto, 1834–1890.' PhD dissertation, University of Toronto, 1982

McGinnis, J.P. Dickins. 'From Health to Welfare: Federal Government Policy Regarding Standards of Public Health for Canadians, 1919–1945.' PhD dissertation, University of Alberta, 1980

Morrison, Terrence R. 'The Child and Urban Social Reform in Late Nineteenth Century Ontario.' PhD dissertation, University of Toronto, 1971

Tomic-Trumper, Patricia. 'The Care of Unwed Mothers and Illegitimate Children in Toronto, 1867–1920: A Study in Social Administration.' PhD dissertation, University of Toronto, 1986

Papers

Findlay, Deborah. 'Professional Interests in Medicine's Construction of Women's Reproductive Health.' Presented at the Annual Meeting of the Canadian Sociology and Anthropology Association, Winnipeg, June 1986
Grahame, Kamini Maraj. 'Setting Standards: The Social Construction of Mothering in *Chatelaine*, 1928–1938.' Course paper for the Ontario Institute for Studies in Education.
Lewis, Norah. '"No Baby – No Nation": Mother Education, A Federal Concern, 1921 to 1979.' Presented at the Canadian History of Education Conference, Vancouver, BC, October, 1983
Peters, Suzanne. 'Reflections on Studying Mothering, Motherwork, and Mothers' Work.' Presented at the Motherwork Workshop, Val Morin Quebec, October, 1985

Index

Illustration Credits